T0272432

More Praise for

# *Hannah's Children*

"The birth dearth is the most important story of our time. Most analysts fail to explain the causes, and most politicians propose hopeless 'solutions.' That's why *Hannah's Children* is a crucial book. Combining the rigor of an economist with the insight of a mother, Catherine Pakaluk opens readers' minds and hearts to the birth dearth's real causes, and exactly why some women are inoculated against this cultural malady."

> —**Timothy P. Carney**, senior fellow at the American Enterprise Institute and author of *Family Unfriendly: How Our Culture Made Raising Kids Much Harder Than It Needs to Be*

"A beautiful celebration of motherhood showcasing the rich complexity—social, economic, and personal—of human love. Catherine Pakaluk makes the compelling case for having a large family in a modern context of adult autonomy and hyper-individualism. Informed by a multidisciplinary study canvasing economics, history, sociology, and philosophy, *Hannah's Children* joins the slim ranks of other groundbreaking ethnographic studies on marriage, maternity, and demography. Within the narratives of human natality, Pakaluk reveals the possibility of greater gain within self-sacrifice, advantage in accepted opportunity costs, and expansion of self within the gestation, growth, and gift of other persons."

> —**Janice T. Chik Breidenbach, Ph.D.**, associate professor of philosophy, Ave Maria University; member of the Aquinas Institute, Blackfriars Hall, University of Oxford; senior affiliate, Penn Program for Research on Religion and Urban Civil Society, University of Pennsylvania

"'In a two-child world, an eight-child choice begs for an explanation.' So begins *Hannah's Children*, Catherine Ruth Pakaluk's intrepid exploration of the reasons why some mothers of many are rejecting the temptation to limit their fertility to few. With exceptional sensitivity and clarity, she untangles the incentives behind a contraceptive culture that regards self-sacrifice as senseless at best. *Hannah's Children* is a tour de force in qualitative economics, as rigorous as it is deeply moving."

> —**Helen Roy**, author of Ladies' Late Rome Journal on Substack and host of the *Girlboss, Interrupted* podcast

"*Hannah's Children* is a powerful look into a countercultural movement being led by—of all people—mothers. But this is not another book touting girlboss culture or a sentimental tale about a woman who leaves her family to 'find herself.' No, the women in this book are bucking the status quo because they believe children (and large families) are blessings from God to be enjoyed, not the 'consequences' of casual sex to be overcome. In a world that often requires children to sacrifice in order for adults to fulfill their dreams, it is both refreshing and inspiring to read the stories of dedication and devotion Catherine Pakaluk brings to life in this book."

> —**Delano Squires**, research fellow, Richard and Helen DeVos Center for Life, Religion, and Family at the Heritage Foundation

"Catherine has greatly advanced our understanding of the decision bear and raise children by sharing the beautiful stories of moth who contradict the grim trend of declining global birth rates."

> —**Clara Piano, Ph.D.**, assistant professor, Department of Economics, Austin Peay State University

"Our world is unwilling to produce enough of the greatest reso of all: the human person. Yet some women defy that trend continue to bring large numbers of children into that same w

In *Hannah's Children*, the economist Catherine Ruth Pakaluk takes us into the dynamics that lead some families to make these radical choices, and shows us what can be done to save our civilization from the birth dearth that threatens to kill it. Read and learn."

—**Samuel Gregg, Ph.D.**, author of *The Next American Economy*, distinguished fellow in political economy and senior research faculty, American Institute for Economic Research

"Economics usually doesn't do much to help us understand our human condition. *Hannah's Children* is the rare exception: it successfully focuses on an essential choice that is offered to almost all people, to be concretely open to the affirmation of the gift of life. This choice is unlike most other choices, and *Hannah's Children* understands this choice in profound ways that situates it at the heart of any possible resolution to the problem that is modernity."

—**Richard Spady**, senior research fellow, Nuffield College, Oxford University; research professor, Department of Economics, Johns Hopkins University

"There's a growing consensus—contrary to long worries about overpopulation—that developed countries are not even reproducing themselves. Policymakers, especially on the right, have started talking about what can be done about this coming demographic disaster. Yet few have asked the question: Why do some people still get married and have lots of children? Catherine Pakaluk asked that question and searched for the answer. If you're concerned about our demographic future, and the state of the family in the twenty-first century, you must read *Hannah's Children*. No public policy response and no campaign for cultural renewal that ignores Pakaluk's findings in this book has a chance of succeeding."

—**Jay Richards, Ph.D.**, William E. Simon Senior Research Fellow in Religious Liberty and Civil Society and director, Richard and Helen DeVos Center for Life, Religion, and Family at the Heritage Foundation

"This is a very special book. It gives flesh and blood to people our culture tells us aren't supposed to exist: women who are happy, healthy, interesting, real, and smart—and who have chosen to have large families. Catherine Pakaluk artfully weaves the lives of these mothers into a bright and insightful story one wants to just keep reading. The testimonies of these women reveal in a fresh way that motherhood is beautiful in all its sacrifice, wonder, tenderness, and joy."

—**Carrie Gress, Ph.D.**, author of *The End of Woman*, fellow at the Ethics and Public Policy Center, and mother of five

"The stories in this book are as beautiful as they are inspirational. *Hannah's Children: The Women Quietly Defying the Birth Dearth* contains profound wisdom on how to live family life well, the blessings of children, the benefits of siblings, and how a renewal of family may get us out of our civilizational mess. My wife and I will be benefiting from this book in our parenting for years to come."

—**Ryan T. Anderson, Ph.D.**, president of the Ethics and Public Policy Center, and author of *Truth Overruled: The Future of Marriage and Religious Freedom*

# HANNAH'S CHILDREN

# HANNAH'S CHILDREN

*The Women Quietly Defying the Birth Dearth*

## CATHERINE RUTH PAKALUK

REGNERY
GATEWAY

Gateway Editions books may be purchased in bulk at special discounts
for sales promotion, corporate gifts, fund-raising, or educational purposes. Special editions can also be created to specifications. For details,
contact the Special Sales Department, Regnery, 307 West 36th Street, 11th
Floor, New York, NY 10018 or info@skyhorsepublishing.com.

Gateway EditionsTM and Regnery® are imprints of
Skyhorse Publishing, Inc.®, a Delaware corporation.

Visit our website at www.regnery.com.
Please follow our publisher Tony Lyons on Instagram
@tonylyonsisuncertain.

10 9 8 7 6 5 4

Library of Congress Cataloging-in-Publication Data is available on file.

Cover design by John Caruso
Cover photograph by Tyler Neil

Print ISBN: 978-1-68451-457-1
eBook ISBN: 978-1-68451-569-1

Printed in the United States of America

*For Ruth's children*

# CONTENTS

# *Author's Note*

What you are about to read is a narrative account of the first qualitative study of the American women resistant to the trend of low birth rates. The findings in this manuscript are the fruit of a multi-year research initiative at the Catholic University of America, in partnership with the Wheatley Institute at Brigham Young University. In 2019, I and my colleague Emily Reynolds of the Wheatley Institute, together with assistants Mary Robotham (née Bathon) and Sierra Smith (née Breshears), visited fifty-five women with five or more children in ten American regions. We interviewed subjects in pairs: I interviewed 80 percent of the subjects with Mary assisting; Emily, the remaining 20 percent with Sierra assisting. As mothers of many ourselves, Emily and I led the interviews. In this volume, I sometimes use the first-person plural "we" as I recall observations from our interviews—since we were always present as a "we." For everything else—my impressions, inferences, and analyses making sense of the data we heard—I narrate in the first-person singular. The views I express in this volume are mine and do not necessarily reflect the views of my team members or our institutions.

Our research initiative, "Motive and Meaning among High Fertility American Women" (Protocol No. 18-083), was certified on November 16, 2018, by the Committee for the Protection of Human Subjects at the Catholic University of America as meeting the requirements of the federal regulations governing protection of human subjects. Research subjects were informed of the nature and purpose of the study, of their rights as subjects, and of the possibility that their remarks might be included in presentations, articles, and books. Subjects signed written consent forms at the time of the interviews. Identifying information and factors unique to the subjects have been removed from all descriptions. Pseudonyms are used throughout this book, unless a subject specifically requested that she be identified by her true name—as in chapter 7. Because our subjects have such uncommon family sizes, I was generally unable to provide their state of residence without risking identification. I ask the reader's forbearance in this matter.

# PART ONE

## *"The Meaning of Everything"— Introducing Hannah's Children*

# CHAPTER ONE

## *"He Still Wants You"—Stranger on a Train*

"Besides wanting and choosing and being moved to do
this or that, men may also want to have (or not to have)
certain desires and motives. They are capable of wanting
to be different in their preferences and purposes...."

—Harry G. Frankfurt, "Freedom of the Will and the
Concept of a Person," 1971

Returning home from a trip, backpack at my feet, I settled into
a seat along the side of a Virginia Railway commuter train
from D.C. to Manassas with my infant son snuggled at my
chest. It was the spring of 2010, after I defended my dissertation but
before I graduated in June of that year. He was three months old,
downy-soft head peeking out from a front wrap. I had never ridden
that train before, and I have never ridden it since. I was surrounded
by working professionals headed home for the night, and the pas-
sengers noted my baby with surprise. A middle-aged woman asked,
"Is he your first?" I have no idea why this is such a common question

to ask a mother with an infant, but over the years I spent traveling with babies it was easily the most common icebreaker. The question poses a dilemma for those of us with lots of children. Like the canned "How're you doing?" to which no one ever expects a negative response, "Is it your first?" is supposed to be answered with a "Yeah," and then followed up with some kind of rejoinder along the lines of "Enjoy it while it lasts," or "Don't worry, eventually he'll sleep."

What no one expects, not anywhere and least of all on a rush-hour train, is "He's my sixth!" At that answer, there was murmuring among the train riders. But above the din I heard one response that I never expected. The woman who had questioned me gave a swift, plaintive reply: "Six! I guess your husband still *wants* you." She was right, of course. He did, and he still does—we've since had two more children, eight altogether. But I had never considered his desire for me as causal in relation to our family size—even though, in some sense, it clearly is. Nor had I ever wondered whether having a lot of babies might make us love each other more. I still don't know. But no other response to my family in public has struck me with the same tragic force as that one fourteen years ago.

In a two-child world, an eight-child choice begs for an explanation. What I chose is unusual, rare, maybe a little crazy. But I certainly didn't choose it for those reasons. I like to be on trend. I always know where denim is going, and I spend more on shoes than I should. Why not be on trend with my number of kids? Why have all these children? I had every door open in front of me. *Why this choice and not another?* I get asked this question a lot, and it turns out that other women with big families get asked too.

I know what the answer isn't. It's not because I don't believe in using artificial birth control—even though I don't. I know when every one of my kids was conceived, and we could have avoided any one of them. Natural family planning has its problems, but so do IUDs, condoms, and pills. Knowing how to avoid getting pregnant is easier than most things I do. Besides old-fashioned wisdom, there are apps to track fertility, wearable wristbands, and simple at-home fertility tests with red lights and green lights. None of my kids was an accident or unplanned in any strict sense. We always said, "Let's go—we're ready for another one if we can conceive."

And it's not because I'm a Catholic and the Church says that I should have a big family—because it doesn't. One might describe the Catholic Church as "pro-natalist" because of its stance on abortion and birth control or the history of large Catholic families among Italians, Irish, and other immigrants. But whatever the Church teaches officially, Catholics nowadays use birth control at about the same rates as everyone else.[1] And in my forty-seven years as a practicing Catholic, I have never heard a sermon on the value of having children. I have never been urged in the confessional to have more kids. There's no doctrine that it's holier to end up with more kids.

Of all the Catholic women in history with big families, the Church has canonized precious few of them, the American educator Elizabeth Bayley Seton being one of them. The childless Maria Goretti, my confirmation saint, is more typical. She was canonized for forgiving her attempted rapist (and murderer). Meanwhile, her mother, Assunta Carlini, a devout woman who raised seven children as a widowed sharecropper in desperate poverty, isn't a saint.[2] Whatever we might say about the Catholic Church and natalism (and that would be a separate book), it would be difficult to make a case that there is any kind of social norm among Catholics to have big families. Nothing to my mind sums this up better than Pope Francis's airplane quip that women don't have to breed "like rabbits" to be good Catholics—a comment I found deeply offensive.[3]

Then there is another more personal reason that isn't the answer. When I got married, my husband was a widowed father of six. He didn't "need" more kids, we had our hands full, and we could have counted ourselves happy if we had raised those children and dedicated the balance of our lives to research and teaching. He already had tenure in philosophy, and I hoped to follow in an academic job. I was a graduate student in a top economics program. I had a promising "career" in front of me, and the sensible thing would have been to finish that program on time and seek a tenure-track job like my husband. And yet—we had more children anyway. By the time I finished my doctoral work, we had six more kids. A tenure-track job seemed out of the question.

So if those are not the answers, what is the answer? It's hard to say. I suppose it boils down to some sort of deeply held thing, possibly from childhood—a platinum conviction—that the capacity to conceive children, to receive them into my arms, to take them home, to dwell with them in love, to sacrifice for them as they grow, and to delight in them as the Lord delights in us, that that thing, call it motherhood, call it childbearing, that that thing is the most worthwhile thing in the world—the most perfect thing I am capable of doing.

But that is not easy to say. Not on a train, not in a dental chair, and not in the checkout line at a grocery store. That day on the train, I began to wonder if other women who shared my choices had ideas about why they do this, and better ways of explaining it. I began to wonder if it was a common experience, and if so, whether it had a common expression. Did it have a story? Did it have a name? So I went in search of reasons, perhaps to know my own for the first time. *Hannah's Children* is the result of this search. In summer 2019, I and my colleague Emily Reynolds traveled to ten American regions and interviewed fifty-five women with five or more children to find out why they do what they do and what they think it means—for themselves, for their families, and for the nation.

As it happens, in a two-child world trending to a one-child world,[4] the desire for children and how it is charted in relation to competing human goods isn't a small thing. It's a really big thing—the thing that ultimately says how many of us there are and what kind of people we will be. Birth rates and childbearing are not a question of merely personal interest. There is no more economically significant question than where people come from, and nothing more deeply informs the way we order our lives together than the first society we experience: the family. So *Hannah's Children* sits squarely at the intersection of personal and professional interests for me.

I will make the argument for the economic importance of this work in chapter 4, but my method notably breaks with Nobel economist Gary Becker's seminal approach to the economics of the family.[5] Becker argued that the childbearing desires of a household are properly outside the scope of economic analysis. The "economic" approach, he argued, assumes "that individuals maximize their utility from basic preferences that do not change rapidly over time. . . ."[6] In Becker's work, household demand for children is modeled like a "consumer" preference: a simple taste for a good that is informed by things outside the analysis of the economists. We take desires as given. This isn't the whole of the story, but in general economists have moved away from qualitative work, preferring deterministic models with fixed preferences and quantitative studies using samples large enough to make statistical inferences based on probability models.

In contrast, the heart of the project of this book is conversations with a small number of women about the nature of their childbearing decisions. Since my sample is not large enough to be representative of women with large families in general, each subject is herself, $N=1$. The narratives that make up my data do not yield descriptive statistics or causal inferences. But as MIT economist Michael J. Piore has pointed out, "What open-ended interviews do yield, and yield consistently, are stories the respondents tell. The story is the 'observation.' The stories are basically narratives. The question is thus what to do with the stories. Typically, stories are not analyzed as statistical data; stories are 'interpreted.' ... The stories [act] not as data points but to suggest particular revisions in theory."[7] It is in this spirit that I took up this work: to find the stories that may ultimately assist in a revision of economic theories about birth rates and population growth.

The wholesale abandonment of qualitative work in economics, especially open-ended interviews, has been a mistake. Economists should still take $N=1$ seriously. This is not the time to make that argument in full except by giving witness to the fruits of its method. For today, I do not see this book as an exercise in doing economics. But I understand it as an economic exercise. In a minimal sense, I want to understand household demand for children better than our current theories, not one of which can really explain the macro trends in birth rates that now puzzle the world. I also want to understand the supply of children better than our current theories. Families don't "demand" children in the way that consumers demand goods and services; they are both demanders and suppliers of the same good. What is wanted, if it is wanted, is not just any child but a child of one's own. The upshot of this is that it is hard to know whether falling birth rates are more of a demand shift (fewer children wanted) or more of a supply shift (fewer children produced) or both. And if we expand our analysis to suppose that children are not "consumed" in a single period of time but experienced over a longer horizon, these demand-and-supply questions become even more fraught.

It doesn't take long puzzling over the problem of childbearing desires to see that there are Gordian knots to be untangled, the threads of which have monumental significance. In times past birth rates were mostly governed by things very far from personal preference, such as famines, disease, crops, sex, marriage, death—fortune and fate. But with modern economic growth and efficient birth control, household fertility desires become an object deserving of study apart and aside from mere sexual appetite. In a contraceptive age, children will not come unless the capacity for childbearing is switched "on." Their existence is dependent on our willingness to let them in, on our motives and desires. This is a book about those desires: not sexual desires, but desires that now change the course of nations.

Of course, we don't merely desire and choose. We evaluate our desires and choices, making judgments about and revising them. American philosopher Harry Frankfurt called these evaluations "second order." He wrote: "Many animals appear to have the capacity for what I shall call 'first-order desires'... desires to do or not to do one thing or another. No animal other than man, however, appears to have the capacity for reflective self-evaluation that is manifested in the formation of second-order desires."[8] The woman on the train connected the size of my family to the character of my marriage. Such a connection would give rise to the second-order desires that Harry Frankfurt described: regrets or satisfaction, shame or pride, sadness or joy. In short, second-order desires arise from the meaning we attach to our choices, looking back.

So a book about motives for having children would be incomplete without the meanings that women attach to the choices they have made—the reasons they wanted kids and the reasons they kept wanting them. To that end, I asked the women in my study to tell me how it started and how it's going. I have presented their stories in as raw and unedited a form as possible. It was an unqualified privilege to hear the reasons of the heart I am about to share with you.

CHAPTER TWO

## *Reasons of the Heart—Hannah's Chain*

"The heart has its reasons, which reason does not know."

—Blaise Pascal, *Pensées* 277

"We know truth, not only by the reason, but also by the heart, and it is in this last way that we know first principles."

—Blaise Pascal, *Pensées* 282

I met Hannah, age forty-four, and Esther, forty-two, in a small Chabad House[1] at a large state university in New England. They wanted to be interviewed together. Hannah hardly sat down, preferring to stay on her feet while she tended to her delightfully plump twelve-month-old daughter, her seventh. Esther, in contrast, never got up from the sofa where she nursed her littlest one, just born, two weeks old, her ninth. "Do I feel like my children are my accomplishments? I more feel like they are who they are," she said.

## "We Were Searching"

Esther grew up in a big family and always envisioned having kids, but Hannah didn't plan for this life. "I didn't even want to get married at one point in my life. At one point in my life, I could not see myself married. I thought I would be like that aunt, or you know, the medicine woman person who doesn't get married." She laughed and continued:

> Where I was in my early twenties, where I was just doing my own thing for wherever I was at that point in my life...most people [who] are [in] their academic years or their professional careers are doing their own thing. And having children was not something that I would...if you're a somewhat level-headed person in the world, you'd say this doesn't fit into this lifestyle. You couldn't do this. It doesn't make sense. Because people think on rational levels, and I think maybe a little bit more super-rational [thinking] has to infiltrate the masses to know that things are possible. Like possibilities of expansion in your life.

The seventeenth-century philosopher Blaise Pascal defined eloquence as "a painting of thought," the capacity to present what is real through a conversational sweetness drawn from truth that captivates the listener.[2] Hannah was a paradigm of eloquence. Like a modern Pascal, she traced out her journey:

> We met in Israel in a city called Safed. We met in a friend's garden. We were introduced through a number of people, mutual friends and teachers who knew both of us, but it was an arranged meeting. Not an arranged marriage, but an

arranged meeting and there was a lot of background already. We have similar backgrounds. We both come from a Reformed Jewish background. We both [went] through a series of life journeys—physical and spiritual—after high school with other religions like Native American and Sufi, et cetera. *We were searching. My husband and I were searching.*

For us, we had both been around the block. We had both explored, we had dated in our public-school secular life. We were both very clear and very focused that one of our main goals of getting married was to begin a family right away and...to have a large family. That was something that we were attracted to with the teachers that had turned us on and inspired us as we returned to our faith. And we talked a lot about that in our first dates.

That, but also on a deeper level, in my own kind of quest for meaning and purpose, I was very into the concept of infinity. I did a lot of Indian meditation and things like that, nirvana. Kind of like this search for reaching this point, like the essence of "What's the meaning of everything?" And I kind of feel like it all came down—like the core of the answer—was that children are this key to infinity. And especially being Jewish, how much more so because this is a link and a chain that we've had from Moses and from Abraham and from Noah and Adam. This link, continuing this legacy by having children is a way to be a part of this chain of infinity. And to me that was it. There is nothing else that is going to do that.

Hannah remarked that, "if you're a somewhat level-headed person in the world," having a lot of children could seem irrational. But she preferred to think of it as super-rational. She had reasons for what she was up to, but reasons that had to do with higher things, ultimate ends, Pascal's reasons of the heart. For Hannah, those super-reasons gave meaning to ordinary reasoning about material possessions and life choices, directing them toward what is eternal.

I opened this narrative with Hannah's story because her contrast between two ways of life provides the best possible introduction to the women in this volume. My subjects described their choice to have many children as a deliberate rejection of an autonomous, customized, self-regarding lifestyle in favor of a way of life intentionally limited by the demands of motherhood. In general, they were motivated by a deeply religious worldview characterized by trust in God and hope in his providence. Faith enabled and dignified costly personal sacrifices—enabled, these women argued, because the gains and losses of childbearing are assessed differently on religious grounds than on secular ones; dignified, they argued, because true wealth doesn't come from what the world offers.

Like Hannah, many of my other subjects groped for descriptions of the customized life they had rejected, where the number and timing of children were fitted to a narrative of self-identity. They, in contrast, fitted themselves into a greater narrative of childbearing. They spoke of self-sacrifice but not of losing themselves. My subjects believe they have *found* themselves in having children. They believe their personalities and capacities have expanded—indeed, superabounded so richly as to give rise to other persons. This expansion has, in turn, somehow opened them to receive gifts of love and sacrifice from their own ancestors, gifts whose meaning had remained inaccessible until unlocked by their own choice to participate with those ancestors in reaching toward the infinite.

Like Hannah, the other women I met extended this contrast to their marriages, to their children, and to social order more broadly. They believe that the sustained effect of living with needy young children for an extended period of life fosters other-regarding virtues necessary for egalitarianism and civic friendship: empathy, generosity, solidarity, and self-denial. Like Hannah, my subjects typically described a life of religious seriousness in which they allowed their beliefs about God and the meaning of life to shape their own hearts and desires. Finally, like Hannah, they had adopted a posture of openness to children as a way of life and not a mere season.

Hannah's contrast between her old "self-regarding" secular life and her new "other-regarding" religious one raises the issue of individualism—people "doing their own thing," as she put it. One might think of Alexis de Tocqueville, who defined individualism as "a mature and calm feeling, which disposes each member of the community to sever himself from the mass of his fellows, and to draw apart with his family and his friends; so that, after he has thus formed a little circle of his own, he willingly leaves society at large to itself."[3] Like Hannah, Tocqueville used the imagery of a chain. He argued that aristocratic societies, replete with class and title, tied people together, with everyone playing a role defined in relation to others. "Aristocracy had made a chain of all the members of the community," he wrote, "from peasant to king: democracy breaks that chain, and severs every link...."[4] Tocqueville worried that democratic orders necessarily initiate a degenerative shift toward individualism. For Tocqueville, individualism isn't the same as selfishness, that "exaggerated love of self" that is "as old as the world." But individualism, proceeding more from "erroneous judgment" than from "depraved feelings," can give reign to selfishness in the absence of a countervailing force.[5]

## "This Chain of Infinity"

Hannah argued that not only the aristocracy but also the ancestral family links everybody like a chain. The family works against individualism by asserting a communitarian reality. In a single generation an individual has parents and grandparents, brothers and sisters, aunts and uncles, cousins, nieces, and nephews. These are the real, flesh-and-blood human beings who make up society outside of your immediate family. You don't have to wonder whether you care about your "fellow man." You do care because your fellow man might be your actual brother, uncle, or son.

Moreover, across generations, individuals have ancestors to whom they have debts and also offspring toward whom they have responsibilities. Childbearing cancels the debts, as it were, while giving rise to new obligations. Paying it forward, we would say now. Having children confers an eternal status on any one individual in the chain, making her equal in dignity to her kin for all time. "Continuing the legacy by having children," Hannah says, "is a way to be a part of this chain of infinity." The family is egalitarian, communitarian, and hierarchical—all in one. On this account, ties to family redeem our freedom and direct its powers. The self-imposed duties of an abundant, generative family life provide the ballast against selfish forms of individualism. With strong stable families, democracy in America might have a chance of fostering the private and public virtue that Tocqueville worried about.

Hannah's chain is a perfect image of the paradox she and my subjects described. A single link can't "do its own thing." But the link is never alone. She knows where she has been, and she knows where she is going. She finds her meaning in the strictures of the ties she has adopted. Hannah found her identity in the ancestral chain—a place of rest, and the end of her searching. "You know," she said, "everyone's searching for identity. Tattoo yourself, pierce yourself, take on another religion.... [But] everybody's got an ancestry. What a way to honor your legacy and your line. What a way to connect the past and the future. That to me is being a part of infinity, to continue a chain. So, what a better way to form an identity, you know?" She added, "No regrets. Not a one. I mean like this is way harder now than [life] was then, but I have inner peace in my life that I didn't have then. I was searching. I'm not searching now."

CHAPTER THREE

# "Red-Diaper Babies"—Political Fault Lines

"During the [first demographic transition] the issue
was to adopt contraception in order to avoid pregnancies;
during the [second demographic transition] the basic
decision is to stop contraception in order to start
a pregnancy."

—Ron J. Lesthaeghe and Johan Surkyn, "When History Moves On"

I n December of 2004, shortly after the second Bush 43 victory, *New York Times* columnist David Brooks drew attention to a phenomenon he dubbed "the new red-diaper babies." He highlighted the "natalists," as he called them, who are found all throughout the country, defying falling birth rates and the retreat from marriage. "[The natalists] are having three, four or more kids. Their personal identity is defined by parenthood. They are more spiritually, emotionally, and physically invested in their homes than in any other sphere of life, having concluded that parenthood is the most enriching and elevating thing they can do."[1]

Brooks's interest wasn't limited to curiosity. He wanted to draw attention to the fact that people having big families were associated, as much then as now, with "red America." They were Republican voters. Brooks cited scholars who noted that "Democrats swept the largely childless cities—true blue locales like San Francisco, Portland, Seattle, Boston and Manhattan have the lowest percentages of children in the nation—but generally had poor showings in those places where families are settling down, notably the Sun Belt cities, exurbs and outer suburbs of older metropolitan areas."[2] Brooks urged his readers to see the "true motive forces behind" the political divisions. The real fault lines of consequence, he argued, were familial.[3]

Just how consequential? More than Brooks knew. Two years later, Ron J. Lesthaeghe and Lisa Neidert, demographers based at the University of Michigan, published findings about the relationship between red and blue voting patterns in 2000 and 2004 and family-related data by state and county.[4] They included birth rates, marriage and divorce rates, cohabitation, and more. What they found was nothing short of remarkable. Birth rates and marriage behavior correlated powerfully with voting.[5] Places with high fertility and more traditional marriage were vastly more likely to vote for Bush; the converse was also true—low-fertility locales favored non-Bush votes. The authors stated that the robust "correlation found in the United States between [traditional family formation] and the percentage of votes for George W. Bush in 2000 and 2004 is to our knowledge *one of the highest spatial correlations* between demographic and voting behavior on record" [emphasis added].[6]

Between 1800 and 1900, the total fertility rate of American women halved from 7 to 3.5.[7] Birth rates continued to decline during the World Wars, rebounded a bit after the Second World War, and nearly halved again between 1960 and 2000, from 3.5 to 2.0.[8] The United States recorded its lowest-ever total fertility rate in 2020, at 1.64 lifetime expected births per woman.[9] The first decline, in the nineteenth century, is generally thought to have resulted from the economic shift away from agricultural and home-based work to non-home-based work, which rendered children a net cost to the household. There is also the fact that as infant mortality decreased in the same time period, families could have fewer births for the same number of surviving children. But demographers debate how to interpret the decline of the second half of the twentieth century. Is it a continuation of the trend that began in the early 1800s or something new, a "second" demographic transition? Some, including Ron Lesthaeghe, began making the case for the latter theory.[10]

These scholars pointed out that rising rates of cohabitation and divorce since the 1960s had not been prominent features of the earlier demographic transition. The first shift, they noted, had favored improvements in the lives of children—marked by better nutrition, health, education, and family stability. In contrast, modern trends marked an unwelcome reversal of that trend. Today fewer than 50 percent of children live with their own two married parents in their first marriage. That number is down from nearly 75 percent in 1960.[11] The scholars also stressed the changing social norms for the pursuit of adult happiness:

> The idea of the *distinctness* of the [second demographic transition] stems directly from Philippe Ariès's analysis of the history of childhood (1962) and particularly from his Bad Homburg paper (1980) on the two successive and distinct motivations for parenthood. During the [first demographic transition], the decline in fertility was "unleashed by an enormous sentimental and financial investment in the child" (i.e., the "king child era" to use Ariès's term), whereas the motivation during the [second demographic

transition] is adult self-realization within the role or life-style as a parent or more complete and fulfilled adult.[12]

The contrast calls to mind the two ways of life highlighted by Hannah: fitting oneself into a narrative of childbearing versus fitting children into a narrative of the self. What would it mean for demographic patterns to be shaped by the quest for a more complete adulthood? To answer this, it helps to examine the history of marriage before modern times.

Sociologist Andrew Cherlin has documented patterns of marriage in America from 1650. His findings converge neatly with the demographers' hypotheses about the second demographic transition. Looking back to the Founding era, he notes that if something like rugged individualism characterized the American temperament, it was a feature of the household rather than the individual man or woman. The household was understood to be self-sufficient and independent, or mostly so, from the larger community, and certainly from the state. This seems to be the kind of individualism that Tocqueville had in mind, an individualism *of the family* with respect to other groups—not an individualism *within the family*. "Within the family, then," Cherlin wrote, "there was little individualism. The husband and wife were engaged in a joint enterprise, struggling to subsist in the New England climate."[13] However, that attitude began to change in the twentieth century. Cherlin describes the emergence of an expressive individualism in the mid-twentieth century that is about the self in contradistinction from the family. Individuals increasingly rejected the idea of fitting themselves into roles in the traditional institution of marriage, such as breadwinner or housewife. They began to look for satisfactions outside of the family, and even began to ask how the family itself suited their well-being. This transition placed a new tension on marriage, a threat from within. No longer engaged in a joint struggle against *merely* outside forces, now the other spouse may be the very force to be defended against. Cherlin explains,

> The shift [in how people viewed their marriages] was part of a broader increase in expressive individualism in American culture—the kind of individualism that involves growing and changing as a person, paying attention to your feelings, and expressing your needs. Expressive individualism encourages people to look inward to see how they are doing, and it encourages them to want personal growth throughout adulthood. It is not incompatible with lifelong marriage, but it requires a new kind of marriage in which the spouses are free to grow and change and in which each feels personally fulfilled. Such marriages are harder to keep together, because what matters is not merely the things they jointly produce—well-adjusted children, nice homes—but also each person's own happiness.[14]

Cherlin's work connects the dots from the pursuit of "self-realization within the role or lifestyle as a parent" to the demographic patterns of the second demographic transition: cohabitation, divorce, and lower lifetime fertility. If the demographers are correct, then expressive individualism, the cultivated habit of adult self-regarding lifestyles, lies at the heart of the current demographic trend in the West. And, moreover, if their correlations are right, expressive individualism, Hannah's "doing your own thing," was a determining factor in the 2000 and 2004 elections. David Brooks was onto something. "The people who are having big families," he wrote, "are explicitly rejecting materialistic incentives and hyperindividualism."[15]

But what if the 2000 election and 2004 reelection of George W. Bush were singular events in American cultural history, decided by a greater focus on family values after the Clinton White House scandals?[16] In 2009, Lesthaeghe and Neidert extended their voting analysis to the 2008 election, where the dominant issues were apparently economic ones. But the correlation between traditional family demographics and voting for the conservative candidate (John McCain, in that election) was "replicated in 2008."[17] Finally in 2017, the demographers looked at the same relationships going back to 1968 and forward through the Trump election of 2016. They showed that "the spatial patterns of … [family demographics] and voting start converging in the 1990s," with a steady and "substantial correspondence after 2000 and continuing through the latest 2016 elections. *More specifically, after the turn of the century, correlations were observed between [0.83] and [0.90] for no less than 5 successive elections.*"[18] These are whopping associations in statistical terms. The authors conclude that "*family behaviour and composition by the turn of the century becomes an excellent predictor of a state's position on the Republican-Democrat continuum for all subsequent elections.*"[19] Statistical controls do little to change the association, they tell us, noting the correlation "*cannot be considered spurious or merely the result of effects of major structural or cultural common predictors.*"[20]

What conclusion should be drawn from the striking association between voting on the one hand and marriage and fertility on the other is not entirely clear. At a minimum, the authors urge caution about supposing that the Trump victory marked a new political era since voting in the 2016 election was consistent with demographic patterns crystallizing since 1996.[21] Indeed, it was apparent to me that Hannah and Esther's families were Trump voters, in spite of living in an area of the Northeast that went overwhelmingly for Clinton in 2016. Esther's husband had greeted us, sporting a classic Jewish beard and hair—and a bright red MAGA hat. Upon our arrival he grinned and asked whether the point of the study was to "make fertility great again."

The causal channel from lower or higher lifetime fertility to a Democratic or Republican vote is only now emerging as a demographic fact pattern. But the research raises the question of just how we come to find certain first principles intuitive. Are our families, perhaps, the source of those reasons of the heart of which Pascal said, "reason does not know"? Where do Brooks's natalists, so unusual and so consequential, come from? Why do some people become like Hannah and Esther, living a life that is "way harder now" without compensation or social encouragement? And what does it mean for them to be the kind of person who can have nine children almost disinterestedly, taking on all their burdens but celebrating their otherness: "I more feel like they are who they are." These are the questions that sent me in search of Hannah, Esther, and dozens of others like them.

CHAPTER FOUR

# *The Future of Humanity—Economic Demography*

"The edict of Louis XVI in favour of marriage,
awarding pensions to those parents who should have
ten, and larger ones to those who should have twelve
children, was attended with no better success. The
premiums that monarch held out in a thousand ways
to indolence and uselessness, were much more adverse,
than such poor encouragements could be conducive, to
the increase of population."

—Jean-Baptiste Say, *A Treatise on Political Economy*

A merica is in the midst of a population collapse. The year
2020 marked the lowest general fertility rate ever recorded—
56 births per 1000 women aged fifteen to forty-four—and
the lowest total fertility rate ever recorded: 1.64 projected lifetime
births per woman.[1] Virtually unchanged since 2020, these trends are
not explained by the arrival of COVID. They are the culmination of
a decades-long implosion. In 1920, and again in 1960, National Vital

Statistics recorded 118 births per 1,000 women aged fifteen to forty-four; there were 87.9 in 1970, 68.4 in 1980, 70.9 in 1990, 65.9 in 2000.[2] A total fertility rate of 2.1 lifetime births per woman is required for a population to replace itself. The CDC reports, "The U.S. [total fertility rate] has generally been below replacement since 1971 and has consistently been below replacement since 2008."[3]

But academics and experts have long overlooked the possibility of demographic collapse. Stanford professor Paul Ehrlich's 1968 blockbuster, *The Population Bomb* (co-written with wife Anne Ehrlich), forecasted exploding birth rates and a grim Malthusian scenario of famine, disease, and premature death.[4] Today it is regarded as a failed statement. Even its authors admit it got the future of food supply and birth rates wrong.[5] Nevertheless, the book helped ignite an international population control movement with appalling consequences—China's One-Child Policy among them.[6] Other academics offered less dismal scenarios, including a theory about alternating waves of growth and decline.[7] But none of the prominent experts predicted what did happen: a steady decline in domestic and global birth rates since the 1960s without abatement. It was an outsider to the elite academy, a Bronx-born son of Jewish immigrants without a Ph.D., Ben Wattenberg, who challenged the prevailing alarmism after more than a decade of statistical forensics. In his 1974 *The Real America*, he argued for a profoundly unorthodox position: that a "birth dearth" had replaced the "baby boom."[8] His analysis received little attention. Continuing fears of population explosion so obsessed leaders and intellectuals that President Carter commissioned the *Global 2000 Report* in 1977, whose findings, now as laughable as *The Population Bomb*, propped up the dire myth of overpopulation.[9]

The tide began to turn during the Reagan administration. Ben Wattenberg was appointed to the U.S. delegation to the Second International Conference on Population in Mexico City in 1984, and he helped to formulate the position that the United States would adopt—that population growth was a "neutral phenomenon" and ought not be reduced through forced measures or incentives when it would fall organically in response to fundamentals of economic behavior.[10] While this position shocked observers at the time, inviting scorn from global elites, it had a growing number of adherents. Michael Teitelbaum and Jay Winter published *The Fear of Population Decline* in the following year, and in 1986 even the National Academy of Sciences raised doubts about the prevailing alarmist orthodoxy.[11] Wattenberg's *The Birth Dearth*, published in 1987, established the heterodox view more firmly and raised more consideration than any prior attempt for the view that population decline, not explosion, would be the future of humanity.

Wattenberg passed away in 2015, but he is remembered as a "prophet" of demographic winter.[12] He had argued early that total fertility rates, rather than crude birth rates, were the best measure for forecasting population growth and decline.[13] Sustained fertility rates below replacement inevitably lead to an aging population, economic recession, depression, and ultimately to depopulation—a decline in the number of people living in a country. Japan has been shrinking since 2010.[14] China experienced its first year of depopulation in 2022.[15] Dozens of countries will follow suit in the next ten years—including Italy, Spain, and Russia. Around the globe, countries that had high birth rates just a few decades ago, such as Mexico, India, and many African nations, have displayed rapid convergence toward the low fertility rates of Japan, Europe, and North America—without population-control interventions. Mexico accomplished a demographic transition from seven births per woman to two in a mere half century. It had taken the United States two hundred years to do the same.[16] South Korean fertility fell from six births per woman to less than three in just eighteen years—compared to the United

Kingdom in a hundred years.[17] Convergence to low birth rates is an iron fact of modern demography.

The political and economic consequences of these trends cannot be overstated. Below-replacement fertility in the United States imperils every New Deal–era entitlement program, every state pension program, and the future of economic prosperity as workers become scarce. Social Security trust funds will be depleted as soon as 2034; deficits are already underway and projected for all future years, to depletion.[18] Medicare Part A will be insolvent even sooner, with its trust fund exhaustion expected by 2028.[19] State budgets are already straining to meet entitlement liabilities. School district finances are bowed under the weight of low or flat student enrollment growth, rising teacher pensions, and state and federal budget cuts.[20] All these and many other programs and institutions will become crippled artifacts of a golden age when we were rich enough, and there were enough of us, to entertain collective transfers from a broad base of young and middle-aged workers to a smaller group of retiring and aged generations. One in six people in the United States is over sixty-five today, compared to about one in twenty a century ago.[21]

Worse, the very transfer programs imperiled by population implosion may have been the cause of their own undoing—deleteriously vitiating a major incentive to form families. Children can be an economic benefit to a household in two primary ways: by providing labor or wages to the family when they are still young, mostly a thing of the past, and by providing support and care for aging, retired parents. A guaranteed pension will tend to reduce the interest in having enough children of one's own to rely on in old age. Births will go down. This is not a mere theory: Italian scholars Alessandro Cigno and Furio Rosati estimated that "as much as three-quarters of the reduction in the total fertility rate which occurred in Italy between 1930 and 1984 can be ascribed to the expansion of the public pension system."[22]

If tomorrow's pension is funded by today's children, when births go down funds available to pay the pension will also go down. Tax-and-transfer pension programs make the economic benefits of childbearing public and push them into the future, while the costs of childbearing remain private and immediate—setting up a free-rider problem. A free rider is someone who receives a benefit without paying for it. In the United States people are eligible to receive Social Security if they contributed earnings when they were younger, but it makes no difference to their benefit if they contributed no future taxpayers. The solution to ordinary free-rider problems is to make the contributions of beneficiaries non-voluntary. Taxation isn't optional. But childbearing is. The disincentive effect of modern old-age programs on childbearing can only be solved in one of two ways: reducing or dismantling them, leaving families to again plan their children with a view to requiring their future financial support if parents cannot save enough; or increasing retirement payouts for women in proportion to how many children they have, not only in proportion to wages they earn.[23] Old-age programs that will be funded in the future by today's children but that reward only working but not having children contain a fatal flaw: the assumption that the propensity to have children does not respond to incentives.

The propensity to have children has been central to economic theory since its beginnings. While Adam Smith, David Hume, and their contemporaries all wrote on population, it was the Reverend Thomas Malthus, an English economist and cleric born in 1766 who is remembered for offering the most famous, though inaccurate, account of the relationship between population growth and the wealth of nations. Beginning with the idea that food is a natural limit on the growth of an animal population, Malthus compared the tendency of the population to increase with the tendency of the food supply to increase. Noting that agricultural production tended to increase slowly and that human reproduction tended to increase exponentially if unchecked, he advanced as a "principle" that human population growth would always tend to outstrip growth in food supply: "Taking the whole earth instead of this island, emigration would of course be excluded; and supposing the present population equal to a thousand millions, the human species would increase as the numbers 1, 2, 4, 8, 16, 32, 64, 128, 256, and subsistence as 1, 2, 3, 4, 5, 6, 7, 8, 9. In two centuries the population would be to the means of subsistence as 256 to 9; in three centuries as 4096 to 13, and in two thousand years the difference would be almost incalculable."[24]

Malthus predicted cycles of famine, disease, and death followed by brief periods of prosperity after those disasters had reduced population. Malthus's *Essay on the Principle of Population,* first published anonymously in 1798, was such a success that he soon claimed it and subsequently released several editions, the sixth and last in 1826. The ideas advanced in the *Essay* appeared to have an unassailable logic. Even if adjustments are made for a larger growth of food supply than his work anticipated, surely no means of subsistence could grow fast enough to supply for exponential growth of the human population. At the root of the Malthusian paradigm is the idea that people are a problem to be solved. Each new man reduces the stock of what is available, competing for resources that come from some unspecified supply outside the system, without relation to human reason, capacity, and ingenuity.

It is hard to overstate Malthus's influence. His *Essay* on population was the single biggest inspiration for Charles Darwin's *On the Origin of Species.* Via Darwin, Malthus gripped the thoughts of racists and eugenicists everywhere, including the front-running progressive activists, politicians, and economists in Europe and the United States. Malthusian-inspired eugenics infected American leaders in the Progressive Era, informing immigration policy and labor proposals such as the minimum wage, pitched to keep "the most ruinous" people from competing for jobs by working for low pay.[25]

But his influence didn't end there. Hitler was obsessed with Malthus,[26] stating in *Mein Kampf*, "The annual increase of population in Germany amounts to almost 900,000 souls. The difficulties of providing for this army of new citizens must grow from year to year and must finally lead to a catastrophe, unless ways and means are found which will forestall the danger of misery and hunger."[27] Hitler's revolting "solution" was as much motivated by his concern to reduce the population as it was by a quest for racial purity. Malthus was also an enormous inspiration for English economist John Maynard Keynes, whose *General Theory of Employment, Interest, and Money* was so influential as to have basically set the framework for government management of the economy since its publication in 1936.[28] Keynes read Malthus with devotion as a young scholar, wrote a dissertation on eugenics in 1907,[29] published a bibliographical essay on Malthus in 1933,[30] and was for a time chairman of the Malthusian League.[31] Keynes scholar James O'Leary remarked that "Malthus deserves first rank as a forerunner of Keynes."[32] Keynes's ideas are now so thoroughly pervasive—taught in every introductory economics course everywhere in the world—that it would be difficult to exaggerate the abiding influence of Thomas Malthus on contemporary economics.

The late University of Maryland economist Julian Simon devoted the majority of his life's work to understanding where Malthus and Paul Ehrlich went wrong. His conclusion: in the short run, resources are limited, just as Malthus assumed. But in the long run, not so. Resource pressures that arise from population growth, far from spelling doom, lead to substitution, discovery, and innovation through human ingenuity. Forego the resource pressures, forego the new sources of abundance. Simon wrote, "Greater consumption due to an increase in population and growth of income heightens scarcity and induces price run-ups. A higher price represents an opportunity that leads inventors and businesspeople to seek new ways to satisfy the shortages. Some fail, at cost to themselves. A few succeed, and the final result is that we end up better off than if the original shortage problems had never arisen."[33]

In a major work titled *The Ultimate Resource*, first published in 1981, Simon argued that "the standard of living has risen along with the size of the world's population since the beginning of recorded time. There is no convincing economic reason why these trends toward a better life should not continue indefinitely."[34] He painstakingly laid out the economic facts, as he put it, against the neo-Malthusian theories, stating, "Minds matter economically as much as, or more than, hands or mouths."[35] The world today supports over eight billion people, with more food per person than in the time of Malthus, and at a standard of living unimaginable to him.[36]

Though Thomas Malthus was as wrong in his day as Paul Ehrlich was in ours, most accounts focus on how they got the future of food supply wrong, failing to foresee spectacular increases in abundance and the resourcefulness of human ingenuity. But just as critically, Malthus and Ehrlich got the future of population wrong too. The equally massive changes in birth rates since the time of Malthus (and Ehrlich, for that matter) demonstrate that they also failed by taking the tendency to have children as fixed and certain. Benjamin Franklin quipped that "nothing is certain except death and taxes."[37] But for animals that reproduce sexually, sex is pretty nearly certain too. And if babies result from sex, then babies are certain too. But neither Malthus nor even Paul Ehrlich imagined the speed with which humanity would adopt a new contraceptive regime with the advent of the Pill—a regime in which childbearing is not the default activity of adult years, but the exception.

In such a world, sex may still be certain, but babies are not. How big, in such a world, is the propensity to reproduce—to have children? Present-day fertility patterns give us an answer—and it is a lot smaller than the one that Malthus envisioned. Children are no longer a necessary by-product of a certain activity. Modern contraceptives "unbundled" sex and babies in the household decision set, making each an isolated, separate object that is subject to isolated, separate human desires. So we can speak of "demand" for children just as we can speak of demand for housing, demand for education, and demand for status, lifestyle, or wealth. Children do not need to be planned *around*. They need to be planned *for*. What Malthus and Ehrlich missed is that when children can be chosen (or not chosen) independently from sexual activity, the standard for the right age to have a child begins to rise. After that degree, after that certification, after that job, after that trip, after that house—after making partner, getting tenure, and so on. And there isn't anything wrong with that, except that time is a rival good, and more time spent on other valuable things necessarily squeezes out time for having children. In short, the propensity to have children responds to incentives like all other human activity.

Countries that were at the forefront of demographic decline—Austria, Spain, France, Italy, the Nordic countries, and Japan—provide troubling models of what we might expect in the United States if the downward trend continues. Falling birth rates appear very difficult to reverse using the standard policy levers of tax incentives and subsidies. Economic demographer Lyman Stone wrote in 2018 that across countries "there is no association between increases in family benefits and fertility.... Nordic-style policies just don't budge fertility all that much. Similar results show up for other Nordic countries. While some policy interventions do have limited, especially short-term, effects, the average Nordic-style policy intervention doesn't do very much for age-adjusted fertility."[38] Sweden's various attempts to increase births going back to the 1970s failed: the country has birth rates indistinguishable from countries that did not have pro-natalist programs.[39]

Similarly, Australia's highly touted $6,000 cash "baby bonus" program caused a temporary increase in births, but by 2020, six years after it shut down, the fertility rate sat at a dismal 1.6, lower than before the program.[40] The reason that generous cash incentives can give an impression of success is simple: women and households that already intend to have children *at some point* rush to have children immediately to "grab" the bonus. They don't have more lifetime births. The apparent baby boom is just a baby "re-timing." More recently, in 2009, Hungary's right-wing leader Viktor Orbán launched the most aggressive pro-natalist policies in modern history, including massive cash subsidies, income tax forgiveness, and even travel and housing benefits at certain birth parities. Hungarian fertility rates have risen from 1.2 to 1.6 in the decade since the program started. But this apparent gain is also likely a mirage of re-timing.[41]

Birth rates are falling because of tradeoffs women and households are making—tradeoffs between children and other things that they value. Tradeoffs enabled by the new contraceptive regime—a "new calculus" of childbearing. It is hard to believe that cash payments will dissuade couples pursuing dual professional degrees to give one up, or to forego a second income. Nevertheless, we are entering a policy twilight zone, with politicians and party leaders getting out ahead of anything that sensible research or a close reading of history would suggest. It has been the universal observation of political economists and historians that fertility cannot be encouraged by policy, even if it can be very successfully discouraged.

Taken together, the political and economic consequences of population collapse provide reason enough to devote time and attention to the women who defy these trends. But a tour of contemporary demographics suggests at least one more reason. A recent global economic report states that "in all countries the number of children women intend to have is far above the actual number they already have...."[42] In other words, achieved fertility seems to be below the level that women report wanting to have. Harvard economists Claudia Goldin and Larry Katz reported the same finding as early as 2002, saying that even while the fertility desires of college women plummeted with the advent of the Pill, neither the 1963 nor the 1973 cohort of college women "had as many children as 'desired.'"[43] The fact that achieved fertility tends to undershoot desired fertility has been euphemistically called the "fertility gap" in the academic literature. A recent study looking at nineteen European countries and the United States finds, "In all countries, women eventually had, on average, fewer children than the earlier expectations in their birth cohort, and more often than intended, they remained childless."[44] Goldin and Katz conclude that the gap "reflected trade-offs [women] were willing to make between family and career."[45] The "new calculus" of childbearing doesn't just leave whole nations wanting for more children. Women too, want for more—about one child more than they get.[46]

Worse still, the fertility gap itself may be related to the phenomenon called "the paradox of declining female happiness." In a 2009 paper, labor economists Betsy Stevenson and Justin Wolfers documented that subjective measures of women's happiness have been declining since 1970, both absolutely, and also relative to men.[47] The scholars stated that "this decline in relative well-being is found across various datasets, measures of subjective well-being, demographic groups, and industrialized countries."[48] They went on to say that the erosion of a "gender gap in happiness" counts as a paradox, since "the progress of women over recent decades has been extraordinary."[49]

Stevenson and Wolfers do not propose an explanation for the mysterious downturn in female happiness, but they argue that it must be driven by "an aggregate change that is impacting women differently than men...."[50]

It may be related to the fertility gap. In a 2005 paper "Partner + Children = Happiness?" a team of researchers found that children contributed to the happiness of male and female partners in different ways. Using gold-standard monozygotic-twin data (controlling for genetic components of happiness), they showed that "children *directly* contribute to happiness for women but only *indirectly* for men through increasing the probability of a current partnership" [emphasis added].[51] Having a sexual partner matters a lot for men. For women too, they found. But having children provides an additional boost to women's happiness not observed in men already coupled. So if birth rates are falling below women's hopes for kids, and if kids matter more to women's happiness than to men's, the paradox has at least one explanation: the birth dearth may be the aggregate change impacting women differently than men.

But the fertility gap is not a rallying cry for feminist progressives who complain about the gender pay gap with nearly single-minded preoccupation. That's a shame. New work by Claudia Goldin, who was awarded the 2023 Nobel Prize in economics, shows how today's pay differentials are often downstream from the same work-family trade-offs that likely lead to the fertility gap in the first place. She explains that the gender pay gap hardly exists when workers begin their careers. It expands over time as women select into more flexible positions to balance work and family. Goldin says, "A flexible schedule comes at a high price [in terms of pay], particularly in the corporate, financial, and legal worlds" where workers are not perfectly substitutable.[52] This means that the gender pay gap and the fertility gap probably have a common cause: the "new calculus" of childbearing, in which babies must be desired for their own sakes if they are to come, evaluated as a separate good among other goods valued by women and men. For most people with ordinary preferences, a mixed bundle—some work and some family—is the solution to wanting two things. The trouble is, that strategy doesn't get you as much family as you might have wanted if the competing good wasn't on offer. It doesn't mean it's bad to have the new option—but it does mean that how you rank the desirability of the goods in front of you will make all the difference.

Ironically, a birth rate closer to women's desired family size would solve the most pressing fiscal problem of the modern state. Having so few babies isn't something that women seem to want, and it isn't something that nations can afford. Any way we parse the facts of economic demography we come to the same point: the regime change characterized by the demographers in chapter 3, from a world where the "issue was to adopt contraception in order to avoid pregnancies" to one in which the "basic decision is [when] to stop contraception in order to start a pregnancy"[53] is not giving women what they want—or society what it needs.

CHAPTER FIVE

## The 5 Percent—What We Did

"One reason why economists are increasingly apt to forget
about the constant small changes which make up the whole
economic picture is probably their growing preoccupation
with statistical aggregates, which show a very much greater
stability than the movements of the detail."

—F. A. Hayek, "The Use of Knowledge in Society"

"There must be an objective basis for the [social]
sciences beside the clarification of method, an ontology
of the mind corresponding to the ontology of nature."

—Edith Stein, *On the Problem of Empathy*

T he project of this book was motivated by a single intuition:
that if a phenomenon is sufficiently consequential, then its
absence must also be consequential. Vaccination for smallpox

was discovered when it was noticed that some people had an uncanny resistance; the deadly effects of the disease were strangely absent among cattle workers and milkmaids.[1] And though most Americans are having fewer children, the birth dearth is not the whole story. Averages hide a lot of variation in the lives of actual women, some of whom are doing something very different. I undertook this research convinced that the study of high birth rates could shed light on the problem of low ones.

Largely hidden from popular view, there are women around the country having five, six, even seven or more children. The Census Bureau estimates that 5 percent of women aged forty to forty-four have five or more children today. This works out to about half a million women, without counting the ones who are older, aged forty-five to fifty, my own age bracket. Five percent of my age bracket also have five or more children today. Nearly 1 percent of each age bracket has seven or more. While the number of women having five or more declined from 20 percent in 1976, it did not continue to fall after 1990; the 5 percent has remained relatively constant since then.[2] "The 5 percent" are strangely immune to the trend toward below-replacement fertility. Why they exist in a two-child world is as much of a puzzle to scholars as is the plunge of the general birth rate to below replacement.[3]

Some posit that women with large families are just ignorant or undereducated, with nothing better to do with their lives but have kids. French president Emmanuel Macron seems to have been thinking along those lines when he declared at the United Nations that women who are "perfectly educated" will not go on to have "seven, eight, or nine children."[4] Macron's view likens women with large families to the handloom weavers of old, unwilling to modernize, destined for extinction with education and time. While he is not very generous to women with large families, there is a shred of reason to his analysis. Education is one of the strongest predictors of low birth rates.[5] Even still, education can hardly be causal. Rather, the evidence points to "career" (or at to least work outside the home) as the mediating variable. Education raises the opportunity cost of foregoing the labor market to have children—both financially and personally. More education means you're more likely to spend time in the labor market, squeezing out time for children. It's work, not schooling per se, that crowds out kids. Macron confuses correlation and causation.

It's also possible, and you hear it a lot, that women who have a bunch of kids are "religious suckers," irrational, or victims of patriarchal religious beliefs. This view supposes that women don't make up their own minds, but follow religious doctrines or leaders mindlessly. Plenty of voyeuristic television and social media fuel this narrative, but there is little research to say whether the eye-popping fringe cases are in fact representative of the 5 percent. I doubt it. In any case, the popular association of religion and big families is based in part on the historical case of Catholics and Mormons. To be sure, immigrant Catholics tended to have more kids than native-born Protestant women, but as in the case of other immigrants, Catholics' birth rates converged to the norm after a generation. Mormon birth rates were higher than average for a century thanks to an assertive pro-natalist ethic and strong socialization, but the differences remaining today hardly merit the continuing strong association.[6] Birth rates for Catholics and Mormons have followed the same declining trend as those of the population at large.[7] Already by 1980, Catholic fertility rates "were about one-quarter of a child *lower* than Protestant rates (1.64 vs. 1.91),"[8] and demographers had announced "the end of 'Catholic' fertility" [emphasis added].[9]

While Mormon fertility rates are still higher than average, about 2.4 children, they are not even a whole child above average.[10] State of Utah birth rates bear this out. Fertility rates in Utah declined over 40 percent from 2007 to 2014 alone—and exhibit some of the largest absolute and relative decreases in birth rates since 2000.[11] Like the "uneducated" explanation, the "religious" one depends on a confusion between correlation and causation. Even if all women today with large families are religious, not all women who are religious have large families. Religion is correlated with total fertility, but not obviously causal.[12] That is, something else mediates the association between religion and fertility. We don't know what that is. So I went in search of the 5 percent of American women quietly defying the birth dearth—to find out why they do what they do, and what they think it means for themselves, for their families, and for the future of the nation.

## The Study

From January through September of 2019, I traveled to eight of ten locations[13] across the continental United States accompanied by my research assistant Mary Robotham (née Bathon). My colleague Emily Reynolds of the Wheatley Institute at Brigham Young University visited the remaining locations accompanied by Sierra Smith (née Breshears). Between four and six visits per location, we conducted fifty-five interviews altogether with American-born, college-educated women who had five or more children with their current spouse. I sought women who would describe their childbearing as purposeful—because we wanted to ask them about their purposes.[14] Our selection process followed established practices for human subjects research under the oversight of an ethics review board at the Catholic University of America.[15] We relied on public announcements in target areas, sometimes online via social media, sometimes in print via church bulletin boards, and sometimes by email through moms' groups or homeschooling cooperatives identified by word of mouth. Interested women were directed to a survey tool to apply for the study anonymously. From the applications in any region, we picked between 5 and 10 percent of the women who applied, making inclusion decisions with a view to obtaining a balanced sample overall in terms of religion, race, and ethnicity. I personally conducted 80 percent of the interviews and Emily conducted the others. We followed identical interview guides. Interviews were held in a location of the subject's choosing, usually in her home but occasionally in a quiet public location. The open-ended interviews lasted from 90 to 120 minutes. Since the women recruited for the study did not constitute a representative sample, it may be said that each subject is herself $N=1$.

I chose college-educated women because I wanted to know what it looked like to face the "new calculus" of childbearing with the difficult trade-offs between work and family and still choose to have several children. How did women think about themselves and their families in light of choosing a different path? Practically speaking, for a small study this meant limiting my sample to women who had faced those types of decisions. An extra benefit of limiting my sample—I could get a cleaner sense of the role of kids in subjects' descriptions of self-identity, marital quality, and life satisfaction without confounding variables from poverty and financial worry, since college education makes those things less likely.[16] Even still, I did intentionally interview women at or below the poverty line in four of the ten regions.

The decision to interview women with five or more children as opposed to four, or three, was somewhat arbitrary, but not wholly without basis. I wanted to find women who were clearly up to something different. I could have interviewed women comfortably above average with three or four. But there is still a chance that such a family might have been merely "trying for a girl"—I myself had three boys before a girl came along. But if you raise the bar to five children, that possibility is greatly reduced. Another value of interviewing women with a lot of kids is that the dose effect of childbearing is pretty high at that point.

As I wanted to understand how women navigated the desirability of children in relation to other important goods, such as self-identity, career, marital quality, and life satisfaction, I hoped that women with the "most" kids—the upper "5 percent" of the childbearing distribution—might illustrate the tensions more clearly.

I want to say one final word about sample selection, as this is the only appropriate place to say it and it must be said: some of what is related in this volume may be hurtful to women and men with smaller families. They may feel judged by me, or by my subjects. This is not my intention, but I know it is a possibility. I apologize for any pain my text may cause. My role as a social scientist is to relay with as much truthfulness as possible what I heard. These stories have not been told, and I make the case for the public importance of this work. My full and real view is that women with much smaller families or no children at all may share the purposes, values, and virtues of the women I interviewed, even though life did not hand them the same opportunities. My five-child selection criterion was designed to ensure that I found out the ways people are motivated to have children against the norm. That required ruthlessly selecting by observed family size, since motives are unobserved. The bar for selection was not designed to pass judgment on those below it. My closest friend, a brilliant legal scholar from a large family in Kansas City, was never able to carry a child to term. After years of trying, she adopted three children at birth, and later another one from foster care. She would not have made "the cut" for my sample any more than millions of women with families of all sizes who nevertheless share reasons of the heart with the women in this book. There are many Hannahs missed by this study.

It is also fitting here to say something about the interviews. I cannot claim to be free of sympathy for my subjects. We made similar life choices. I love my life, am blessed by my children, and would not trade my family for a more prolific career. So I have a lot in common with the women I interviewed, and that may have cost me some objectivity. But my sympathy was rewarded by the openness of my subjects. When sociologist Sudhir Venkatesh ventured into the ghetto streets of Chicago to learn about the urban poor, he was immediately confronted with the problem of being an outsider. It wasn't until he met and befriended JT, a notorious gang member, that Sudhir gained "insider" access to the life of the street.[17]

Rapport makes or breaks an interview. So, in this understudied population, it seemed to me exactly right that interviewers should fit in with their subjects. We didn't want them feeling judged; we wanted them to feel comfortable. And the stories of censure they had faced that we heard in the interviews themselves seemed to validate that approach. Together, Emily and I represented two different religious traditions (Mormon and Catholic), two different generations (she is a Boomer born in 1954, I am a Gen Xer born in 1976). We live and work in two different regions (she the Utah Valley, I the mid–Atlantic Northeast) and two different disciplines (she is a psychologist, I am an economist). But we are both mothers of many: she has seven children, I have eight. We will not be the last scholars to attend to this overlooked group of women, but we were the best ones to be first.

My personal inspiration to take up qualitative interviewing first came from reading Kathryn Edin and Maria Kefalas's groundbreaking *Promises I Can Keep* almost twenty years ago.[18] Elegantly designed and beautifully written, their book focused on stories—but not easy ones, stories it took them years to glean. In one compact manuscript they showed that poor women have babies before marriage because kids offer the prospect of a steady relationship in a universe of broken promises. Kids offer meaning and purpose—even if the timing isn't right. Their book changed the conversation on nonmarital births and revealed the humanity behind the numbers. It also exposed cheap policy solutions for what they are: solutions for the wrong problems. I was still a graduate student in 2005 and very far from an opportunity to do this kind of work. But they demonstrated a mode of social science that was, to use the words of one reviewer on the dust jacket, "a revelation." *Just go talk to people.* From that time on I knew that I would incorporate qualitative work into my social science, disciplinary boundaries be damned. Later, manuscripts by my friend the University of Texas at Austin sociologist Mark Regnerus continued to point in the direction of a project like this one. There are truths that cannot be captured by statistics, no matter how fancy. And these truths are still the purview of social science, whether or not a century of quantification has worked to push them away.

In her 1958 reverie on *The Human Condition*, another Hannah, the Jewish philosopher Hannah Arendt, wrote that "the miracle that saves the world, the realm of human affairs, from its normal, 'natural' ruin is ultimately the tact of natality...." She continued, "It is, in other words, the birth of new men and the new beginning, the action they are capable of by virtue of being born. Only the full experience of this capacity can bestow upon human affairs faith and hope...."[19] Demographic collapse is a statistic, a trend, a "phenomenon." But it is also an apostasy, a despair, a "natural ruin." Social science must have a language for the latter. It must learn to recognize the spirit in the nature and affairs of men. Natality belongs to the domain of the spirit. In light of the seriousness of demographic decline, one might argue that the failure of the social sciences to apprehend the nature and causes of low birth rates amounts to an ipso facto judgment against them. I do not agree with this assessment. But I do believe the relentless secularization of research universities has produced massive blind spots for inquiry into fertility. The ethos for *Hannah's Children* arises from that chasm of missed chances.

# CHAPTER SIX

## Different in Kind—The Biblical Hannah

"Two roads diverged in a wood, and I—
I took the one less traveled by,
And that has made all the difference."

—Robert Frost, "The Road Not Taken"

W hat do they mean to me? Everything. And nothing compares. I almost feel like [saying] this will hurt my friends
that can't have children. *Nothing is as good.*" I wouldn't
meet Hannah, who talked about the "meaning of everything," for six
more months, but Amanda gave a solid preview of what I would hear
in my travels.

Her fifth baby just three months old, she welcomed us into her
home in yoga pants, apologizing for her postpartum appearance. As
if I cared. Her picture-perfect house was situated in a leafy, upscale
suburb of Washington, D.C. Family photos taken on the U.S. Capitol
steps graced her home. Dozens of similarly magazine-ready family
pics lined her entryway, sent by her friends at the holiday season. Pics

she'll take down and replace next year. Surveying the wall of cards, I could see that many of her friends have big families too. Amanda worked in the nonprofit world and intended to go back into it later. She's Mormon, a member of the Church of Jesus Christ of Latter-day Saints, and a motivational speaker. Her flair for the dramatic was not lost on me. When I asked her to say why she chose this life, she gestured at her infant sleeping in a swing and said,

> But for me, if you are a mother, after you've had a baby and it's so physical and it's the most hard thing you've ever done and you can feel their body and smell them and you look into their eyes and it's like it's another person and nobody—fathers are so important—but no human will have a better impact on this soul than I will, as a mother.
>
> So, when I think about all the work, go out and speak or start a charitable foundation that helps people—which I want to do, and I'm going to do—but nothing I ever do will ever be more purposeful, meaningful, and have more impact on a human than giving them a body and then nurturing them as a human.
>
> And because of my religious beliefs, I also know that that relationship is eternal. So, for me, it's the *most worthwhile thing* that I will do in this life.
>
> Is that making sense?

From Philadelphia to Los Angeles, Seattle, Houston, and Denver, the women we met told us that they valued childbearing—and children—more than the other things they could do with their time. Our subjects had more children because they valued them more. More than their careers, their passions, and getting a good night's sleep. They valued them so much that when they sized up their own capacities and found them lacking—in strength, or money, or health—they often prayed to be able to have more children, and their prayers were answered. "They're everything. They're like the purpose," Amanda said. Talking about her fifth, she went on: "The timing of him was just awful. His middle name is Atlas because that is the name of the Greek god that had the weight of the world on his shoulders and that's how my husband and I felt. So, having him is because we really wanted him because it didn't make any sense in our timing. And I think it's because I started identifying what my children mean to me and what I'm doing."

Her words reminded me of an interview I heard with legendary Lakers basketball player Kobe Bryant, tragically deceased in 2020. "I had a purpose," he said, "I wanted to be one of the best basketball players to ever play. And anything else that was outside of that lane I didn't have time for." He told how his purpose helped him summon the grit to finish a game with an excruciating Achilles injury:

> I tell this example, and I think this is the best way to explain it. You know, you have a hamstring injury. You pulled your hamstring really, really badly, you can barely walk, let alone play anything. You're at home, all of a sudden a fire breaks out in the home. Your kids are upstairs, your wife is wherever she may be, you know, shit's going down.
>
> I'm willing to bet that you're gonna forget about your hamstring, you're gonna sprint upstairs, you're gonna grab your kids, you make sure your wife's good, and you're gettin' out of that house.
>
> And the reason is because *the lives of your family are more important* than the injury of your hamstring.[1]

Kobe concluded that the injury was just "another obstacle." It would not determine when he would be done with basketball. "I'm gonna step away on my own terms," he said, "and that's when the decision was made that you know what, 'I'm doin' it.'"[2]

*"There Is Nothing That Will Compare"*

Amanda had her own version of that story. "For me," she explained,

> I had to have another one, even though my body was done, because I thought, well there is nothing that will compare or be more worthwhile, so I want to do it as many times as I can.
> Because when it's over, because this is one part of our life, when that time is over and I miss it, I can say, "I did it, though"—I had as many as I could in the right way, in the way I wanted to... "I did it, though." And no, this charity isn't as fulfilling, it's still good.
> But—"I did it."

The life of her little ones was her game, her purpose—like Hannah's super-reason, the reason that provided a reason for everything else.

The women in our sample ranged in age from thirty-two—born in 1987—to seventy-one, born in 1948. The number of children they had ranged from five to fifteen, with an average of seven. Seventy-five percent of them were white; 25 percent reported something else—black, Hispanic, Asian, Filipino, Jewish, mixed race, or another. They were Baptists, Evangelicals, nondenominational Christians, Presbyterians, Mormons (Church of Jesus Christ of Latter-day Saints), Jewish, and Roman Catholic.[3] Forty-five percent came from families of origin large enough to fit the study sample, with four or more siblings, while 55 percent came from smaller families. Twenty percent had just one sibling growing up, and 7 percent had none. They came from all walks of life, some living in Charles Murray's "super-zips"— the nation's wealthiest, most elite zip codes[4]—and others living paycheck to paycheck in the foothills of the American Rockies. They were musicians, doctors, lawyers, scholarly academics; they were educators, nurses, doulas, graphic designers; they were former aspiring opera singers, lit majors, and social workers. They had not always jettisoned careers—some worked full time, others part time, and some not at all. Their husbands held all manner of jobs: blue collar, white collar, and everything in between—IT workers and engineers; musicians, doctors, and lawyers; teachers and professors, therapists, salesmen, and pastors; music producers and accountants. One dad worked on an oil rig—and one stayed home full time while his wife worked as a pediatrician. The moms had kids ranging from adulthood down to Esther's ten-day-old baby. Some of the moms we interviewed were expecting. Two who had fully raised their families were already enjoying grandchildren—lots of them.

Their narratives taught us that falling birth rates are not a cost problem, at least not the way we normally think about a cost problem. The relevant obstacle to choosing a child, they said, was the cost of missing out on the other things you could have done with your time, your money, or your life. The expected cost of raising a child wasn't the main thing—because that cost, future and uncertain, was also in terms of what else you could do with money in the future. The women in our sample at every income level talked about giving up other things to pay the expenses of a child. They also talked about the expenses being a lot smaller than people thought. And about unexpected turns of fortune that had made paying for children easier after they had them. But the "price" they really leaned into, the real "cost" of children, was what they had to give up. They talked about sleepless nights. About giving up comforts, plans, hobbies, status, a clean house. Giving up alone time. Giving up achievements. Giving up freedom. Giving up meeting your own needs. "Having children and parenting is all about living for someone else, not yourself," one mom named Jenn opined.

These costs, they granted, were big and consequential. But they saw those obstacles the way Bryant saw his hamstring. They would not be defined by what they had missed out on because the reason for missing out—the purpose—was so much bigger than the losses. Yes, the losses meant parts of yourself had to die, they said, to be unrealized, as it were; but they were only dead for a time. They would be transformed, brought forth in the crucible of suffering, and redeemed by the very children they would bear. They would give up something of themselves, but their children would give it back to them with interest. If these notions seem biblical, they are. The women defying the birth dearth had a reason to have children big enough to give up their lives more than once or twice, and that reason came from deep trust in God, or love for their spouses, or love for their children—often, all three. Like Bryant had said, "When the game is more important than the injury itself, you don't feel that damned injury."[5]

And anyway, the losses weren't the end of the story, they insisted. Their children were their greatest blessings. They told us in so many words how their children had saved their lives, saved their marriages, and saved their souls. By their own accounts they had been saved from immaturity, loneliness, selfishness, and uselessness. And so had their kids and their husbands. The women told stories of healing and growth. "We've seen miracles," Esther told us. The upshot of all this? They believe the nation would be happier and more virtuous if we spent more of our adult lives taking care of children—and if our children grew up with more siblings.

Taken together, these narratives sorely challenge family policy pre-scriptions, particularly pro-natalist policies. Cash incentives and tax relief won't persuade people to give up their lives. People will do that for God, for their families, and for their future children. If you want to find a policy angle to improve the birth rate, expanding the scope for religion in people's lives is the most viable path. Make it easier for churches and religious communities to run schools, succor families, and aid the needs of human life. Religion is the best family policy.

### *"I Have Asked Him of the LORD"*

Chapter 1 of the first book of Samuel tells the story of Hannah, the favorite but barren wife of a man named Elkanah. The Bible tells us that Hannah was distressed to be without child, wept bitterly, and prayed to the Lord at the sanctuary in Shiloh: "Oh LORD of hosts, if only you will look on the misery of your servant, and remember me, and not forget your servant, but will give to your servant a male child, then I will set him before you as a nazirite [consecrated to God] until the day of his death."[6] The priest Eli observed and heard her plight. When she returned home, she "conceived and bore a son. She named him Samuel, for she said, 'I have asked him of the LORD.'"[7] Hannah's story is so intricately bound up with being graced to receive Samuel that her name itself comes "from a Hebrew word meaning 'He (God) has favoured me (i.e. with a child).'"[8] So Hannah means *God has blessed me*. Our own Hannah had said confidently that "each child brings a blessing into the family, comes with their own source of divine flow of sustenance, and it brings benefit to the family and to the world." The biblical Hannah, keeping her promise, left the young Samuel in the temple after he was weaned, to be in the service of the Lord.

The second chapter of the first book of Samuel opens with the Song of Hannah, read on the first day of Rosh Hashanah and the inspiration for one of the greatest prayers in Christian history, the Magnificat of Mary the Mother of Jesus, uttered upon Mary's greeting of her cousin Elizabeth when the latter was pregnant with John the Baptist. Hannah's prayer begins, "My heart exults in the LORD; my strength is exalted in my God" and continues, "The LORD makes poor and makes rich; he brings low, he also exalts. He raises up the poor from the dust; he lifts the needy from the ash heap, to make them sit with princes and inherit a seat of honor."[9] Hannah's song connects the fate of the nation of Israel to the gift of Samuel—through whom, unknown to Hannah, King David would be anointed. Mary's prayer echoes Hannah's: "He has brought down the powerful from their thrones, and lifted up the lowly; he has filled the hungry with good things, and sent the rich away empty. He has helped his servant Israel, in remembrance of his mercy, according to the promise he made to our ancestors, to Abraham and to his descendants forever."[10] Holding her newborn, our own Esther, steeped in these traditions, said serenely,

> You know, my understanding is that all blessings come from God. And the three big blessings that we talk about in Judaism are children who bring us pride and joy and follow in tradition, good health, and financial sustenance.
>
> I don't feel like you could ever have too much of any of those things. These are blessings. They're God's expression of goodness. We can put up roadblocks to not get the blessings, but those are blessings.
>
> And sometimes we need to ask God to make ourselves proper vessels to receive the blessings, but those are the biggest blessings.

We are told that Hannah was rewarded richly for bringing Samuel back to live in God's service. "Then Eli would bless Elkanah and his wife, and say, 'May the Lord repay you with children by this woman for the gift that she made to the Lord.'"[11] She who had been barren went on to have three more sons in addition to Samuel, and two daughters—*Hannah's children.*[12]

In the chapters that follow you will read about a small but not insignificant demographic group: women in contemporary America like the biblical Hannah who see their children as their purpose, their contribution, and their greatest blessing. Women like them may never be a majority, but their stories have profound relevance for the domestic policy questions related to demographics, as well as for the deeper public dialogue about lifestyle patterns, individualism, rootedness and connectedness, deaths of despair, the character of our political order, and the future of the American experiment. The women in our study gave witness to another sort of reply to the crisis of the West. Not a plan, or a policy, but a message—the salvation of the world is in the birth of a child.

For all of his insight, David Brooks got one thing wrong. He argued that "the differences between [natalists] and people on the other side of the cultural or political divide are differences of degree, not kind."[13] That can't be right. People who think you can't have too many children are certainly different in kind. One mom named Ann, with six kids, told us about a time when Nigerian contractors came into her home, saw her family, and exclaimed that it "was the first time they saw in America something that they wanted." Only 5 percent of Americans agree with them. That's a difference in kind. What you are about to read is a narrative account of that difference. The testimonies from mothers we met, only a fraction of which appear in this volume, make up the evidence collected from the first qualitative study of the 5 percent of American women quietly defying the birth dearth. And while it isn't an exercise in "doing economics," it will inform a lot of what economics will be doing in the future.

# PART TWO

*How It Started—Motives*

CHAPTER SEVEN

## "It's Just a Wonderful Life"—Kim, Twelve Kids

"I didn't want any children.... [My husband] wasn't sure either."

—Kim, mother of twelve

‎H‎arris Park Bible Church sits in the Elk Creek valley on the southeastern side of Mount Rosalie in the Colorado Rockies. We drove there from downtown Denver early on a cold, drizzly Sunday morning in June. Kim Probst[1] had invited us to attend the 10:00 a.m. service preached by her husband, Pastor Alex Probst. We were thrilled.

The drive itself was memorable. Mary and I made the trip in a rented Jeep, stopping for a cup of coffee and a bag of sugared donuts at one of those tiny drive-through-only locales that you find in the West. The Jeep was almost as big as the coffee joint. Before the pit stop we had dropped into a Catholic mass at Saint Mary of the Rockies in Bailey, where I very much regretted not having a warmer coat and a pair of boots.

We got waylaid between donuts and the final trip into Elk Creek when we lost cell phone service and had not thought to download our map in advance. We had to backtrack, save the map, and start again. The drive up from the 285 into the valley made us wonder more than once if we were on the right track. When we finally got to the tiny church, at least fifteen minutes late, we deliberated if we should go in. I think I almost opened the door three times. The last thing you want to do as a researcher is draw attention to your presence.

Fear of missing out finally overcame my aversion to making a scene. We opened the door and stepped quietly into the vestibule area where, off to the side, we could see plates of wrapped food intended for the community potluck that Kim had invited us to share with the congregation after the service. Moments later, one of Kim and Alex's children was sent to greet us, and we were welcomed warmly and ushered into the worship space where their dad was preaching on King Nebuchadnezzar. I couldn't help but think that Pastor Alex Probst looks a little like what I think an Old Testament king might have looked like: tall and stocky, strong and bearded, with a cheerful grin and a big voice. His wife, Kim, is petite, relatively short, and youthful looking, with medium-brown shoulder-length hair. Both have a cheerful, open demeanor.

Kim and Alex talked to us about their twelve children, whom they explained that they homeschool, ranging in age from five to twenty-five. They believe the Bible is "the only infallible, authoritative Word of God."[2] Once, Kim told us, when they were at the grocery store, "Somebody said, 'Are they all your kids?' which is what they always say. And then they said, 'You should be spayed'—*to my husband.*" Between them, the Probsts defy almost every stereotype you might have had about a big Christian family homeschooling in the foothills of the Rocky Mountains. But you'd have to get past appearances to know it. Take Alex's background. When we saw that he boasted two advanced degrees, we assumed these were in divinity studies or religion. Our mistake. The Probsts explained that Alex has a master's in engineering from McGill University and a Ph.D. in computer science, mathematics, and statistics from the Colorado School of Mines—both elite programs—and that Kim had double majored at McGill in music composition and education. They told us how they both became fluent in Portuguese: Alex was raised partly in Brazil, and Kim traveled the world growing up going on sabbaticals with her academic parents—professors of organic chemistry and political science, respectively.

Kim recounted how she had been raised in Montreal, Canada, in an agnostic, unreligious family. She recounted, "There was a cultural clash...because we got engaged on my eighteenth birthday and then my parents discouraged us. I mean, I love them, and they are wonderful, but they didn't want us to get married...until I had finished my degree and maybe a master's. Maybe further is what they were really envisioning."

Kim described how she and Alex had wanted to honor her parents by getting their consent before marrying. When "they basically said no," Kim and Alex began living together instead, and "they were fine with [that] which is kind of funny...you know. But we wanted to get married, so I kind of wish we just had. We've since changed our mind about [cohabitation before marriage]."

### *"We Just Fell in Love with Babies"*

Kim related that sometime later "we went to them as living together and said, 'We would like to have children. Can we get married now?' And they said no. And there were even like 'economic sanctions'—like if we got married then I would have to pay for my whole college." She laughed and explained that it took getting pregnant to force a change: "And then I came to them and said, 'Okay I actually am pregnant,' which I was...and then they were like, 'Okay you have to get married in six weeks.' So, all of a sudden, that was okay. So, then we got married.... It was in the middle of my music degree and he was in the middle of his engineering degree."

Their first child came soon after.

She brushed off the idea that they wanted twelve at the time. "No," she says, "I actually told my husband's mom that I didn't want any children.... Alex wasn't sure either." It came in stages. After her first, Kim told us, "I had an IUD put in right away and then I didn't like it. I felt it. I had an infection and had it removed within like a month. *And we just fell in love with babies.*" Later in the interview she described it as "a joy that's more internal" and doesn't need validation. Kim elucidated: "The world is not always very positive. Sometimes they are. You get surprised. But sometimes they really aren't. So, it's not like I'm seeking what the world thinks. It's more like you're happy with what you're doing and with your kids and time together.... I don't care what anybody else thinks. My joy doesn't come from that."

So, Kim and Alex had a second baby, a girl. "At first, I had said I only want two [kids]." But then "we came to know the Lord." She explained:

> We were living in Ontario...but basically nobody shared the gospel with us. I was reading the Bible myself and actually I was afraid. I went into a Bible store and bought one. We weren't going to church, but we actually felt like we wanted to get married in a church. We just felt like that's what you should do. And then we started attending the church. Actually, they said they would marry us if we attended the church because they were like, "You need to know about what you're making your vows into." So, we did.

Neither one of us knew the Lord at the time; we did go and church became part of our lives. So, we went to a church, and I had started reading the Bible. One day I pulled over my car as I was just thinking and pondering what to do. I was about to finish my degree and I said, "I know there's a one true God. Reveal yourself to me." And that's what He did.

And I started reading His word and I didn't understand it and I was like, "I'm college educated. Why can't I understand this book that's supposed to be so simple?" So, I just prayed and said, "Well, I know you wrote it so help me understand it. Give me the wisdom." So, I took my questions to God and that was that year. It was '98 and then she was the first one born after that.

She told us that Alex had a similar change of heart, though initially he was put off by her intense conversion: "He has a funny story about me being [too] Christian...and then finally I read the verses about the quiet and gentle spirit of the wife, and I totally stopped [nagging him about religion] and served him and loved him and cooked for him and did stuff. And then he was like, 'I got my nice wife back!'"

She laughed and continued: "And then the Lord himself spoke to him, so he came to know the Lord that way."

As extraordinary as Kim was for her family size—the average woman in our study had half the number of children[3]—and for the intensity of her conversion, her story was like many that we heard. Our subjects, in all but one case, attached religious significance to their childbearing. And a significant portion of them described a conversion or reversion[4] on the way to those convictions. Like our Hannah introduced in chapter 2, Kim was one of the many women we met who had not wanted children at all, or had wanted a small family, before a religious change of some kind. We heard dozens of comments like this from Tina, who said, "Well, we wouldn't have started having kids if the whole Catholic thing hadn't come into question. So that was a big part of even us entering into parenthood." Each of our subjects, however, had a story to tell about just *how* their religious experiences influenced the decision to have so many children. The path was never straightforward.

This stands to reason. Almost all the women in the United States with big families are religious—in our sample it was 100 percent. But not all religious families have lots of kids. Some scholars point to frequency of church attendance as the mediating variable, as women who attend church more tend to have higher ideal family sizes and completed fertility.[5] For Kim and Alex it was more isolated, and personal. Embracing a lifestyle of childbearing, she said, felt like a private calling "for us individually, for us uniquely, not as something that others need to do." She expanded:

> God started working on my heart when my husband and I came to know the Lord. [Alex] tells the story that he felt like the Lord putting on his heart that God needed to be in charge of the amount of kids in our family, and I had the same impression, but he [didn't know that] and was afraid to come and tell me that because how do you tell a wife that? [She laughed.] So he came and told me that and I was like, "I've been feeling the exact same thing." And so, we did and just ever since, whatever, open to it all the time.

She told us later, over a plate of potluck lunch, "Well, it's just a wonderful life. I feel very fulfilled. I love them. We love each other.

And now they're people. They're growing into adults that I love, that I enjoy, and they love each other.... So absolutely no regrets about that."

Many of our subjects shared Kim's attitude of letting God "be in charge of the amount of kids," but Kim's particular approach, "whatever, open to it all the time," was not the norm among our subjects. When I probed for more, she clarified: "[Letting the Lord be in charge] means not using contraceptives and it also meant, for me...normal spacing of 18–24 months and usually we were just excited to have the next one and we tried. So, it was probably active trying, not just 'we'll see' but really wanting."

Kim and Alex had come around to seeing children as desirable for their own sake. They viewed childbearing as something God was doing for them. She even hoped for another. "They're a gift," she said, "I mean, I would like one more." If her approach to family planning was not the norm in our sample, her expressions of joy were 100 percent typical. For Kim, the enjoyment of her children early on seemed to be an additional motive to have more kids: "We just fell in love with babies."

Kim described children as something of an experience good. Other women concurred. "You can't really know what it is until you experience it. You fall deeply in love with your first baby," said Moira, a mom with five in the Northeast. "Experience goods" is the economists' label for goods whose total costs and benefits cannot be fully assessed in advance, before being acquired and experienced. An example would be a vacation in a new place, or a meal at a restaurant. You have a rough idea of what you're getting, but you must make the decision before you know the most important things about it. So, the idea that the benefits of having children turned out to be more substantial than expected came up frequently.

Before we left Harris Park Bible Church, we met most of the members of the church who had come in for the potluck—and almost all their children. Kim finished her story about the "you should be spayed" comment in the grocery store. "Other people around us said, 'Do you know that person?' And they supported us, and they were kind, and the guy started yelling about carbon footprints and stuff like that." With a shrug, she continued, "That was the strangest [thing] probably. And that someone could be that aggressive about, yeah, it's funny that they're worried about that now that we're at 1.7 [kids per woman]—it shouldn't have made everybody scared about a carbon footprint, which ours is very small because we buy used clothes and drive used cars and take the smaller vehicle."

### "They Feel Useful"

Despite buying used things, Kim didn't seem to fixate on the deprivations of her life. She didn't even seem to count them as missing. Instead, she talked about the unseen benefits of having so many kids, for her personally, and for her family.

> Up until I had four or five who were under [age] 5, that was the hardest time. And then they help. I don't know if you've ever read *The Rabbit and the Gold Shoes*?[6] [The mother rabbit] took the time to train and care for her children when they were young and everyone was laughing at her and saying, "You can't do anything." And then when [the kids] are older and they could do all the chores and help, they want to.
>
> There's nothing wrong with that. They contribute and they feel much more positive, welcome. They feel useful. You see suicides around in people who don't feel useful.

And so it's funny because our culture wants to not have kids do [hard] stuff so that "they can have a childhood" but then when they don't feel useful then they don't know what to do. They feel depressed.

The moms we met were universally enthusiastic about the effects on kids of growing up with many siblings. But among our subjects Kim's phrasing stood out: "They feel useful." She surmised that being needed protects children from depression. She's probably on to something. High levels of social connectedness reduce symptoms of anxiety and depression in children and adults.[7] What's more, loneliness causes irritability, depression, self-centeredness, an increased risk of premature death—and is "emerging as a public health problem."[8] So the organic connections arising from a houseful of siblings present a welcome contrast. Rosalie, a Filipino mom on the West Coast, remarked that "just to be with each other I think for them is a big deal, and I never realized that because I only have one sibling. But for them, when I start moving them [to different rooms] somehow, they magnetize to one room even though you're trying to give them more space—they find it better to be sardines, because that's what they want." Rosalie continued, echoing Kim's sentiments: "Now we see so many kids who are in depression, and committing suicide, because they're on social media looking at what so-and-so did and what I didn't do, and they're comparing. I don't think my kids have time to compare. They just have time to play, they have time to be with one another.... You don't really need much when you have a big family, because you have each other. And that overfills the cup, so to speak.... You don't need stuff, you just need one another."

Kim rounded out her comments about connection by suggesting, to my amazement, that American schooling tends to undermine family ties rather than support them.

Some of it is just putting your kids in school for eight hours a day, honestly. Because your child, you bring them to the school. The kids cry. They want to be with their parent, and they feel rejected almost. It's not the normal thing to do to bring your kids to school, but they start getting connected to their teachers instead, and they change their teachers every year.

So, they learn not to connect, and if they connect at all, it's with their peers instead, which can be good or bad. It's often bad.... And even the siblings. They're in different grades and they learn not to play with anyone that isn't their exact age.

Kim believes that the forced separation in schooling—parents from kids, and kids from siblings—has led to a failure to connect at home, and to less satisfying family relationships. "You don't put the gift on the shelf," she said, implying that unexamined habits of ordinary life might be the overlooked roots of larger personal and societal problems. We choose disconnection without thinking about it, she seemed to say—and then lament that our teens struggle with a fractured life. "It takes vision and imagination" to see it doesn't have to be that way, she reflected. "Because the problem is every movie we see—it's like there's these teenagers and they're rebellious and they hate their parents. They don't want to be around them. You just have to say, 'That's not what I believe. [We] can have something different.'"

Kim linked her experience in the grocery store checkout line to a "coldness to children in general" arising from our tendency to avoid disabilities. "If we abort or don't welcome kids that have special needs then our heart of compassion as a country, everything changes, I think. Because if you see a family, if they have one special needs kid in that family, it changes the heart of everybody."

She spoke from personal experience. Her second daughter is autistic.

"But if you go down south like to Brazil or Mexico, they welcome families. They are [like], 'Hey, there's your baby!'"

Soberly Kim said, "It's not always like that here." Nevertheless, she is optimistic about the future. She believes that hitting a cultural rock bottom is planting seeds of change: "We went through existentialism, nihilism, and we see where it went. I mean, look at the school shootings. People are asking now, 'What is there? It can't be that I just become dust.' And I think people are not satisfied with that and they're asking. *And there are answers. . . .* It's a result of just letting the culture play out and see what's going on. You can't say you don't see it."

Her hopes are driven in part by what she described as rapid growth in the network of Evangelical churches and Christian home educators in the Rocky Mountain region: "God is doing something really special up [here in the mountains]. A lot of us are feeling that there is a big revival coming in. All the churches up here are feeling that. . . . And we're all coming together and things, praying for each other."

But it was hard for me to resist feeling that part of her hope comes from her great marriage. Earlier in the interview, Kim had laughed off the suggestion that kids were bad for her marriage: "Not at all. My husband's part Brazilian, so he's very romantic and we're not shy. So, he'll hug me or kiss me, and the kids think that's fine. But when we have time together, we do guard our time together, so sometimes we'll all watch movies on our bed together but then it's time for the kids to go up and we just tell them it's time for kids to go out. So we never have a problem with that. We guard our time. We like that—it's a big part of our lives."

Their warmth spilled over. There was no coldness in the parlor of their humble family church. From potluck lunch to grinning children, we were blanketed in care and affection that chilly morning. By the time we left, the sun was out, and I almost forgot that I had been cold at all.

CHAPTER EIGHT

## "You Believe It's Good"—Miki, Five Kids

"We were either going to have to move apart or we were going to get married.... [Kids] was the deal-breaker for us."

—Miki, mother of five

We asked all our subjects if they knew from the beginning, when they met and got married, that they wanted to have a lot of children. For Kim the answer was no. For Miki, eight months pregnant with her fifth, the answer was a hard no. Japanese American, Miki had grown up in California. Chin-length black hair fell loosely around a middle part, framing her round youthful face and dark eyes. She wore a loose cardigan over a plain maternity tee shirt, a scarf draped effortlessly around her neck.

Miki recounted being asked recently, in an elevator at the university where she teaches, whether she was expecting her first. She shrugged. "I said, 'No, it's my fifth' and they said, 'Oh, you don't look like someone who has five kids.'" With an inquiring expression, she continued, "I thought, 'What does that person look like?' But I've heard that several times. What is that comment about?"

Miki's journey began with an unlikely academic romance. Although neither she nor her future husband was religious at the time, religion quickly came to the forefront:

> So, we met in graduate school, in [elite college town]. We were at the [university] and we both came in as master's students together. At the time, he was not a practicing Catholic. He was very adamant about not being a practicing Catholic having grown up Irish Catholic. And I was not raised with any religion but then as we started dating, we started basically arguing about fertility because he is one of seven kids.
>
> And his sisters that he's closest to both have large families and I wanted to be an academic and had gone to a very liberal women's college and had some strong opinions about how many children I was going to have.
>
> So, when we were dating we started the conversation about how many kids we would have if we were going to get married. We argued about [it] . . . for two or three years.

Despite having scorned Catholicism, at least one tenet of her husband's former faith stayed with him, Miki explained:

> We talked a lot about fertility because even though he had rejected the Church for like ten years, he grew up with a worldview that he couldn't shake, which was that he had a certain idea of what sex was and how fertility worked and what it means to a relationship and a marriage.
>
> So even if he wasn't a practicing Catholic, he was not going to budge on that. Which, that was where the conflict

came in. So, it was one of those things where, to me it was linked to our marriage because we were either going to have to move apart or we were going to get married. That was the deal-breaker for us.

Her husband had come from a large Irish-Catholic family that, following the official teaching of the Catholic Church, didn't use artificial birth control. While he had fallen away from the creed of his youth and his family, he had made that particular belief his own—ironically, since the teaching on birth control is often touted as a reason that people leave the Catholic Church (and, among those who stay, hardly anyone bothers following the teaching). A mere 13 percent of weekly Church-attending Catholics believe that contraception is morally wrong. And among Catholics who attend Mass less frequently, a bare 6 percent view it as morally wrong.[1] This data highlights just how unusual Miki's husband was. Who leaves the Church but *keeps* the prohibition on birth control?

She recalled that it was difficult working through these questions within the secular bubble at her elite research university. "I remember one of the things I struggled with when I was at [grad school] was when I was having these arguments with [my husband] there were very few people to talk to about that who wouldn't perceive him then, if I complained about it, as being crazy or oppressive or something." Amidst this confusion, remarkably, Miki and her husband began going to church together. She described their religious evolution:

Yeah, so part of what happened was I think on his side, as we got more serious, he thought, "Well if I'm going to be seriously involved with this person and wanting to start a family with her, how am I going to raise my kids?" And that took him back to the Church.

And for me it was partially this intellectual thing because at the time I had been working in Holocaust Studies and I was doing a lot of work in ethical theory. So, I was thinking, I need something intellectually consistent.

So, I had an adviser who had actually converted from Catholicism to Judaism, but he was very supportive of the idea that you might convert to a religion and so there was that, but it was also inevitably because [my husband] was Catholic. And so, I ended up converting [to Catholicism] in graduate school before we got married.

Like other intellectual converts, Miki resisted the change that she knew she wanted to make.

I fought it for as long as I could, basically. I just recently read [Evelyn Waugh's] *Brideshead Revisited* and I hadn't read it for a long time and Julia at the end made so much more sense to me now because my conversion was not a surprised-by-joy moment.

It was definitely this experience of painfully having to let go of myself and the ideas I had about the world around me basically because I couldn't argue with [my husband].

I tried, I tried really hard. And part of it was not entirely intellectual. But I realized I can't actually defend most of these ideas that I [used to] have because they are mostly feelings.

I asked her about what she meant by saying of her conversion that it was "not entirely" intellectual. She replied, "There's that intellectual part of me and there's this huge part of me that I consider to be very Japanese, which Japanese people are extremely superstitious.

And that was actually a huge help. We're also very hierarchically minded.

"So, I remember the Church hierarchy was no problem for me because I had a friend who was converting from Protestantism at the time. And he was like, 'No.' But I was like, 'Jesus seems like a weirder idea to me than just a pope.' I'm okay with authority."

Miki described how she came to accept the resurrection of Christ:

[But] what is this crazy thing you're trying to tell me happened?

I tipped over [to the Jesus stuff] when I decided to embrace the notion of mystery. I was like, "Actually I can do that." That is something that is deeply ingrained in me that there are things that I can't explain rationally.

### *"I Can Be Open to Three"*

At the beginning of Miki's relationship with her husband, religion came up mostly in the context of their disputes about kids. But slowly it became more of a focal point in their lives. So I asked if she finally knew when she converted that they would have a lot of kids. She answered, "Oh no. We were not going to have a large family. I was like, 'Look, you're one of seven. Are you expecting to have seven kids?' And he was like, 'No, definitely not.' But he was like, 'I don't know, maybe like three?'

"And I was like 'I was thinking maybe one or two.' But I thought, 'Okay, I can be open to three.' So, it wasn't until things moved along that it became something that we thought about."

When she said she was "open to three," Miki could have spoken for most of the women in our study. Their reasons for wanting children more frequently led to a posture of *openness* towards children, rather than to one of *demand* for children. Kim used the language of "just whatever, open to it all the time" and Miki found herself "open to three." Demand in the economic sense represents a desire for a specific quantity, a want in relation to a perceived need. For instance, I *want* to own another pair of shoes; I *want* to have two cars.

Miki's conversion didn't leave her wanting lots of kids. Instead, she still wanted about the same number of children as she had wanted before—"maybe one or two"—but it left her *open* to a third, and committed in a minimal sense to not closing the door on kids permanently. The Church's "official" position on birth control (which Miki and her husband adopted before marriage) does not allow sterilization; but it does allow, and even encourages, prayerful consideration about the number and timing of children, and the use of natural means to space children.[2] This is usually called natural family planning—even if the word "planning" carries connotations that many women in our study explicitly rejected. Medical scholars refer to natural approaches as "fertility awareness–based methods," or FABMs, since they help women know the days on which they are likely to conceive—approximately six days per cycle.[3] Evidence-based FABMs, unlike calendar-based methods,[4] are just as effective as hormonal contraceptives.[5] Thus a couple can be in agreement with the Church but still want a limited family size: this is exactly where Miki was when she and her husband got married. For her, being "open" to a third meant merely not closing the door. It wasn't a preference for a third. And it was that sliver of openness that made refinements in her thinking—second-order desires—possible later on.

Miki's openness could not have been more different from Kim's "whatever, open to it all the time." At no stage did Miki arrive at a blithe "as many as possible" attitude. Nor did she ever use the language of "letting the Lord decide." At forty-two she is unlikely to consider having another child, even if she is able. She still finds herself amazed by the five that she has. At one point she exclaimed,

> I was just emailing my sister about this. I still cannot believe that you can make people with your body. I was just like, "How crazy!" No matter how many kids I have, it gets crazier and crazier, I think.
>
> Earlier I never gave it much thought. I never thought about being pregnant in my twenties. It seemed horrifying. But now, I think the more I experience it, the whole thing becomes more mysterious each time. It's amazing. I can't believe it works.

The posture of openness to more children was commonly expressed by the women in our sample, even if it operated differently for each of them, as for example for Kim and Miki. Women in our study had adopted a lifestyle of never say "never"—even if they were actively avoiding children when we spoke to them. They often struggled with the language of being "done," which they saw as problematic. Beth, nine kids, in the Pacific Northwest said, "The babies came. We thought it was great. It was a miracle. You know, they just show up. There was no calculation anywhere." Rosalie, also with nine kids, put it this way: "I think in the back of my head I know whatever happens, God will provide, if it's a monetary thing, or a mental chaos, God will give you peace.... As a family, as a big family, we really work together, and that in itself has kept us going. So, there hasn't been a question to like, 'That's enough.' No, I think we're so far still open to life." June in the Southeast, eight kids, said, "And I think we began to see life differently and we enjoyed our children so much that it seemed like after we had one rather than closing the door we said, 'Well, let's go for another one.' So really it was one at a time."

The implications of "openness" for fertility surveys and social research are profound. Questions in surveys aim to get at one or more of the following aspects of the fertility issue: the number of children wanted, the number of children expected, and the number of children a respondent thinks ideal for a family to have. Women with a posture of "openness" to another child will have difficulty answering every one of these questions. First, it may be that their own "wants" are highly variable. If Miki had been asked how many children she wanted in year one and again in year ten of her marriage, she would have said one or two the first time, and then later four or five. Expectations are similarly problematic for these women—either variable (changing with their current desires at different times) or undefined, since women who practice "openness" may be unwilling to use current desires to benchmark future expectations. Finally, ideals don't work at all. A woman who believes that "whatever happens, God will provide," like Rosalie, or that the Lord is in charge of her family size, like Kim, will be unwilling to provide an ideal number for herself or any other family. Ideal is what God sends, or what they are led by God to choose over time—no less, and no more.

## "A Conscious Decision to Shift My Energy"

Three things eventually moved Miki to be open to more than three. The first was related to the progression of her academic career. She said, "It has something to do with the timing of when I left the tenure track. At that moment I did make a conscious decision to shift my energy away from research. Not that I don't do research, but I certainly don't do as much as I was trained to do. But that energy doesn't go away. So, I think there is a substantial amount of that that I have now channeled into having a family."

When asked if she experienced that shift as a loss, she responded, "I did at first. I mean, I think it wasn't until after the third [baby] that I was like, 'This is how I'm challenged.' But at first it was a hard adjustment."

The second factor was the addition of social supports to her life, at work and at home. When she and her husband had moved to their second university position (when she left the tenure track) they "finally had an employer that was really supportive of [their] having a family." Soon after, they moved to a parish and neighborhood with lots of big families. "Just imagine having community support for a family, which we had never had before. So, part of it was that, but it also started to feel like a norm. I had never had that as a norm where there are large families around." She stressed the contrast with her graduate school community. "So then moving into [this] neighborhood and meeting other moms [and] wives who find it a struggle to be married and have kids but where that's just life and it's not endless suffering, made it easier because you have people to talk to about that and understand. And so, it's less alien, the idea that, 'Oh right, it's actually hard,' but also there's a joy in that."

Miki expounded on the importance of social support: "When I think about it I often think in the context of my experience as an academic that I've been forced to move places away from family. I think about how difficult it is to have a large family if you are afloat somewhere, and increasingly that is what is happening to people. They move away for jobs. There's something about the way we live modern life that is making this."

She's not wrong. The U.S. Census Bureau reports that the average American relocates more than eleven times in a lifetime, compared with an average of four times across most of Europe.[6] Miki connected the experience of being physically uprooted with less support for having children. If she and her husband hadn't moved into their particular neighborhood because "we were looking for a school for [my son]," Miki isn't sure whether they would have gone on to have their fourth and fifth babies.

But there was something else she mentioned, a third factor influencing her choice to have more children: "The other thing about being friends in this community—and this happened between the decision to have three and four—in communities where there is more fertility you also see more mortality among children and babies. And that used to terrify me. But now seeing that that is a part of life makes a huge difference in terms of my being able to accept life and being more open to it. Because one of my good friends when we first moved here lost a young child and seeing how that worked out made me much more open to life in a way that I hadn't anticipated."

Here Miki touched on a theme that we heard in various permutations: that the direct experience of loss of life—a miscarriage, or a death in the family—could lead to greater appreciation for the possibility of new life. One of the moms we interviewed, Jenn, lost her first baby to miscarriage. She told me, "I think because the Lord took the first one away, I was really able to treasure the second one." And Mary, who lost her fifth, a little boy, to leukemia at age four, said, "Life is never as precious as when you realize how brief it is, how fragile it is." Mary went on to have several more children after losing him.

It would be well beyond the scope of this book to cover the relationship between child mortality and fertility more deeply. They generally are correlated, with lower fertility occurring where there is lower child mortality, and vice versa.[7] The usual explanation is a simple overshooting story: with high child mortality, a family that wants four kids needs to have five or six to ensure a final count of at least four. As the French historian of childhood, Philippe Ariès, points out, before modern medicine, "There were far too many children whose survival was problematical. The general feeling was, and for a long time remained, that one had several children in order to keep just a few."[8]

Miki's story seems to illustrate an alternative theory also touched on by Ariès. She says that the idea of losing a child "used to terrify" her, and seeing another woman endure the loss, in a Christian community, made it a "part of life" that she could accept. Objectively, and I can say this as a mother, the idea of losing a child *is* terrifying. One response to that fear is avoidance. So Ariès separately traces out a line from high infant mortality to callous indifference towards children, of a piece, he says, with the ancient Roman and Chinese exposure of infants. Indifference, he argues, obliterated the very concept of childhood and was a "direct and inevitable consequence of the demography of the period."[9] Families did not become attached to their infants, he claims, and entire cultures did not develop a concept of childhood, or children, as lovable. It is hard to love what you must repeatedly lose. But, Ariès points out, this indifference was in deep tension with Christianity, which provided both a rationale for lovability—the child made in the image of God—and the hope of immortality: "He has conquered the grave."

### *"This Is Actually My Life and What I Believe Now"*

Returning to the subject of her conversion, Miki told us, "Over time I gave up the idea that [the religious conversion] was an experiment basically. Like no, this is actually my life and what I believe now." But as an academic she felt the sting of being judged irrational:

> Thinking about how I used to think about large families, the few large families I knew [growing up] were either Mormon or Catholic or Filipino.... I don't fit that type of

stereotype that I used to have, and there's something to be done with showing people that it's not all one thing.

I definitely feel that [stereotype] at work a lot. . . . I think it has something to do with the fact that, I mean, it's more of the sort of rhetorical structure of saying you [have kids] because you're Catholic, which implies again that blind adherence rather than that you've actually considered something. Not that it's all about choice—but that you're actually doing something because you believe it's good.

She continued:

I guess part of me is annoyed as an academic. . . . I remember when I converted there was a lot of pushback from my colleagues in the grad program because they were like, "Oh, someone brain-washed you." And I was like, "We are supposed to be a lot more . . . than this."

It is just insulting on that level, like, "Oh it's because you're blindly following some kind of thing." Because part of me is looking at my colleagues and I think, "You have no idea the level we are operating on constantly because we have all these small children."

She laughed. And I laughed. She's right—they don't know. How many people have firsthand experience juggling three or four little ones and two jobs? She recalled, "We had our first when we were both still in grad school and we were both writing our dissertations. . . . [But] at [an elite university], that was not a thing.

"People did not have kids. Faculty didn't even really have kids."

Her program may have been an extreme example, but across academia it certainly seems as if women with children are hard to find. None of the senior-ranked women in Harvard's economics department had children when I was taking classes there in the late nineties. Only 40 percent of female faculty are married with children within twelve years of Ph.D. receipt, compared with 70 percent of their male colleagues.[10] And while women make up about half of the tenure-track faculty in the United States, they fade at higher ranks, shrinking to just 40 percent of tenured faculty, and only a third of full professors.[11] Miki remembers a valued female adviser who was kind enough to share her doubts about the typical academic paradigm: "When I went to tell her I was pregnant she was really supportive. She said, 'You know, it's really hard for women in academia. You either have kids before you get a job, or you wait until after you get tenure.' And she had decided to wait, and she said, 'You know, I don't know if I made the right decision.' She was really helpful to talk to."

This seemed ironic to both of us, since there are some ways in which academic life is more compatible with childbearing than professions where hours are not so flexible and work is not aligned with kids' school schedules. But Miki notes there has been a "very rigid narrative about what success in academia looks like, and it's wrong." She continued, "I teach a 2-2 because it means I have a heavy administrative load. My schedule is very flexible.... [So my husband and I] are able to actually provide childcare for our kids because we wouldn't be able to afford to otherwise."

Though Miki started her family later in life than I did, our careers in academia have been similar. Like her, I have a deep sense that I was made for it. But the academy as established is not "made for us," and that is a reality as painful as it is ever-present. We've both made personal sacrifices to remain attached to an academic life. "It's true," she said, "that if I did not work that would probably be better in a lot of ways for our family—but I would be so personally unhappy. The balance is not as clean as that." For my part, the opportunity to *begin* a tenure-track job at the age of forty was an unexpected blessing. Now, as my kids are growing up, it's like a second spring. The children need less of my time now; and I can redirect my energies into other forms of fruitfulness and creativity.

Miki envisions the possibility of "retraining people in academia to think about what success is and what is fulfilling in an academic career." She thinks that the trend toward maternity leave for faculty is "moving in the right direction." I'm not so optimistic. Gender neutrality has made maternity leave prematurely stale. When leave can be taken by both mothers and fathers, men use the time to write papers, advancing toward tenure. Women use the time to care for their infants—widening the publication gap that makes it harder for women to get tenure.[12] It's not hard to see that gender neutrality and feminism are on a collision course, within the academy and without. Women in academia who want to be open to children may need to build new institutions, or to seek work at universities that value motherhood as part of what makes you suited to join the ranks of the senior faculty: teaching, research, and motherhood. But so far, that's uncharted territory.

## "It's Just Surprising How Traditional Things Have Turned Out to Be"

Thinking back to her relationship with her husband in grad school and their academic lifestyle as a couple, Miki thinks their work life takes its toll on their marriage. Children complicate that picture, she said, but she wouldn't "isolate it to just having children."

> When my husband and I think about what causes tension in our marriage, it's work actually. And obviously having kids is part of that, like how do you balance both of our

careers and the commitments we have? I don't know. We tend to think actually work is the bigger strain.

Developing this thought, she reflected on how kids had made her marriage better:

> I think our marriage has gotten a lot stronger and it's a lot easier for us to negotiate our marriage actually since we had like the third kid.
>
> It took us a long time to figure out what the marriage was with our jobs and with our kids. I think the key thing for us was that we stopped trying to act like we could implement the ideas we had before we started having kids in our marriage after we started having them. We had this idea like it was going to be fifty-fifty. And we had this idea that we were going to prioritize my career.
>
> And then none of that worked and in different ways we had to figure out how to let go of all of that and we've had to embrace things that seemed stereotypically gendered. And not that we're hugely ideologically opposed to that, but it's just surprising how traditional things have turned out to be on some level.
>
> And so, I think that the increased flexibility [helped], which intellectually we knew was necessary, but we hadn't had to actually do that before. I think having more kids forced us into that on some level.

CHAPTER NINE

## *"Family Is . . . Eternal"—Shaylee, Seven Kids*

"I think I always knew I wanted to be a mom and I think being an older sibling in a large family probably played a part in that. I know religion does too."

—Shaylee, mother of seven

Women like the eponymous Hannah and like Kim and Miki never wanted to have several children, or any at all, before a conversion of some kind. Their stories, to be sure, were some of the most memorable we heard. They helped to dispel certain misconceptions. Women with large families didn't necessarily grow up in what we would call pro-natalist, fundamentalist, orthodox, or otherwise *serious* religious families. They weren't always from large families. And every one of the women we interviewed, without exception, whatever background they came from, had very clear reasons why they had chosen the life they had chosen. Nobody stumbled into it. As Miki said, "You're actually doing something because you believe it's good."

But a downside to starting with these narratives is that it risks
overemphasizing the role of religious conversion. For many of our
subjects, like Hannah's friend Esther nursing her ninth, the choice to
have many children was more organic, like "the cloth we're cut from,"
as another mom said. So now I'll introduce one of the many women
who were more like Esther, a woman who grew up in a big family
and always envisioned herself having children. If her story seems
more ordinary, it's only because the women like her don't think of
themselves as doing anything extraordinary.

At thirty-seven, Shaylee would still strike you as a young mom if
you met her. She was a special education major in college, loves children, and seems very put together even though she admits to having
"plenty of meltdowns and bad days and exhaustion and times when
I wish my kids would listen better." That's no surprise. She had seven
kids in fourteen years of marriage, all still under the age of twelve at
the time we interviewed her. She was holding her youngest, a
four-month-old baby boy, when we got together for the interview.
The favorite dumb comment she gets about her kids? "I get a lot of
like.... 'Do they all have the same dad?' So, my husband's Filipino,
Hawaiian, so we expected all our kids to look like this [points to her
baby], like dark skin, dark eyes, dark hair. But our first and third
kiddos are blonde and blue-eyed. Which was a surprise to us. But it's
just funny that people...would be comfortable asking that of a complete stranger." She laughed.

Shaylee met her husband at church. They are Mormons, members
of the Church of Jesus Christ of Latter-day Saints:

> We met at church in a single adult ward. So, I grew up here
> [in a state in the Northwest]. His family moved here from
> California while he was serving a mission for our church.
> So, he never went home to California. He just came to [my

city] where he had never really been before. But I'm forever grateful. It's not really an exciting story. We just met at church. I was the choir director. He started coming to choir. So, I was grateful, and we liked each other, and we met in October, started dating in December, got engaged in May, and married the following September. So little less than a year. Nothing too crazy.

We both came from big families. He's the third of eight and I'm the second of nine. So, we've both experienced life in a big family, but we've never had an aspiration to a certain number or we've just kind of taken it one at a time. I never saw myself having just one or two children, but I was never like, "I need to have nine kids," you know? We just kind of take it one at a time. . . . It's always been a prayerful decision and one that we've not taken lightly.

Shaylee is understated about her life choices. But she is actually an outlier. Despite the stereotypes, seven kids isn't exactly average for the Church of Jesus Christ of Latter-day Saints anymore. Mormon families are still larger than the national average, but the difference is much smaller than it was when I was a kid. Back then, Mormon families had a total fertility rate of about 3.06 children per woman compared to 1.76 for the nation.[1] Today's Latter-day Saint adults grew up in families of about 4 children. In contrast, 57 percent of Mormon adults surveyed in 2016, mostly Gen Xers born between about 1965 and 1980, had 0, 1 or 2 children. What's more, most Mormons today think 3 children is ideal, and the median Mormon family size is only about 2.42, or half a child above the national norm.[2] Utah, with a fertility rate below replacement, like all other states, nearly leads the nation for the biggest decline in birth rates in recent decades.[3]

But the collapse of Mormon fertility isn't remarkable. Birth rate convergence to below replacement is a global phenomenon. What *is* special is Shaylee's path. She credits her family background, in part:

> I think I always knew I wanted to be a mom and I think being an older sibling in a large family probably played a part in that. I know religion does too.
>
> I had a lot of little siblings that I got to help take care of.... We were in a car accident when I was young and...three of my siblings passed away. So, I don't know that [my parents] would have had all nine kids if that hadn't happened. They had six and then three of them died and then they had three more.
>
> And so, there's kind of a big gap between me and my younger siblings. And then my dad had some pretty major health issues when I was in high school, which had my mom—instead of being like a stay-at-home-mom piano teacher—suddenly she was scrambling to [be the bread-winner], it was like a total role reversal for them. Things were different and I think I had the opportunity to... [help] a lot more at home than I think I would've needed to if that hadn't happened. And it wasn't bad. I liked it.

Here Shaylee touched on that mysterious connection between child mortality and births that Miki had first raised for us. We didn't probe for why Shaylee's parents had three more children after the accident, but the thought that the three were mere replacements seemed absurd—especially since Mormons believe that family is eternal. Those kids weren't lost to them any more than their living kids. It seemed more likely a result of valuing what they had lost more. Shaylee also mentioned a point that Kim had raised: growing up she was needed more than normal, even for a large family, since her dad became disabled. She didn't look back with resentment. She "liked it" and believed that it shaped her character in a fundamental way.

### *"My Greatest Joys"*

Like many moms that we interviewed, Shaylee feels the weight of the religious stereotype. She tried to lay out—as a contrast—her central reason for action: the joy she derived from having children.

> I don't know… our church has the stereotype false reputation that… the church like says you should have as many kids as you possibly can or that birth control is bad or something. And that's not the case. I don't feel like I've ever been pressured into having children.
>
> I feel like I've just, that I've experienced that, that my greatest joys growing up happened in my family and my greatest joys in my adult life have happened in this family that we've created that it's, it's just *good*.

She mentioned that religion played a part, and we asked what she meant. She told us,

> Our church teaches that family is sacred and that it's eternal. That it's not just a relationship that is for here and now on this earth. We believe that our spirits live on after our bodies die and that our family relationships can also continue after that, which especially, is a truth and a hope that has been

really important in my life ever since my siblings passed away when I was a kiddo. Like that was something that my parents found a lot of hope and comfort in was that belief that our families go on and that they're just important.

Compared to the women like Hannah, who found childbearing at the end of a long search for meaning and purpose, Shaylee's story seems straightforward, almost boring. She isn't struggling with her past. She hasn't left the faith of her parents. She didn't have a big "wham" moment when it hit her. She and her husband are both living a life similar to the lives of their parents. They were happy growing up, they loved being part of a big family, and they wanted to do the same. And they didn't meet any major roadblocks along the way. Women like Shaylee came to having a big family organically. It is where they were from and where they were always going.

Growing up in a larger-than-average family was common in our sample. Just under half of the women, 45 percent, came from a family with enough kids to be in our study (five or more). If you include subjects from a family of origin of four kids or more, that percentage rises by a third, to 62 percent.[4] A large family of origin is the demographic I belong to. Like Shaylee, I'm the oldest of nine, and like Shaylee, my greatest joys as a child were when a new baby came home from the hospital with mom and dad. Nothing else I experienced as a child came close. Not by miles. Shaylee and her husband felt the same way and set out to recreate those joys in their own family: "I feel like motherhood is the hardest thing I've ever done but the most rewarding thing I can imagine doing. I enjoyed working with other people's children when I was doing special ed, that was really rewarding too. And I like that I've been able to take things from that, from my education, and apply them in my home. But I feel like it's true joy here."

*"A Matter of Prayer"*

Shaylee didn't have an "aspiration to a certain number," but she didn't have Kim's attitude of "whatever, open to it all the time." She described it as a process of discerning "one at a time," waiting and praying to feel ready for the next. Her discernment process was a version of the most common approach we heard from our subjects.

> We just, we've always made it a matter of prayer when we felt like, assuming that we wanted our kids to be about two years apart, right around the time our babies [were] about one year old, we start praying and asking the Heavenly Father if we should have another kid. And like at first I know that I'm not ready to have another kid, or like especially before we start that process, I'm like, oh my goodness, I'm so deep in this new babyhood and I can't even wrap my brain around having another child and there's no peace, and there's no, like, it's only fear in those moments.
>
> But then as we get further down the road and make it a matter of prayer together and independently and or individually and, and just keep thinking about it and talking about it and I don't know, eventually peace comes and we just feel good about it. Or we each have our "Aha!" moment, which sometimes comes separately, but we ended up in the same place where we're just like, "Yeah, we're doing it again."

So after a baby was born, Shaylee always knew she wasn't ready to have another one right away. There was "only fear" at that stage. Most of the women we spoke with used some form of family planning, natural or otherwise. But then, she says, time would pass, and she would take it to prayer. Would she get to peace about it again?

Six times after her first child the answer was yes. When we spoke to her, she was still figuring out if there would be an eighth—but at that point she didn't think so. Regarding the growing sense that she and her husband might be finished having children, she said, "We've been doing a lot of reading and a lot of praying and a lot of talking and we feel like [the] Heavenly Father trusts us to make this decision.... It's up to us. It's always been up to us." The whole process—from peace and readiness to conception and birth, to *not being* ready and only fear, to praying and feeling ready again—was entrusted to God's providence, but with her active participation. She had to feel ready. If readiness never came, it would be a sign her family was complete.

Shaylee's language of readiness paralleled Hannah's, as if they had been sisters from another mother. As Hannah explained,

> There's like this moment that *that* happens after every kid. There are definitely clear moments where it's like, "I am so not ready yet." And you're nursing or you're having issues mentally and you're like, "I am not ready." And there's a vessel that is not ready for it.
>
> But then there's a shift. And... after that, that's usually when I would be like, "Okay, I can handle this again." Or it wasn't even me saying that it was God saying, or putting, that thought or those feelings into my psyche. But "I'm ready for this."

Hannah, a forty-four-year-old Jewish mom, and Shaylee, a thirty-seven-year-old Mormon mom, with seven children each, never walked in the same social circles. Hannah lives in the Northeast, Shaylee in the Northwest. They never listened to the same preaching. Shaylee always wanted kids. Hannah only came to it later in life. They were interviewed by different researchers. But they described their discernment of family size in nearly identical terms. Each wanted to be ready and made that their prayer. Each trusted that God would answer by putting a desire into their hearts different from the one they were presently experiencing. They aimed to fit their own desires for children into God's plan for them. These are a kind of second-order desires.

Although they didn't use the language of "openness" that Kim and Miki used, Shaylee and Hannah are up to something similar. They take the approach of "never say never," but there is a very clear standard for conceiving another child. They have to feel ready. They seek God's guidance. And there is mild anticipation, wondering whether God will change their own sense of readiness. They defer ultimate planning to God, but they trust God to govern sweetly. If God wants to give you the gift of a child, he will give you the desire for the gift in his time. But he will wait for your free collaboration.

### *"I Love Seeing Them Care for Each Other"*

Shaylee was visibly shocked when we asked her why she thought birth rates were so low among her peers. "That blows my mind. I haven't thought about it. It's new information to me. I don't think I can answer that question." Although she feels that her family stands out, she didn't know they were quite so different. Still, she isn't always sure how she wants to present herself in public: "There is a sense of pride. [And sometimes] I don't want to talk to people about it. [But] sometimes I want to like shout it from the top of someplace very high that I have all of these beautiful miracles, and sometimes I'm a little bit more, almost even self-conscious about it, but it's just the best thing, I don't know.... I love seeing them care for each other, I think that's my favorite."

She wasn't kidding. Shaylee mentioned her children's care for each other again and again. She continued:

> That's one of my favorite things about having all of them is seeing them interact with each other when they're not pushing each other's buttons or, I mean, I don't want to paint this picture of like always getting along and listening and being kind. They have those qualities in them, but that's not always what they choose.
>
> But I love it. I want for them what I have...all of my siblings, they're like my favorite people in the world. We're not all the same. And we have our moments when we drive each other crazy too. But we stay in touch and when we have big family gatherings, it's like it's just big and comfortable and there's somebody for everybody and, and I want that for my kids and they're getting it.
>
> I love that it worked out that my two oldest are boys and then we have our three girls and then our two youngest are boys. So, everybody's got buddies. Somebody close. And, and now that we have a bigger spread in ages, our older kids, well even the younger, older kids take care of the little kids. I feel like, it's different than if there were only one of one or two of them.

Shaylee believes that having a lot of siblings fosters virtues in children organically. Not just, she insisted, virtues regarding things. But more complicated virtues like compassion and taking responsibility for the vulnerable. She continued:

> They're learning things like of necessity. They're having to learn to share or to be patient or to be independent or to

be more compassionate and look out for each other and be more responsible and take care of each other and of themselves more than they would if I...were there to give them everything they need.

And that's something my mom taught me too, has told me sometimes when I'm feeling bad about or stressed about not being able to...do the twenty minutes of reading with every single kid for school every night when the afternoons are so short after school.

She said it doesn't all have to come from me. I mean if I can get my eight- or six-year-old to read to my four-year-old for twenty minutes, they're both reading for twenty minutes and I'm keeping somebody else alive or in a clean diaper in the meantime.

She elaborated, describing a recent trip to the playground:

I love when I take them to the park, and they all spread out and go their separate ways.

Just a couple months ago I turned around and saw my eleven-year-old standing up on this rock-climbing wall, like scanning the park and counting the kids.

I didn't ask him to do it, but he's just kind of taken that role upon himself that when we go out places, he's like carrying my two-year-old on his shoulders now or counting to make sure everybody's there, or my eight-year-old hears [the two-year-old] crying in his crib and goes and gets him without being asked.

They're still kids and they're still playing and doing things, but they're also, I think, being given opportunities to love and serve and care and be good at independent play and things that I think are going to be good for them in the long run, that they don't have to be entertained by a grown-up.

I love it. I love it and I'm excited about it for them.

So, Shaylee's eleven-year-old keeps lookout at the playground and carries the toddler on his shoulders. And her eight-year-old checks up on the two-year-old in his crib without being asked. This might not sound ordinary, but in Shaylee's universe this is what ordinary looks like. "I mean, kids can be happy in any family situation," she continued:

> But I feel like . . . the things they're experiencing in a large family are going to help them grow and flourish. That the ability to play independently or to help themselves when they need help, you know, to go get the stool and get the cup out of the cupboard and do it because mom can't come and do it right now.
>
> I mean, it's a small thing right now, but it's a larger principle. I think that it's going to hopefully be a positive when they're in their older years. They need love. They need opportunities to work, opportunities to love other people and try to put themselves in other people's shoes, which is a constant conversation we're having here.
>
> I don't know that they're internalizing it at this point. Work, love, family, support.

*"Focusing Together on These Beautiful Babies That We've Made"*

It isn't all roses. Shaylee admitted, "My body's falling apart now." Seven kids takes a toll. "I miss sleep," she volunteered. She wished she got more breaks. But she differentiated between "a bad day and life being bad. Life," she insisted, "is not bad. Life is good." She continued:

> Even if [I'm] having bad days I feel like I am exactly where I need to be.
>
> I don't feel like they've made me lose who I am. I feel like they're helping me become who I need to be.
>
> It's just this is the most important thing I could be doing with my time right now. And so, what if I'm not sitting down on the couch reading as much as I used to? I can listen to my audiobooks while I fold laundry, or maybe I'm not going on long arduous hikes like I used to, but I can enjoy watching my kids enjoy the short, less intense hikes that we go on and look forward to them enjoying that in their lives.
>
> I don't feel less because I'm just a mom.

Shaylee seemed to want to say that her children made her more by challenging her to grow into who she needed to be. And she highlighted that, whatever the obstacles, those obstacles weren't as important to her as what she was doing.

She applied the same logic to her marriage. The pressures of children, she argued, meant that her marriage had to mature through the hardships, but the result was greater closeness, greater trust. She said,

> There's supposed to be highs and lows and good and bad in everything. Like that's part of the plan. That's part of what makes us…able to appreciate the good.
>
> I mean, do we spend less time like focused on each other? Sure. Do we go on as many dates as we would like

or used to? No, no we don't. And we need to be more purposeful about that.

But I mean...like when we had our miscarriage before we had all of our kids, that was one of the most difficult things I've ever been through in my life. But through that my husband and I grew to know each other in a way that we didn't know each other before and we grew closer to each other and we like developed this new, trust in each other and depend, not dependence, but you know, like we knew that we were there for each other and that we were going through this thing together and so we grew closer together and to [the] Heavenly Father and it was a really sad thing that also had blessings attached to it that benefited our marriage.

And I feel like having kids has been the same way. Like sure. There are negatives. Like we don't, I don't know. We, we haven't traveled the world and...we never get away.

But we're doing this incredibly important and rewarding thing together and we're both in it 100 percent and we're working together, and I feel like we wouldn't know each other as well or be as close or trusting of each other. This has made our marriage stronger than it would've been without it.

Yeah. Like, sure. It's not as centered on us but centered like [on] focusing together on these beautiful babies that we've made.

Shaylee was adamant that she has no regrets: "I wouldn't, if I had it all to do over again, I wouldn't change a thing. It's a worthwhile sacrifice." But a sacrifice nonetheless, she said. "I'm told that I will sleep again...that's probably one of my least favorite things...feel[ing] so frazzled all the time. But they're worth it." Of her baby, her seventh and the one she thinks might be her last, she told us, "He's an angel baby by the way. He is God's gift to me. Like, 'Thank you for being willing to do this again...have an easy baby.'" I knew what she meant. My last baby was an angel too, a little bit of heaven on earth.

CHAPTER TEN

# "Strength and Conditioning"—Terry, Ten Kids

"We got married the summer before my
senior year...and really, I mean, I just knew
I wanted to be a mom."

—Terry, mother of ten

A nother of our subjects who arrived at motherhood organically was Teresa, who goes by Terry. We met in the front living room of her house in a Denver suburb, within close walking distance of her family's Catholic Church. She was thirty-seven weeks pregnant with her tenth. Tall and athletic-looking, she wore leggings and a tunic top. It turns out she had been a college volleyball player, a setter. In a big easy chair with her feet up, wide smile, no makeup, Terry was a natural beauty. We had her full attention except for occasional commotion in the house caused by a miniature poodle puppy.

Terry grew up the eldest of eight kids in a happy family with parents who had a tremendous impact on her view of family life, as she related. More than any of our subjects, she shared specific stories about "things her parents would say or do that influenced" her view of things. One such example related to the grades she received in school growing up:

> My dad would, I'm going to cry, he would do things, we'd get our report cards [voice quivers]—and he's alive, I know, I'm just crying because it's a good memory. He would get our report cards and we all went to Catholic school. And he would expect us to do our best and he'd be proud of us if we got an A but he would make it clear that, if we did our best, that was okay.... But then he'd get to the character section, and it would say "plays well with others" and you could get "exceptional," or "satisfactory," and so on.
>
> And he'd be, "Okay!" And he'd get everyone's attention. "This is what I care about, is your character." And he'd go through and say, "Whatever [name], 'is respectful to the teacher—exceptional'" [and so on].
>
> He was the one that was always saying, "I'm the richest man in the world because I have all of you." So, I grew up with that.

If Terry seems overly emotional, it's good to remember that she was thirty-seven weeks pregnant when we talked. I've cried over far less at that stage. She had powerful memories about her mom too.

> And then one time my mom, so I graduated from [eighth grade]. And they were sending me to [a college prep Catholic high school]. And I did very well, got straight As and all that stuff.

And I just remember she picked me up early cause the eighth graders are done early, so it was the rare occasion where I was alone in the car with my mom 'cause there were seven younger than me and she just, she pulled over and just parked and I was, "What are we doing?"

Terry's mom was about to tell her plainly that she (and Terry's dad) didn't view education as a waste even if Terry wanted to have a family instead of a career:

> She's, "I just want you to know that we're sending you to a Catholic prep school and we're so proud of you for how well you do academically, but we just want you to know that you can, you can do as much as you want with your education, but that we really, we really would value that if you became a mom and all of that education wouldn't be wasted, it would contribute to you as a mom, and remember that your vocation is more important than your career. Because we're worried that [high school name] might be too, career oriented."

I was struck by the story because of the number of college women who have approached me over my teaching years with an opposite story: parents who counseled their daughters against marriage after college because all they had poured into high-priced tuition. I can still picture the women with loving boyfriends, eyes brimming with tears, who have approached me saying, "You have a Ph.D. *and* a family. What can I tell my parents, so they won't be upset if I want to get married?" I never really know what to say. But I hear it enough that it must be common. Enough to know Terry's mom was different. Terry continued: "It just really stuck with me. . . . I guess I kind of took that comment particularly and that's how I kind of approached college.... So anyway, I think that they definitely instilled in us the idea that there was more value in family and being open to life and, your vocation, than there was in money you made or whatever."

### *"Fulfilling to How I Was Made"*

Terry used language about being "open to life" that we heard across the interviews. But she also used the language of "vocation," which seemed to capture a lot of what our subjects thought was happening in their lives. Terry felt that having children was a particular calling in her life, much the way that a craftsman or an artist might say that their work wasn't a mere choice, but a fulfillment of something placed in them. She said later,

> All the natural ideas of how our bodies are made [have] only confirmed the faith that I already had. I guess I'm talking about natural law in the sense of, God created me a woman to have babies. I am made to do that. And it's, I think particularly for me, *I* am made to have babies, I've been healthy and had great pregnancies and, I've been able to give birth and all that stuff.
>
> And so, if you're always asking... "God, what do you want me to do with my life?" Or even just, "What are the clues written into my being that tell me what you want me to do with my life?" So, you may not even believe in God. You may just realize that this is fulfilling to how I was made, or who I am.

All of this helps to explain why, for Terry, finding a husband who wanted a big family was part of the deal. It's what she really wanted, and she knew it. "I remember him calling me [for the first time] over the break, Christmas break . . .we ended up talking for three or four hours, but I remember the first thing I said was, 'He's from a big family and wants a big family.'" So Terry, who had two very Catholic parents, who had gone to Catholic schools, who was serious about staying Catholic, found herself dating a guy who wasn't Catholic because they were on the same page about hopes for a family.

> Dan came along and, I remember even after our first date, it was just, we both knew right away and then we picked out a name, "Therese." We started dating in January and this was maybe March. I was, "Well, if we have a baby girl first, we have to name her Therese...." I was taking French and I said, "Therese is my French name." And Dan was, "Therese, I love it."
>
> And so, for the whole rest of our dating time and being married [it] was, someday we might have a little "Therese." And we did.[1]
>
> So, it was very, it was pretty instant. And I was surprised by it because he wasn't Catholic.... And I remember just praying and saying, "Okay, God, what is going on?" And just feeling a sense of peace that, that it would work out. And it did.

It is difficult to get into words the exact kernel of Terry's story, in terms of motive. Religion is certainly there: her close relationship with God, her determination to understand what God wants her to do with her life. But what emerges more than anything is a picture of a young woman convinced that having a big family was going to be "fulfilling to how I was made, or who I am."

*"It's Almost underneath Religion"*

We didn't find that type of feeling exclusively among women who grew up in big families. Ann is a great example. Ann was a "dropout" from a Ph.D. program at Columbia University. She had a brilliant college career, got married after her first year in graduate school, and had her first baby in the summer after her second year. "I got a master's and then dropped out of the Ph.D. program.... It was a hard decision. But I don't really regret it." When we interviewed her, she had been married for nine years and was expecting her sixth baby. Ann grew up with exactly zero siblings. She was an only child. "I can't remember a time where I didn't think children were a great blessing, so that's always a good thing. But there's also this sort of natural component. I think it's almost underneath religion, like a human thing where you're listening to your body, listening to the scenarios around you, and not necessarily trying to force it, just letting it come."

The phrase "underneath religion" seemed to get it about right. Ann and her husband were Catholics, but she didn't spend a lot of time talking about her faith. It was more like a question of conscience for her. "I don't feel like we're obliged to have large families, but I do feel like it was sort of the thing that was set in my heart and the thing that was placed in front of me. And if I didn't follow it, I think I would feel bad about that." She reminded us of Kim, who felt the call to have a lot of kids was "for us individually, for us uniquely." Ann continued:

> Let's see, for me personally, even as a small child I had these pencil organizers with little acorns drawn on their faces and there would be a big family, like every time there would be a big family. And that was in some contrast to a very small family. And that was before, like, we went to

Mass, but we didn't pray, we didn't do things. I didn't really know about the Faith.

So, I think this is for me, sort of, pre-religious, if that even makes sense. And then certainly reinforced by, I mean the Church believes that children are a great blessing and that just sort of fleshed out a great language for what was already obvious to me.

I asked Ann if she thinks she and her husband are "done." Six kids in nine years is a lot. She looks tired.

No, we aren't done yet. . . . I guess I don't feel done. I kind of feel like we've won the lottery, right? I have a husband who makes a good income that allows me to stay home. I have pretty good emotional and physical and psychological health. We have a great relationship. I don't know, I feel like we've been given the green light.

I guess I see additional children as a greater blessing than travel, than career, than—I mean, I hope we still get to do some of those things, but I think this is more important. Or a greater good, I guess.

For Ann, with no siblings, and Terry, with seven, motherhood felt like who they were long before they were mothers.

Terry continued her story, telling us about how things had gone so well with Dan, her non-Catholic "from a big family and wants a big family" guy, that they dated through college and got married before her senior year.

Let's see, we dated freshman, sophomore, and junior year. Got engaged. Must have been at the beginning of my junior year because we got married the summer before my senior year. And I played volleyball for [my college] with a scholarship. So, I knew I could probably graduate early, but I needed to [play that year] because [my college] has a trimester system, and really, I mean, I just knew I wanted to be a mom, so, I knew I had to get through one season and then I was pretty confident I could graduate one trimester early essentially.

So, I ended up being pregnant right before my season started, or right at the very beginning. I just played. I talked to the doctors a lot about the health of the baby, and they were, "If you've been going this intense, then keep doing it." And so, I did.

Terry played her senior volleyball season, finished school early as planned, and had that baby right before commencement.

I didn't do the full graduation just because I mean, new mom, leaky breasts. And I was in the Phi Beta Kappa honors society, so I went to that instead because I knew it would be a lot shorter. And Dan has this story where I'm up with the people going through the formal stuff and he has [the baby] and [she] starts sucking his arm really strong and the lady behind him is [saying], "What the heck, she's sucking on him!" Anyway.

Terry recalled graduating Phi Beta Kappa, by all accounts a tremendous accomplishment, very casually, as a kind of sideshow to the real story of her first baby latching onto her husband's bicep. There's no flavor of "I am woman, hear me roar" in her story. Her baby is the story she wants to tell. Or just about. She does mention one thing she's clearly proud of, but this too is colored by motherhood.

> One of my funny stories is that I just had [my daughter], so of course I have this postpartum body (and baby) and I was chosen as the, well every senior gets looked at for how well they did on their strength and conditioning work and how much it affected their sport.
>
> And I won that, which is the, it's big 'cause it's every athlete from every sport at [my college] whose strength and conditioning, weightlifting, whatever affected their sport the most, over the four years.
>
> And so, I walk up to receive the award looking nothing like the strength and conditioning winner. But I did.

She grinned, still proud.

### *"How Many More Can We Have?"*

Pregnant with her tenth, Terry wonders out loud how many more she can handle and knows it won't go on forever. "I'm getting older, and pregnancies are harder. I guess I have felt the weight of the sacrifice more.... But we [still] get just as excited, just as thrilled for every baby." She reminisced about the one before her current pregnancy, her youngest baby:

> I will say that having my ninth, I remember having [her] and I mean, instantly I had her and we saw it was a girl. And then I remember turning to Dan and saying, "How many more can we have?"

And it was just this overwhelming sense that it wasn't about me. It was about...bringing souls into the world. And by now I know all my weaknesses. Well at least I know probably a little bit of them. There's probably way more. I have doubted myself and questioned myself and gone through really hard times. "Why God, why are you giving me so many kids when I'm such a bad mom?" and all of that.

But I don't know. There was something about [her] birth where it was just, "It's okay, these things are temporary and you're doing your best and these souls will last forever and ever, and you can't change that."

Lots of the moms we met wanted a big family, but ten was more than most even in our sample. Terry went from being the Phi Beta Kappa strength and conditioning winner to having "the overwhelming sense" that a tenth baby would be worth the "weight of the sacrifice." We asked her to share how she came around to wanting so many.

About having her first, Terry said the experience of motherhood was "as great as I thought." She also said it was "more work than I thought, and more selflessness than I ever thought possible." She continued: "In our case we knew we wanted a big family, so we were pretty much not using any sort of [natural family planning] or anything. But I know at a certain point it was more me saying omigosh I'm so overwhelmed.... And my husband is more laid back and more fun, and he'd just be, 'You're doing great, you're doing great.'...So, I would give in because he was right, we're overwhelmed but there's nothing better."

Her sense of vocation kept her going and helped her push through to where she felt more relaxed about the next ones coming: "Yeah, it was very difficult and hard, and it just felt [like] saying no was saying no to God. And so, at some point I just, I don't know, I just kind of gave in to a much more laid-back approach where it was more... 'Okay honey, I think that I'm fertile and I think I need a couple of months.' And so, we would be more careful, but I wouldn't worry."

Terry didn't use the language of readiness that Hannah and Shaylee used, but her approach seems somewhere in between theirs and Kim's. She felt free to get the space that she needed, when she needed it, but her default—their default as a couple—was openness to a baby, even if it seemed overwhelming at times. Terry elaborated:

> Being open to life, to me, means that it's, it's a gift and you wouldn't say no to a gift.
>
> With children [I've] been forced to learn patience and basically become a better person because I'm accepting the gifts that God is giving us.
>
> And again, there's always the reflection on like I said earlier, that my suffering, my worry, my inabilities...are just absolutely minuscule compared to eternity.
>
> I think once that clicked for me it was more, okay, whatever, we can just...let babies come when they want to come.... If I start to panic about not being ready, "I'm having a baby, I'm not ready," they really just need...a boob and an outfit.
>
> So—me and an outfit—and we're good.

She explained how she and her husband had dismissed other objections to letting babies come:

> We have talked about things like money. Something Dan and I both talked about with this is the fact that, when we

think about money, we're not even thinking about a [developing] country where they are struggling to feed just each other. We're so rich compared to most of the world. So that [objection] was kind of written off the table. . . .

And at one point I said, "Okay, we're sending our kids to Catholic school," I said, "so moneywise what do we want, more kids or Catholic school? What would we choose if we had to balance the budget?" and he was, "More kids, for sure" . . . and so, we kind of took that off the table and then I started homeschooling later.

And I'm healthy. . . . My pregnancies are healthy; my deliveries are healthy. I've done home births, last six babies, so I think all of that being good, it was, how could I say no, that was kind of how it ended up.

She sounded like Ann, who said, "I feel like we've been given the green light." For Terry, having babies was "switched on"; she didn't have a reason to shut it off.

### "Yes, and It's Wonderful"

Like the other women we met, Terry caught a lot of public comments about the size of her family. "The most common is 'You have your hands full.' That's definitely top," she said. "And then, we were at a wedding once for Dan's side of the family, so not Catholic. And it's the first time I was brave enough to respond to the question, 'You know how this happens, right?' And we're sitting there, and I was, 'Yes, and it's wonderful!' And the whole table just laughed. . . ." Terry talked a lot about Dan, and their relationship. "Gosh, how would you describe it?" she remarked about the first moments after childbirth. "Just, yeah, that joy of the love that you share with your husband, you're holding it in a concrete way."

She isn't shy about saying that it is wonderful. "So, the intimacy thing...like my husband knows that there's a possibility of a baby every time we come together. And so, I think because of that love and respect he is giving me, I am much more willing to give back to him.... Yeah, so we are frequently intimate, and I think, really enjoy it and it's not, I mean in a way, finding the time can be more exciting, 'Quick, we have a minute.' So that's there."

She seems vaguely aware that not all marriages work out so well. She wonders aloud if she and her husband want each other more because they don't use hormones to space their kids. "Just from comments I've heard, it's probably easier for me than for women who have been on [the Pill] because my body is doing what it's supposed to be doing." There's definitely evidence to support her speculation. Underactive sexual desire, a common problem reported by women using hormonal contraception, seems to be one of the reasons that women are trending away from the Pill, looking for more natural approaches.[2] Overall, however, Terry seemed more inclined to think about the sexual satisfaction in her marriage as a function of trust and closeness that she attributes at least in part to childbearing:

In general, gosh, I mean, I mean I can't even describe how close I feel to my husband. Right. Especially when I give birth. There's just such a...I can see the love and respect that he has for me after watching me give birth. And then, he takes care of me.

I have this kind of rule [after childbirth], a week in bed, a week on the couch. And he usually takes that first...week off. So, I'm in bed and they bring me food and stuff. And so, then I feel really appreciative to him. And it helps us grow in that service of each other.

Miki, who was about as pregnant as Terry when we interviewed her, also felt that the lasting desire in her marriage was about trust. Miki said,

I've been thinking about this a lot as I've been thinking about going into labor.... I mean I know I can trust him with anything.

I used to think that [kids ruin your sex life]. I used to assume that. Like on a practical level, we don't co-sleep so there's that. Not that co-sleeping prevents marital intimacy at all, but I also think that it's gotten better for us because I feel like the more I trust in our marriage to being open to having this many kids, that makes such a huge difference to intimacy. I used to be paranoid about getting pregnant and having lots of kids. Yeah, no fear [now].

Terry talked about how she and her husband foster closeness by getting out on dates. "One perk to having a big family is we have babysitters. So, we just, we told them every Tuesday night we're going to make sure you have a simple dinner and we're going out. And so we don't plan much. We just go. And that was huge for us. Just having that date night every week and really just reconnecting."

She also credits her husband's success as a breadwinner with contributing to their relationship. "So of course, every marriage has its ups and downs, but I would say that one thing I've noticed is my husband and men with large families, I feel they tend to be more successful at their jobs. Yeah. Just because there's that inward drive to provide. And so, my husband's very good at that. I think that it works because, I mean, it's hard. Sometimes he works too much, but it works in the sense that he's fulfilling that really deep desire to provide for his family, for our relationship."

Married men do tend to have higher incomes—and good evidence says their earnings are explained by working to provide rather than simply by the selection of higher-income males into marriage.[3] But what about being a great provider and relationship quality? In a nationally representative survey of over five thousand couples, sociologists Brad Wilcox and Steven Nock found that women were more likely to report being happy in their marriages when their husbands earned more than two-thirds of the household income.[4] Their result held even when wives reported having more egalitarian views about gender. Terry offered testimony in favor of the notion that male breadwinning fostered closeness, appreciation, and trust. And these in turn fostered greater intimacy and affection.

Terry remarked that it was hard for her to think about what her marriage would be like without kids. At one point she said,

> I have not had a husband *without* kids. We had our first [baby] ten months after we got married. So, it's hard to imagine not having [kids].... we [couldn't] wait to get married so we [could] have children.
>
> My grandpa is a deacon and...he did our marriage prep and he just was very open about that too. He would say things [like], "Don't tell God no [about kids]. That is the fruit of your love. That is the fruit of your marriage."
>
> That is. And to me I think we've lost this idea that the whole point of marriage is to have a family and I think that's really sad.
>
> When you have a wonderful husband, and you have a family...it just works. And I don't know.... I struggle with life in general all the time, but when I look at sort of

everyone else doing sort of the typical thing, getting married, not having kids for a while, having their two kids. I
just feel like there's a, how do I say it? There's a little bit of
emptiness that they're not really following what their
body's telling them to do in a way.

In an earnest, awkward sort of way, Terry voiced what many of our
subjects said. Kids couldn't make your marriage worse: kids were the
*meaning* of a marriage, the "fruit of your love." She thought that curbing
children into a little sliver of your marriage, people "having their two
kids," could hurt a marriage. To be sure, she had a great marriage by any
standard, one about which the woman on the train I mentioned in chapter 1 would have been right: *I guess your husband still wants you.* Terry's
husband, Dan, certainly did. "And it's wonderful," Terry said.

### *"God Will Fill in the Gaps"*

Terry shifted her legs a bit, and we could tell that she was weary-
ing of her position in the easy chair. We'd taken enough of her time,
and the new puppy (with eager kids trailing) had wandered into the
parlor a few times. But we asked her to say more about how she saw
children as a gift from God, and what it meant when she said you
wouldn't say no to a gift. Did she still feel free to decide, like Shaylee
and Hannah? The answer was yes, but it was complicated. Children
were a gift she insisted, but God wouldn't give them without her yes.
Her goal was to have enough trust in God's goodness that she could
say yes to more gifts.

I think that being open to a gift, so it's always a gift, always
a gift to have a child. So being open to a gift means that
you're trusting God and trusting that this gift is going to

come with more than you can imagine. Whether it's the personality of that child [or] what they bring to the family.

This would be a good time to describe what I felt when I had a sixteen-week miscarriage. It was kind of a long process, 'cause it was, "Heartbeat sounds funny." Yeah, okay. Now "We don't hear a heartbeat." Now "The baby is dead." Now "If you want to wait to deliver, that's going to be another week." And then I had the baby, then another week for the funeral.

I remember at my baby's funeral just feeling this overwhelming sense of, I was just honored that God chose me to carry this little baby even if it was just for sixteen weeks, because I said, "The soul is going to live forever and ever and ever."

So yeah, I guess it's a participation with God, which is unfathomable.... That God gives us that choice and by saying yes, there's a freedom that you were mentioning earlier. That gives us that joy in that sense of purpose and that confidence and trust in him, even when it's hard, hard, and hard.

Trusting God didn't mean that it wasn't hard. It meant that God was going to help. Like the rest of the women in our sample, Terry scoffed at the idea of regrets.

No regrets. Yeah, my mom used to say, "Well, which one should I give back?"

...[I] guess I would kind of look at a high school reunion and I kind of feel, I don't know how to say this, but I kind of feel sorry for them because, to me the things that they're excited about are not lasting. They're not eternal. They're not going to take care of them when they're older or be at their bedside or, and I just, I don't know.

I think my parents, I am trying to remember where I got this from, but I think my parents went to a reunion and had so many people come up to them and say, "You guys, you guys did it right." 'Cause they had eight kids. And so many of them just said, "I look back and I wish I'd had more kids."

And that was basically it, so I think that I have latched onto that a bit too, just knowing, people who've been there, who are older, they do [regret]. But anyway, no regrets. And then, I've said throughout this interview, I just—it's hard, and I struggle—but I just have to trust that there's a purpose to all of it, and all I can do is my best and God will fill in the gaps hopefully.

# CHAPTER ELEVEN

# "He Wants Nine"—Lauren, Five Kids

"And he's like, 'Yeah, well I want a big family.' And I'm
like, 'I'm not committing to nine.'...I knew we were
going to have a lot. Like it was no question from the start
we were going to have kids."

—Lauren, mother of five

We didn't check Zillow, but Lauren's home in one of the
wealthiest zip codes in her state would easily boast a
seven-figure valuation. She has a doctorate in special
education but was mostly a stay-at-home mom at the time of the
interview. Her academic training was apparent before Mary and I
had even gotten settled. She asked right away which of us was the
"PI" of the project. (PI means "principal investigator" and refers to
the senior most responsible person on a research investigation.) She
seemed to want to know whether the PI was the one of us with the
eight kids, or if I had been dragged along for the sake of rapport. She
was delighted to learn it was the former. Her husband was an

academic too, teaching at an elite university a short commute from their tony suburb.

Lauren described having "a very Jewish home" and added, "My kids go to Jewish day school.... And we are very observant in our house. We keep kosher and we celebrate all the holidays. We host Shabbat dinners like as frequently as we can. You know, we try to bring in, you know, if there's something going on, you know like using the values to help explain a situation." And yet religious sentiments did not enter her conversation much. Lauren explicitly compartmentalized her family size and her Judaism: "The having a large family is separate from the Jewish piece." Lauren didn't seem to attach religious significance to her childbearing, and in that sense she was an outlier. So it is important to include her story.

## "He Convinced Me"

The other women in our sample reported valuing childbearing as a great good either from their own childhood or after a change in life marked by religious conversion. They also denied having any particular "number" in mind. Lauren, in contrast, did not share the desire for more children in her marriage. It was all her husband. And he had a number. The irony was not lost on us: the only "husband-led" childbearing we encountered was in the marriage with the fanciest pedigrees and the fewest religious motives. "He convinced me," she told us. "I would have stopped after three if he was good after three. He's definitely leading the charge." Though her husband's preferences prevailed, she stressed that "it was an agreement. It was a joint decision." Lauren related the story.

So, his parents came to [the city] for a weekend visit—that was the first time I met his parents...and his mother turns to me...and goes, "You know, [he] wants to have nine kids."...And I'm like, "Huh?" And she's like, "Yeah, he wants nine children. He wants them sleeping in the closets all over."

I can still see like the background of the restaurant because I'm like, "Who, why? What!?"

That night I said to him, I was like, "Your mom told me this really interesting thing." And he's like, "Yeah, well I want a big family." And I'm like, "I'm not committing to nine."

Lauren laughed and continued: "I knew we were going to have a lot. Like it was no question from the start we were going to have kids." She told us,

I mean, dating my husband, my husband's delightful.... I don't want to make him sound like a jerk, but like he wanted to have, he wanted me to be tested for fertility before we got engaged...just to make sure that I can have kids.

And I swear like, I swear that like when you look at our [background] without being gross about it, when you look at our pedigree and where we came from and our families, not never, I swear it was pheromones or something that like he wants a lot of kids [and] that wasn't going to be a problem for me.

So, we got married and, how quick was it? I think maybe...three years later. And so, we got married and I started my Ph.D. program and shortly after, it was when I was done with all my coursework. That was kind of like we were going to wait until that point—and then I can just start.

In another contrast with the rest of our sample, in Lauren's family deciding when to have another child didn't involve prayer or trusting in God's plan. It was her husband's plan—but he had to convince her. He would work on her until she agreed. She explained:

> We both wanted to like bang it out pretty quickly... for of each them except number five, like after they hit the one-year mark, it was, "Let's get it going."
>
> So, we have three and then I was like this close to agreeing to number four and I said like we need to like work on our help situation 'cause I can't manage this on my own. And I agreed to everything... and right after [our fourth child] was born, [my husband] told two of my girlfriends, "I'm going to get another one, just watch."
>
> And in that, not like in a douche way, but like "of course," and my sister, one of my sisters, she's like, "He's going to get you again." She was like, "I don't know what he does, he's going to get ya again."

Lauren was obviously aware that her story might sound sketchy or unbelievable. I might have thought so, if I hadn't heard it firsthand, in her living room, and if it weren't for the balance and humor in how she told it. She was not a wilting flower, and she was not being steamrolled by an overbearing husband. Continuing, she said,

> Maybe it's dickish, but like when somebody says, sort of, "What led you to here?" and I say like, it's sort of a mic drop when I say, "I have a Ph.D." I chose this, I wanted this. I could have done a bunch of other things. I've been out of the game for a little bit, so my options are a little more

limited, but like...this is totally a choice. I'm happy with this choice.

There is also the fact that they have built and protected an incredible marriage:

> We are a team when we're together and we're home, we are a team and we still have our life together. We get up in the morning, we work out together every morning. I don't know if I would say I work out, but I'm with him in the gym. We have a gym in the basement. And so, you know, I'm down there, it's just the two of us and the kids know that they can't come down until a certain time. And so, it's protected. Because you know, after 7:38 p.m., we're zombies.

It comes out that the basement gym is occasionally something more than just a place to hang out. "Without sharing too much, we'll still sometimes, like they'll be asleep, and we'll be like, you know, 'Let's just go to the basement and do something, you know, crazy.'" While she says, "It's not happening often," I can't help thinking there are probably a lot of couples who wish a basement fling was more than a memory from their first year of marriage. She laughed, "You know, it's 'We're not going to put on a cute nightie for you, I'm wearing my gross T-shirt that I've worn for the last month straight.'" Whatever they wear—Lauren and her man are still into each other. And like the other women we met, she doesn't see the kids as a threat to that. It's more integrated. She said,

> My husband loves being a dad. He loves being involved. He loves [it]. He's not around much. He works a zillion

hours. He travels a ton. But when he's home, I call him Santa because he just wants to be the fun guy that does everything.

We spend a lot of that [basement alone] time talking about the kids and talking about like things coming up and [it] serves as our time to like debrief and connect. But it's also our chance to talk about whatever's going on.

And I think that for us that really works, you know, so we have our life as a family, and we also still have our life as a relationship, as a couple.... We just have found balance, and balance in that. Not that we—we share the job and it's not equal, but it's shared.

### *"All Hands on Deck"*

Among the fifty-five women in our study, Lauren's husband was probably the top earner. He would have been a top earner in almost any sample. We didn't collect financial data, but their seven-figure house in a high-cost-of-living city suggested at least the upper quintile of household income nationally. Despite this, we found they had plenty in common with our bottom quintile households. Esther, from chapter 2, told me that her family lives "very, very simply" and that she doesn't "spend money on a lot of things that other people spend money on.... We do activities that don't cost money, like going to the playground." Esther, with her matter-of-fact humor—"fighting with your siblings doesn't cost anything, so it's all here and available"— reminded me of Lauren more than once.

Putting the transcripts of Esther's and Lauren's interviews side by side made me wonder if having so many kids had done the work of bridging a cultural divide between income strata. Esther and Lauren appeared to have more in common than the inhabitants of upper– and lower–income zip codes are generally thought to have. Lauren told us about one of her family's favorite activities:

> So, we go to, we take the kids, we go to Embassy Suites once every couple of months. They have a swimming pool and it's like a hundred bucks for a night and it's actually the best deal in town. You could probably appreciate this.
>
> So, we can still get into one room, you know, like we can make them, you know, the four, four big ones in the beds. The baby goes in the crib and my husband and I sleep on the floor in the living room, and so we order pizza. We take them to the pool, they swim, we order pizzas, delivered for dinner, and they're thrilled to sit on a bed watching TV, eating pizza and, so I don't have to cook.
>
> And then they go to bed and my husband and I get no sleep, but that's fine. You know, the next morning they get up, the next morning they go back to the pool, which thrills them. There's the breakfast and like it's amazing.

I made a mental note. A mini staycation for seven people for a hundred bucks and the price of pizzas? That *is* the best deal in town. I wonder if hotels realize the opportunity there. While this is probably out of reach for Esther and her family, Lauren and her husband could afford a lot more. Their neighbors certainly do. An old friend in the upper quintile recently told me about taking his kids on a cruise to the Galapagos Islands. A once-in-a-lifetime trip? No, for them it was just an ordinary mid-winter excursion. Lauren's Embassy Suites adventure seems banal in comparison. The point is Lauren and her husband have more the outlook of Esther's "the best things are free" than that of my old friend whose kids have seen the seven wonders of the world.

Lauren talked about what else she wasn't going to do for her kids:

> Well, even like the happiness thing like this is one of my biggest pet peeves when people talk to me about how like they just want their children to be happy. "All I want is my child to be happy."
>
> [For me] I could care less if my kids are happy. That's their job. You figure that out. Like you need to find out what makes you happy and you got to go out and find that. I'm happy to give you whatever tools you need. I'm happy to give you whatever instruction to help you out. But that's, that's on you.

In chapter 2 we saw how Esther talked about having nine children in an almost disinterested way. "Do I feel like my children are my accomplishments? I more feel like they are who they are." It seemed to me that Lauren might have said the same. "Your happiness is on you, kids. You are who you are."

We heard nothing during our interviews that could have been described as helicopter parenting. Quite the opposite, and this seemed notable. It would be crass and unfaithful to our data to suggest that the moms paid less attention to their children on account of having more. Rather, what emerged was a picture of overlapping caregiving, characterized by older children helping younger ones, and mothers freed up by children who stepped in to help. Lauren related,

> I don't know if it's the influence of having an infant around or just being a part of a big family, but there are definitely some characteristics I absolutely think are a result of so many kids. Everybody has to help. It's always all hands on deck, and they'll help with the baby.

Like the other night, I asked the ten-year-old to take the baby upstairs because I was helping with someone else. And so she took him upstairs and I could hear her in his room over the baby monitor, and she's talking to him, trying to read to him. And then she's like, "Okay, baby, good night," and then closes the door.

I come upstairs; I was like, "What?" She's like, "I thought he was ready for bed, so I put him in the crib." She just jumped in there, you know what I mean?

It would take a separate book to contain all the stories we heard like this one—like Shaylee's son, in chapter 9, who kept lookout at the playground, all on his own. The upshot of having children who "jumped in there" seemed to be that the whole project of keeping kids safe, or entertained, or happy, did not depend solely on the moms. It depended as well upon the other people around their children—chiefly, their other children.

Lauren said that growing up "all hands on deck" changed the character of her children. She explained: "I think they all have a level of patience, not necessarily with each other, but in total, you know, when they're out and about that, and flexibility with people that I think is just a result of constantly having to negotiate with others and be around people. They are not shy around people at all and will happily talk to anyone. I'm assuming that comes from just being in a large, loud house.... I think there are more direct characteristics that are a result of just being a part of a big family."

Interview after interview, we heard versions of Lauren's "there are more direct characteristics" that come from having a lot of siblings. Among these were the abilities to take responsibility from a younger age ("she just jumped in there"), to get along with others who are different, and to share space, material things, and time. The moms didn't think these characteristics were just nice to have for the "havers." They believed their kids' pro-social virtues would be a benefit to their future families, places of work, and communities.

Lauren and Esther's almost arm's-length approach to their children's happiness—"they are who they are"—ultimately indicates a kind of detachment from how their kids are turning out. That stands to reason. If you have five, or nine, you probably can't be overly invested in any one kid being a certain way, having a certain job, or achieving anything for certain. Maybe that's why we heard so little that sounded like over-parenting. The moms were forced by the nature of things to let go of micromanaging the organic process of growing up. "I'm happy to give you whatever tools you need," Lauren said, but happiness, "...that's on you."

## "The One Thing That He Asks For"

I asked her if she thought there was going to be another one. "I mean, he's working on it," she said. "The IUD just came out just a couple of weeks ago, so there's a pretty good chance that there will be another one." I probed to figure out why she goes along with it, and why she has gone along with it. Why does Lauren have five kids? "I think it was after number two or number three. We had just gotten home from the hospital and he's sitting at the kitchen counter holding the baby and I don't even know what I'm doing, but I'm on the other side of the counter. He's like 'God I can't wait until we have a house full of these.' And I was like, 'Fuck you.... I'm like you know, barely upright right now. Like screw you.'"

She laughed and went on. "It's hard to like [explain what] we have without again painting him as being a monster, like we have a great life. There really isn't, we have everything that we need, and this is the one thing that he asks for.

"You know what I mean?...I rarely do his laundry; he makes most of his meals.... And so this is really the one thing that he asks for. And so there is a little bit of guilt in *not*. Or in saying no and pushing it off and pushing it off."

Ultimately it feels like that's our answer. "It's the one thing that he asks for." Or at least it's as much of an answer as we were going to get from Lauren. She laughed outright when I asked whether she agreed with other women we had interviewed who said children are blessings from God. "Heck no, no they're not. I mean, they're all blessings in their own way. They're also pains in the ass in their own way. And we've been very fortunate. We've had five, I've had five very straightforward pregnancies, and they're all relatively healthy. They have their issues, nothing too extreme. And we're very fortunate that way."

For Lauren, having more children than she had wanted was about giving something deeply valuable to her husband. She was the one woman in my sample I could not have likened to the biblical Hannah without doing some gymnastics. She chose children—and she did choose—not out of a sense of meaning or purpose, not because "she was made for it," but because her husband wanted them so much.

Husbands are not the focus of this narrative, but nevertheless they play an important role. These are not the stories of women who persuaded their husbands to have all these children, least of all Lauren. But also, except for Lauren, these are not the stories of women who were persuaded by their husbands. Among our other subjects, both husbands and wives had mutually adopted a routine openness to another child, conditional upon their discernment: *Are you ready? Are we ready?* The door wasn't closed for these couples. Never say never was the unspoken position—even if it might take a while for them to be ready. This openness to a child—this attitude of not being "done"—makes the women in my sample unusual, to say the least. The 5 percent, I've called them. But it makes their husbands even more unusual.

Data on fertility desires says that women tend to report wanting two to three kids even if they end up having just one or two (the so-called "fertility gap" discussed in chapter 4). But for men we don't know as much. Men get ignored, or treated as incidental, in research about family planning and fertility intentions.[1] The Census Bureau released its "first ever" report on men's fertility just a few years ago, in 2019,[2] revealing that completed fertility for men aged forty-five to fifty is significantly lower than it is for women (1.83 versus 2.01) and that the percent of men who are childless at forty-five to fifty is substantially higher (24 versus 15 percent).[3] Though men can have children after their forties, very few do,[4] so these numbers won't change much as men get older. The National Survey of Family Growth provides some clues to male attitudes about fertility. Only 25 percent of men said they would be bothered "a great deal" if it turned out they never had a child, compared to nearly 40 percent of women.[5] So, today men have fewer children than women, are more likely to be childless, and are more likely to report not being bothered by childlessness. Do these differences explain any part of the female fertility gap? That is—do birth rates tend to reflect men's or women's preferences, or something in between? We don't know because it hasn't been studied. The general assumption seems to be that in countries with greater gender equality, childbearing will be resolved in favor of women's preferred family size. But the general assumption has also been that men want more children than women. It is hard to find reliable evidence for either of these stories. Current trends can be construed as challenging both assumptions. Surely, at least, men willing to have five, six, or more children stand out for investigation as much as their wives.

## "We Got to Look Good and Drive Our Nice Cars"

Returning to Lauren—she was frank about how her gift to her husband had cost her something, personally. Yes, there were financial costs. She had gotten help at home at a certain point. The kids went to expensive schools. But on the list of obstacles, the personal costs had more weight. First, there was the shift in how she thought about herself—not unwelcome, ultimately, but costly because she had to give up her old self. "Identity is a really hard thing after having kids. And, I would say my identity is totally changed. I'm a mom. Like that's who I am. That's what I do. And I still have things that are mine. Like I work very little, but it's mine. It gives me purpose. It gives me something outside the house, away from the kids. And so, I would definitely say that [my identity] changed and shifted."

Second, the motherhood shift had placed her outside the norm for her peer group, leading to a type of isolation:

It's just not normal [now]. But if you go back forty years you know, it was not, you know, it [was] not abnormal. With that I also feel sort of, a loneliness 'cause like I'm doing that. You know what I mean? And people don't get it and that's fine.

I don't care if you understand or not. But like, don't ask me, "How did you get everybody to school with their lunches today?" And I was like, "Well it was ugly, but I did it." Like you know, that's life.

And so, yeah. So, there is a little bit of loneliness, but I think…that's not the identity piece. That's just sort of the lifestyle piece. Right?

Finally, she talked about the challenge to social status—also a lifestyle factor:

> We're so sensitive and self-conscious and you know, we got to look good and drive our nice cars.
>
> And I think there's this world with social media that you see everybody posting—look how beautiful everyone is dressed and with their, you know, cute last day of school picture or whatever, and that's just not reality.
>
> And when you're looking at that all the time and competing a little bit with that and kids are expensive and we're humans, we're selfish, you know what I mean? And like I look at that kid and you know, you're my vacation to wherever I want to go.

Altogether, Lauren felt that she had walked away from the comfort of a professional identity, a normal lifestyle, and a desirable social image. These were real costs—what she had given up having five kids. And so she wasn't hard on people who had picked a different path. She probably would have done that herself if she had married a different guy. "I think people are overwhelmed," she said.

> And it can be overwhelming. And it's hard to see past that.
>
> Yeah, like the village doesn't exist. The in-house help and even the community, like communities don't exist.
>
> We talk about building community and it's bullshit. Like that just doesn't exist. And so that's, you know, everyone's out there on their own.
>
> And yet we're all doing the exact same thing.

For Lauren, the benefits had overcome the costs because of her husband's desire for children and what it meant to their relationship. For most of her peers, it seems, there just isn't much to balance out the sizable costs she had outlined.

CHAPTER TWELVE

# The Road Not Taken—Cost and Choice

"Costs are equal to the value attached to the satisfaction which one must forego in order to attain the end aimed at."

—Ludwig von Mises, *Human Action* (1949)

"At the moment of choice itself, cost is the chooser's evaluation of the anticipated enjoyments that he must give up once commitment is made. . . ."

—James Buchanan, *Cost and Choice* (1969)

With Lauren's story behind me, it's possible to formulate a reply to the first question I set out to answer in this study. Why do women defying the birth dearth do what they do? Before setting out to do this research, I had expected religious motives to play a large role. And indeed, nearly every subject had a narrative thick with elements of faith. From this perspective it looked like Lauren was the exception who proved the rule when she said that "the having a large family is separate from the Jewish piece." But I couldn't leave the analysis there. To say that motives have a religious source still leaves the question of desire and choice unanswered. It leaves religion in the black box I wanted to unpack.

Miki had drawn a distinction between "saying you [have kids] because you're Catholic, which implies . . . blind adherence" and having kids because you've "actually considered something...because you believe it's good." There was also Ann's comment that the motivation to have a large family was "almost underneath religion," and Shaylee's explanation that "being an older sibling in a large family probably played a part in that. I know religion does too." To group all this together under the heading of "religious childbearing" was to leave the question I had set out to answer unanswered. Lauren's story—the outlier—helped me see the structure of my data more clearly.

And so did Dave Skarbek's research on social order in prison gangs. Skarbek, an economist at Brown, spent years studying the phenomenon of gangs in prisons. "Prison gangs appear baffling," he wrote. "Many people associate their lifestyle, organization, monikers, activities, rituals, and customs with non-rational forces. The oddities of the criminal underworld seem attributable only to psychopathy or pure evil."[1] But Skarbek believed he could gain insights by assuming instead that prisoners, like the rest of us, make choices for intelligible reasons. Making use of scholarship on prison violence as well as legal records, indictments, court transcripts, first-person testimonies, and historical data on California's inmate population, Skarbek found that prison gangs provide order in a profoundly unstable environment. Prisoners face obscene risks to life and health at the hands of other prisoners. This is true even under the best systems of prison governance, since prisoners cannot be protected from each other all of the time—for example, in the lunch line, or during recreation. In states where prison governance is particularly weak, near daily threats can be impossible to live with. Gangs make sense to inmates because the benefits of joining are substantially larger than the costs of not joining. While gang membership may bring new problems (from opposing gangs, or prison officers), it may offer needed security where there is none. It may also reduce the number of potential assailants, since members of your own gang are not likely to attack you. According to Skarbek, prisoners who join gangs aren't irrational: they just face different incentives from the ones we do.[2]

This type of argument about human action can be traced back to Aristotle, and before that even to Plato, but today it is associated with economics.[3] Skarbek calls it the "economic way of thinking," or the theory of rational choice. Individuals pursue ends that they value, and in pursuit of these ends they weigh the values attached to a choice when picking a course of action.[4] When economists say that "incentives matter," what they mean is that human action results from how people size up the gains and losses. People are motivated not by an "incentive" per se, but by the relative value they assign to the different choices in front of them. In popular use, we use "incentive" to describe anything that adds value to a course of action, something that tips the scale in favor of one choice over another. An incentive can be monetary, of course—a bonus, prize, or subsidy. But an incentive can also be an idea, or a conviction, or a set of circumstances that changes the calculation of loss and gain: for example, the likelihood that I will end up dead or injured if I don't join a gang.

Faced with a choice that is binary—join a gang or not, have a child or not—only one option can be picked: the "cost" of choosing A is missing out on B. So however much B is worth to you is the price you pay for picking A. The evaluation of the choice includes weighing the gains and the losses, present and future, on each side. Losses include the money price you pay, but also the personal and subjective loss you suffer. In this sense, the most relevant "real cost" at the moment of choice is a value determination. How much do you want what you'll miss?

Economists call the costs of missing out opportunity costs. When a fan buys a ticket to a Springsteen concert, she does so because she reckons that the value of attending is more than whatever else she could have done with the price of her ticket—and whatever else she might have done with her time. If attending the concert means missing out on her best friend's wedding, the "price" of the concert goes up. That price is the opportunity cost: the cost of the missed opportunity of attending the wedding. Using the language of opportunity cost, not joining a gang means missing out on protection from injury or death—things you probably care about a lot more than the value of staying more lawful. Rational choice depends upon value determinations—because costs aren't fully assessed until you know the worth of what you're giving up when you choose. The cost of a choice includes all the goods you have to give up with your choice—the money price, plus any other things you count as loss.

Values that motivate action are subjective, not necessarily quantifiable, and not necessarily comparable to one another. To continue with our Springsteen fan, suppose that attending her friend's wedding is worth more to her than attending the concert. That does not mean that other people would necessarily share that preference; it does not mean that she could assign a money value to what the wedding is worth to her; and it does not mean that she could say precisely "how much more" attending the wedding is worth. Value that motivates action need not be "intrinsic" to an option; rather, objects of choice have particular value in relation to our purposes. In fact, "attending a wedding" has no particular intelligible meaning at all until it is personified: Whose wedding, and who is attending? That prison gang members valued protection in prison over other goods in prison didn't mean that they would choose gang life in any other circumstance. That's just the point.

Every choice can be understood as a consequence of assessing gains and losses in personal ways. The idea of opportunity cost did not originate with the Scottish Enlightenment, nineteenth-century utilitarianism, or the marginal revolution; it is a deep truth about the logic of choice that was understood by ancient philosophers.[5] To place the prison gang example on the older philosophical footing: the inmates ranked the good of personal safety (being in a gang) over the good of lawfulness (not being in a gang). The higher-valued good prevailed.

## A Unified Account of Costs and Benefits

Lauren's story opened my eyes to the structure of my own data because it forced me to think about her motives *apart* from the religious significance that my other subjects reported. When Lauren gave the answer that "[having kids is] the one thing he asks for," I understood her to mean that the good motivating her to have five children was the gift she could give to her husband. In choosing additional children, she ranked the gift to her husband as having greater value *to her* than the alternative goods she could have picked, such as fitting in with her peers, keeping her old identity intact, or having more time for professional work. Those are goods that she had "given up" with her choice to have five.

All the features of "the economic way of thinking" are there in Lauren's story. She pursued ends that she valued. She weighed gains and losses, comparing the value of the options in front of her. She didn't have kids out of "blind adherence" to her husband, even if he was "leading the charge." She chose a large family because on consideration she believed that it was a good—just as Miki would have said, although for different reasons. Lauren's desire for the fourth and fifth kids was genuinely her own desire, but it was a second-order desire. For herself, she "would have stopped after three if he was good after three." But because her husband wanted more children, she told us, "I chose this, I wanted this. I could have done a bunch of other things." This is rational choice to be sure, but Lauren's desires were not fixed. They evolved with her changing perceptions of the value of having another child, and her assessment of its relation to the costs she faced—the goods that she was giving up. As in Skarbek's prison example, what might have looked baffling or irrational from the outside falls into place when assessed in terms of Lauren's own personal incentives. The "incentive" that tipped the scale for Lauren was how much she loved her husband—and how much he valued children.

Women make choices about having children based on "costs and benefits"—but not in the way we usually understand that phrase, which is the cash money we give up or get. Rather, women compare the subjective personal value of having another child with the subjective personal value of what they will miss out on if they have one. Both sides of the scale include gains and losses. The choice to have a child is a value determination about the relative size of those gains and losses. The values will not usually be quantifiable for an individual woman or comparable across women—even if a common estimation of things may arise out of our social nature.

Armed with this interpretation, I re-read Lauren's interview for things I hadn't noticed at first. When she said, "We're so sensitive and self-conscious and you know, we got to look good and drive our nice cars," she was saying, in effect, that some people don't have more children because the value *to them* of the next child is not as big as the value *to them* of the other goods they would have to give up: relationship goods (maybe a husband who doesn't want another kid, or parents who will freak out), identity goods (maybe a career, profession, hobbies, or interests), lifestyle goods (maybe more sleep, better health, not being overwhelmed, or not being misunderstood), consumption goods (maybe a better home, more vacations, or eating out more), and status goods (maybe nice cars, or looking good). From rich to poor in my sample, these were the sorts of goods women admitted to missing out on. They were goods deeply connected to identity, well-being, and quality of life. Giving them up, my subjects reported, often felt a little—or a lot—like dying to self.

What made Lauren different, by her own accounting, from women who made different choices, wasn't that she valued those other goods any less. At least, she didn't say she held them in contempt. She had a Ph.D. She was a skilled and talented scholar. She enjoyed looking good, and for all we knew, probably enjoyed driving a nice car. What made her different was that her husband "want[ed] nine"—providing a very high relationship value for having more kids. It was a gift she could give him. She felt the sting of being misunderstood, lonely, overwhelmed, and limited in her future work options. The reason she got to kids numbers four and five was that she had something on the other side of the scale that weighed more than the losses. She had an end that she valued more because it ranked higher than the goods she had to forego.

Looking at it this way, I could see my way to a unified account that covered every woman in my sample. The women who attached religious significance to their childbearing were not fundamentally different from Lauren. Additional children were a good that they ranked higher than what they were giving up. That good was the value of God's plan for them ("letting the Lord be in charge"—Kim, twelve kids); the value of accepting a gift from God ("you wouldn't say no to a gift"—Terry, ten kids); or the value of an eternal human life ("that relationship is eternal"—Amanda, five kids). Each of these women had also talked about the loss side of the scale. Like Lauren, they mentioned the same types of costs and foregone goods: compromises at work, physical and emotional difficulties, being misunderstood by friends or family, financial strains. But like Lauren, they ranked the value of another child ahead of the value of what they were missing out on. The extraordinary value that my subjects placed on another child led them to push beyond comfort to obtain a pearl of great price. I could hear the words of Kobe Bryant: "*The lives of your family are more important* than the injury of your hamstring."

Most basically, the women in my sample went on to have more children because the value of doing so exceeded the value of not doing so. They ranked the next child more highly than the other things they could do with their time and resources. They embraced a scale of values in which something of tremendous worth was attached to having a child; that something was the kind of thing typically reckoned worth dying for: love for a beloved, love of God, love of eternal life, and the pursuit of happiness. No wonder, then, that women reported their losses as the dying of other goods that were truly good. The American women quietly defying the birth dearth had incentives big enough to die for.

## Implications of the Unified Account

This discovery is as simple as it is arresting. It means that women with many children make choices about their families in a manner totally consistent with other human action. They simply have a scale of values tipped in favor of childbearing. What is arresting is that there is nothing mysterious, or set apart, about the role of religious motives. They are powerful incentives for human action. That's not irrational. It's about as rational as anything can be. But love is also a powerful motive. As is a conviction that a child will be a joy. The more powerful the motivating values, the more sizable the difficulties they can overcome. Love and faith can move mountains.

The implications of the role of cost and choice in childbearing are manifold. First, the real costs relevant to choosing a child are subjective and have to be reckoned by asking, "Compared to what?" The modern calculus about family size presented in chapter 4 dovetails with the unified account. As the economic contribution of children to the household eroded, other sources of value were needed to balance out the costs; but the opposite happened. Women's options outside the home swelled, raising the real costs of childbearing even more. So falling birth rates are a cost problem, but not simply in the way that we usually think about costs—as money affordability. The opportunity cost of having a child increased sharply with women's expanded education and professional work. But there was no corresponding increase to the value of having a child. Costs went up and benefits stayed the same or went down. Ceteris paribus, fewer children were born.

A second implication is that applying an opportunity-cost framework illuminates how the binary choice plays out in the lives of American women. For most women, beginning with kindergarten there is an uninterrupted sequence of educational and pre-professional years leading inexorably to a job or career. Women begin their adult years having implicitly chosen not to have a child. Each year that they enjoy their studies, training, or work reinforces the value determination that "having a child would mean missing out on what I have come to know and love." The trouble is, if children are in some way "experience" goods, as the interview with Kim suggested, women will not know in advance how much they might want what they are missing. The value of what they know—their social networks, their successes, their professional goals—easily outweighs the value of an unknown child. Except for the few who grow up around babies, women will not know whether there is joy to be found in children, and how much. Women may desire one or two kids at the start of adulthood, but if their desires change later, they may not have time for three or four. Perforce, their children will not grow up around babies, perpetuating the cycle of ignorance about what is missed.

A third implication is that women defying the birth dearth are not necessarily doing so because it is more affordable for them, or because their costs are smaller. They are having children because their reasons to do so outweigh their reasons not to do so, however large the costs. We talked to women who had battled through depression and mental illness, anxiety and poor health, financial strain and uncertainty, and even older age, to have another child. We talked to women who had children with disabilities, illnesses, and fatal diagnoses, and went on to have more. When our subjects had felt it wise to postpone a child for one of these reasons, they had looked forward with hope to when they could have another again. They had even prayed for obstacles to be removed so that the pearl of great price could be purchased again. And when they sensed they weren't ready for another, or when they didn't want more kids, still "they wanted to want [more]" and hoped that God would change their hearts. Those who are immune from falling birth rates are immune because of differences in demand. They believe that having children is more valuable than whatever else they could be doing with their time, their money, and their talents.

Insights from what happens at the margin of an additional child is a fourth implication of the relative-value framework. Women with large families face similar total costs as other women, but their marginal costs are certainly lower—at some point. Women with more than two or three kids have already given up a lot of big-ticket items: they have adjusted their work life, traded a small car for a larger one, changed their recreational habits, and more. If the real cost of a child is what you give up to have one, that cost decreases with additional children after two or three. That's because by then you've already given up most of what you will have to give up; only smaller, variable costs remain: extra sleepless nights, food and clothing, schooling, health care. Once you're riding around in a twelve-seater van because a minivan only fits eight, the extra child doesn't change much. Taken together, these variable costs aren't necessarily minor—but they are small compared to giving up partnership in a law firm or quitting a private practice or moving to a different neighborhood to get by on less income. The total cost to a woman's identity, status, and lifestyle of having more than an average-sized family was counted as huge by the women in my sample—but the marginal costs diminished.

At the same time, we heard a story of increasing marginal benefits with more children. The rough idea was that the joy of an additional child reverberated among all the members of the family, especially when the older kids reached early teenage years and beyond. With more kids, there were more people to have and share the joy. This fact, superadded to their baseline reasons to keep going, meant that the marginal value they attached to having a child actually increased with more children. For them, children weren't like a consumption good with diminishing satisfaction. Women frequently reported enjoying their fourth, fifth, and sixth babies more than their firsts and seconds—as incredible as that may sound. In my own life that has certainly been true. I loved my first baby more than I thought I could love anybody. But my eighth was a joy to me even bigger, for which I can still find no expression. More so: his older sister, around the age of thirteen, when once rolling around in play with her baby brother, exclaimed, "We didn't know we needed a Finnan, but we did!" The benefit of my eighth wasn't just my joy: it was mine and hers together.

My subjects offered descriptions of increasing joy akin to the progress of being on higher and higher mountaintops—the rewards are spectacular up there, but few of us climb high enough to get to them. Ultimately, the pattern of diminishing marginal costs and increasing marginal benefits helped to explain the outliers of family size in my own sample—women like Kim, with twelve kids; Terry, with ten; Esther, who has nine; and women that we'll meet later. Others would have gotten there too—if they had started earlier.

A fifth implication of seeing costs and choice in childbearing as a value determination about alternatives—"Compared to what?"—is that it explodes the faulty logic behind failed pro-natalist policies. Nudge-style programs offering baby bonuses, subsidies, and other benefits to persuade women and families to have more children aren't likely to work because they don't operate on the right margin. These programs take childbearing decisions to be a function of cash flow, of balancing the household budget. But that is strictly speaking, false. At the time of the choice, a couple must consider the entire bundle of the costs of having a child—and that bundle includes what else a woman might wish to do with her time, talents, and money. It's not just a question of cash affordability. It's a question of lifestyle affordability, career affordability, identity affordability.

Do women and families want to pay the price of giving up the panorama of goods that will be sacrificed to have another baby? Pro-natalist policies assume that they do. But that seems fantastical. People who are cash-flow-constrained in the short run can change any number of things in the medium to long run to alleviate their constraints. If children were worth it to them, they'd do exactly that. Baby bonuses and subsidies don't work because they aren't the kind of incentive needed to tip the scale in favor of taking on big-ticket sacrifices and commitments. Incentives like that have to be big—big enough to give you a reason to die to yourself.

Rather than taking baby bonuses seriously, we ought to dismiss them as the political gimmick that they are—designed to appeal to pro-family voters, with no hope of success in changing the birth rate. Would anyone think you could increase the number of ultramarathoners by offering people a monthly cash payment or a bonus? What you'll succeed in doing is rewarding the people who already want to train for ultramarathons. That's fine, and maybe countries should reward people who want to have kids—if they can afford it. But it won't raise the birth rate. It's not that incentives don't work. It's that they have to be big enough to tip the scales—they have to answer the weight on the other side of the scale. When it comes to having a child, for a woman, that weight is her whole self. That is what she "gives up," in a sense, placing herself at the service of a new life. What can answer the weight of your whole self? Rightly only someone you love as much as your own self: God, your spouse, and your children. This is the simple reason that it is easier for policymakers to discourage fertility than to encourage it. The real resources to have a child never can come from the state.

A final implication of the value-determination approach may be surprising. But it is hard not to notice that the narratives in this book are not about birth control. The women quietly defying the birth dearth are not doing so because they won't or can't use family planning. Across my sample, women had used, or were using, various types of birth control—from the Pill to IUDs to natural methods—to space or avoid children. But when we talked about what got them started having large families, and what kept them going, the mechanics of preventing births was not part of that story. True, we had recruited women who described their families as purposeful, and that may have meant that our sample didn't include the women who got to five children accidentally. But still, there was ample room for the women in our study to say that their motive for having children, their purposefulness, depended upon a conviction that using birth control was wrong. We just didn't hear that.

A few women, mostly Catholic, talked about coming to have a view of sexuality that included preserving its reproductive potential—but they had definitely spaced or limited their childbearing, in natural ways. And they weren't any more likely than other women in the sample to have especially large families. It seemed to us that the causality likely went the other way: women who had come to believe, like Miki, that childbearing was "good" did not have a difficult time seeing artificial birth control as problematic. If, like Esther, you believed children were "God's expression of goodness," why would you put up "roadblocks to not get the blessings"? And yet—rejecting birth control was not the story of *Hannah's Children*.

What the narratives did uncover was a rejection of a conventional attitude towards family planning, where children are fitted into our own lives, our own stories—our own plans for the future. My subjects believed that the value of having children proved itself over time in ways that evaded human design and expectation. They were open to more children not merely because they believed that children were good, but because they believed in a greater wisdom of which children and human generation were a part. "God owns the world," Hannah told us. "And He knows what's good for us." They took the commandment "Be fruitful and multiply" as a manifestation of that wisdom. How openness to children was operationalized day-to-day, year to year, in terms of readiness, assent, and birth spacing varied across my sample, to be sure. But in general, the women took having children to be about a willingness to cooperate with God's plan, a finer plan than their own narrow designs. The gift of their fertility was an invitation into "the miracle that saves the world," which is "the birth of new men and the new beginning...they are capable of by virtue of being born."[6] It was this attitude that set the women in my sample, confronted with "two roads diverged" onto "the one less traveled by."[7] For students of human nature, the contraceptive revolution of the twenty-first century will continue to be a subject of great interest—as well it should. But for students of economic demography, the important question is not whether people do or don't use birth control. The question is why they want—or do not want—babies to come. The tools in our hands have use-value only in relation to our ends.

PART THREE

*How It's Going—Meaning*

# CHAPTER THIRTEEN

# "The Planner of All Plans"—Hannah, Seven Kids, and Esther, Nine Kids

"Yes, it became something through my learning and through my meditation and through my wanting to serve God as a Jewish woman that this is the answer. This is what I was being called to do as a servant of God."

—Hannah, mother of seven

"God's not out to trick us and to send us trouble. He really wants to send us blessings."

—Esther, mother of nine

There was no easy demarcation between how it started and asking how was going. For Hannah, whose story opened chapter 2, motive and meaning blurred together. We learned about her "quest for meaning and purpose," which led first to Israel, then to meeting her husband through "mutual friends and teachers who knew both of us," and ultimately to marriage: "We were both very clear and very focused that one of our main goals of getting married was to begin a family right away and wanted to have a large family. That was something that we were attracted to with the teachers that had turned us on and inspired us as we returned to our faith. And we talked a lot about that in our first dates."

Hannah told us with a laugh that friends had matched her and her future husband up because they both had dreadlocks, loved organic farming, and were drawn to a recovery of their Jewish faith. "The two main things that people knew were organic farming and dreadlocks.... That's not why we were meant for each other, but that was like [the reason we were introduced].... He did [have] red-headed dreads, they called him Raven. He was the shaman of Missoula, Montana."

From a Reformed Jewish background where she "didn't even want to get married at one point" in her life, Hannah's search led her to the idea that children are "the meaning of everything."

Such a conclusion might have been reached on human terms. But Hannah's discernment was nourished by devotion to God after her conversion: "Yes, it became something through my learning and through my meditation and through my wanting to serve God as a Jewish woman that [having children] is the answer. This is what I was being called to do as a servant of God." It was in this part of the interview that Hannah called children a "key to infinity" and described how being a Jewish mother made her part of "a link and a chain that we've had from Moses and from Abraham and from Noah and Adam."

### "I Wanted to Do the Right Thing"

In contrast, Esther—interviewed with Hannah in our only joint interview—was more like Shaylee and Terry. She embraced child-bearing easily. "I really can't say I thought deeply into having kids before it happened. I mean, I'm the oldest of five.... So even though I didn't think ahead much about having kids, I wanted to do the right thing." After marriage, it took her two years to conceive her first. "I have Crohn's disease, so I went through periods of being very sick as a teenager so I wondered if that might have impacted something. So, I was very nervous until we did get pregnant. And when I heard the news, that was a very memorable moment for me.... It was very amazing to hear that news. But it wasn't like, I didn't have that experience of Hannah's where it's like, 'This is a goal.' I just knew I would do the right thing."

Esther used the expression "do the right thing" twice. What did she mean? She explained: "Based on what I've learned and my background, I didn't think it was right to try and not have kids, you know?" As I shared in chapter 6, Esther believes that children are one of "the three big blessings" from God and told me that she didn't "feel like you could ever have too much of any of those things."

Hannah and Esther articulated their reasons of the heart—the great meaning they attached to childbearing, which made it worth the personal costs. In chapter 2, we saw how Hannah talked about "super-rational" thinking that leads to "possibilities of expansion in your life." She and Esther didn't think of themselves as less rational than others—as, say, not counting the costs, or pretending the costs didn't matter. Rather, they knew costs were real, but the goods they were after compensated for the hardships they incurred.

For Hannah, the pain of disapproval and emotional rejection by her more secular parents had been "one of the most stressful experiences of [her] life every time [she] got pregnant." She added that "everything is fine now. They love us, they love our kids." But nevertheless, it hadn't been all roses when she and her husband broke with the way they had been raised. She described the saving help of friends, mentors, and her husband: "You need approval the most from the people who you are closest with. I've had to exhibit an incredible amount of strength. My husband grounded me. And my friends have been so critical in terms of getting through those moments."

"Also, the fact that we believe so much in what we're doing. So that kind of holds strong through everything.... At the end of the day, my mentor was like, 'With time and with grandchildren, everything will be fine.' And she was right. So, I just kind of hold on to that."

Postpartum depression had also burdened Hannah's childbearing experiences. "Not severe," she said, but "prolonged." She had developed strategies for managing it, she said, but she "really struggled in a lot of ways," especially at the beginning of her married life, when she was more isolated and had fewer personal resources. "On a physical level, I was pretty good. But for the mental, emotional stuff it was really hard for me. You can get support for those things. You do. But that could also be something that would be a deterrent for continuing. I guess I was just committed."

### *"Your Heart Grows"*

Hannah and her husband kept going not because having kids was easy, but because it meant so much to them. Still, the hardships gave way to some immediate rewards even while they waited on time and grandchildren. To illustrate, Hannah shared a memory from her early days as a mother:

> I couldn't imagine having a second kid after I had one. [But] one really nice thing I want to share with you about that is after I had my first, I could not understand how that worked. Having a second baby and the amount of love you have for your family.

And I experienced this feeling of your love expanding. I get choked up about it. I was like, "Wow, I really don't get this. You can expand a family and your love grows."

And I really felt more after I had my second that I had a family then. Having a first was like an extension of our marriage, [it] sealed... our marriage. But having two kids really was more of a feeling of like, "This is a family." And that just kept growing, I guess.

Her statement went to the heart of the phenomenon I set out to investigate. Among the moms defying the birth dearth, their reasons for getting started often had to do more with values and principles. But their reasons to keep going were more like second-order desires: joy and happiness superadded to the meaning they already attached to their childbearing. The added joys created a snowball effect in favor of more kids. "My heart is bigger, if that makes sense," said Tina, mother of six children in the Northeast. Amanda, whom we met in chapter 6, said, "With kids... your heart grows." Molly, who had five kids when we interviewed her but hoped for another one soon, put it this way: "[Every kid] keeps adding more color to the family. It's always, 'Like this is better, this is better again, it keeps getting better!' So, I just think we've had such a track record so far with each kid bringing a new source of joy that it's exciting to think that could happen again." And of course, there was Terry's emotional post-birth exclamation: "How many more can we have!?"

Esther, much quieter than Hannah throughout the interview, described some of the difficulties she had had early on.

Speaking of never being the same, that was an awareness that came to me when my oldest daughter was a couple of days old. And we brought her home from the hospital and I couldn't believe they were letting her out with us, you know? And...for the next little while, I slept sitting up staring into her basket. Like I couldn't relax enough to lie down and go to sleep.

And it occurred to me that from now on I'm not going to have a day where I'm not going to worry. Or a moment of worry-free. I definitely tend to be a worrier. I battle against it, and I try to work on strengthening my trust in God.

Esther said that her eldest daughter had special needs, including Crohn's disease like herself. But, "It's managed," Esther said, and "everybody else has been healthy and well. And we've seen amazing miracles." Still, she struggled with anxieties and fear:

I'm always nervous in every pregnancy, you know, is the baby going to be normal? Is it going to be okay?

And part of my fear as we had more and more kids, I had this very severely in my seventh pregnancy, I had fear about if the baby was going to be healthy.

And I asked myself, like, I have six healthy kids—I almost felt like I was playing Russian roulette. Like, "Why am I taking another chance?" But that's the wrong way of thinking about it, and I really, really try as much as I can not to feel like that.

And our rabbi...very much encouraged big families and I saw a video of him speaking. Talking about if parents would only realize how children and more children are their greatest source of blessing, why would anyone want to not have that?

And it's an awareness that children—God's not out to trick us and send us trouble. He really wants to send us blessings. Yes, things don't always turn out exactly the way you might have expected—but children are a source of great blessing. And God wants us to have more blessings and more healthy children and we should definitely ask for that.

### *"Our Finances Don't Add Up at All"*

Esther's view of children as blessings reflected her understanding of God's providence. *Trusting* in God's material providence went together with *entrusting* the size of her family to God's design and plan. She used their financial situation as a clear example of how God was not out to trick them:

> Yeah, we could not have predicted that we would be somewhat afloat with nine kids, two of them in out-of-town schools and a third going out of town next year. Now it doesn't add up. It does not add up at all. But a lot of things that people think are going to be big expenses also don't turn out to be. All my kids are wearing hand-me-down clothing.
>
> We live very, very simply. I don't spend money on a lot of things that a lot of other people spend money on. We don't go anywhere, for the most part. And I work on trying to make our home life fun and happy. We do activities that don't cost money, like going to the playground. And fighting with your siblings doesn't cost anything, so it's all here and available.

She laughed. Her husband, the one who had greeted us with a MAGA hat, grinned from an adjacent room. He was reading, but clearly listening in. Unable to hold himself back, he interjected twice during our conversation. Concurring with his wife, he said,

> This is just one interesting thing, this is from my own perspective, but when someone has twenty cars, no one thinks that they're crazy. You see these billionaires with ten houses, and I'm like, "I can barely keep up with one house. How do they keep up with ten houses?"
>
> But nobody thinks they're crazy. Nobody says, "Are you going to stop buying another house in another place? What's with you?"

Esther picked up on her husband's line of thought. "Let's get people as envious of having more children as they are envious of people buying cars and houses and boats...they don't ask that question, 'How are you going to finance that?' But they do with children."

And her husband continued—in his second and final outburst: "The main rabbi said, '[Kids] is a good retirement plan. If you only have one child, how much can you burden them with your aches and pains and crutches when you get older? [Now] is the best time—when they fight over you.'"

Esther's husband was obviously proud of his wife's thriftiness. And eager to point out that the decision to have a lot of children felt to him more highly scrutinized than the acquisition of material things. And he relished the thought that in his old age his kids would take care of him.

After the exchange, Hannah chimed in, "A lot of people have financial hang-ups about having more kids. That is not one of our considerations. Our finances don't add up at all. If we were to try to make them add up, we wouldn't even have one kid or two kids or three kids." She continued: "Because someone can't afford another child, that in Jewish philosophy would not be a reason not to have another one. The idea is that each child brings a blessing into the family, comes with their own source of divine flow of sustenance, and it brings benefit to the family and to the world."

She seemed to be referring to a Talmudic teaching that "when a male comes into the world, his loaf of bread, i.e., his sustenance, comes into his possession."[1] Presumably through the influence of Sephardic Jewish scholarship in the Middle Ages, the notion became a proverb in the Spanish language: every child is born with a loaf of bread under the arm. The proverb expresses the connection between trusting in providence to provide materially and entrusting the size of one's family to God's plan. Hannah even put the two types of planning—financial and familial—side by side and declared, "We're not financial planning. We're not family planning according to our finances. We're not waiting to have that set and then have our children."

So Hannah and Esther rejected the idea of financial planning as much as they rejected any mainstream norm of family planning. But for the same reason, which had nothing to do with a prohibition on birth control. Rather, it had to do with letting God be the author of what Esther had called "the three big blessings...children who bring us pride and joy and follow in tradition, good health, and financial sustenance." Properly understood, they insisted, these couldn't be in conflict. They believed, and their experiences had confirmed—"our finances don't add up at all"—that God would provide for more children since children and sustenance belonged to God's provident care. "God owns the world," Hannah said, "and he knows what's good for us."

### *"I Want to Want"*

Letting God be the author didn't mean for Hannah what it meant for Kim—"just whatever, open to it all the time." Rather, it was more like Shaylee and Terry, where after each baby was a time of waiting and discernment. This was the point in the interview at which Hannah had talked about "moments where it's like, 'I am so not ready'" for another child. As she explained,

> There's a vessel that is not ready for it.
>
> But then there's a shift...all of a sudden it begins to creep in. Like the question, you ask yourself, because in general I want to have more. So, I would pray to have the ability or be the vessel to have more. I want to want more.
>
> I would pray to want more because sometimes I'm like "I don't want"—but I want to want, you know?

"And so, then there would be this shift where...I would be like, 'I can handle this again.'"

Hannah described a mode of being open to another child that was typical across our sample. Between children the door wasn't closed permanently. Readiness involved deep introspection, and an awareness of their changeable second-order desires. It was good to have another baby, they felt certain; there would be great joy, and God would provide. But personal limitations, health problems, challenges of the day might hold you back. Even the certainty that God wanted you to feel ready might hold you back. If you didn't want another one yet, you'd wait and avoid conception—some used birth control, others natural methods. But when the time was right, you expected God would work through your desires and not against them. You would "want" by then, you would "feel ready." Overall, your desires had a meaning, and God might change your heart later if you weren't ready now. God would wait for you until you were "the vessel to have more." As Hannah put it, finally,

I would say "I'm done," I personally know my limits and I've pushed my limits like big time—I don't feel like I can push my limits anymore, so I have that personal statement that I contend with, like "I'm done."

[But] do we ever really know what's going to happen? I also hold that. "Am I really in charge?" No, I'm not in charge. But on a personal level, I am like, "I can't handle any more"—like honestly.

Does God have something else in store for me? I hope not. But I also know that I'm not the planner of all plans.

Having more children and providing for them took on the character of an active relationship with a living God who "owns the world" and "knows what's good for us." Hannah felt free to declare her limits, but she also wondered what the future might hold. Planning for that future and bringing it about was ultimately God's responsibility, but she was a partner in that. "I wouldn't say it's *not* our responsibility," she reflected. But "these children are given to us temporarily. We're partners with their godly parent and somebody besides us is watching over them and helping guide them and take care of them."

### *"What a Better Way to Form an Identity?"*

Hannah's expression "I am not the planner of all plans" recalled the biblical Hannah's exclamation that "the pillars of the earth are the LORD's; and on them he has set the world."[2] The song of the biblical Hannah might even have been her own: "The barren has borne seven."[3] Our Hannah had not been barren of body, but barren of heart: "I didn't even want to get married at one point in my life." But she found her identity in bearing children and taking her place in a chain going back to the biblical Hannah. "And I feel like even more on a personal level, being Jewish, what more could I do to perpetuate the life of the Jewish people after all the persecution then and now? What else could I do? This is it. This is it." She continued: "You know, everyone's searching for identity.... What a way to honor your legacy and your line. What a way to connect the past and the future. That to me is being a part of infinity, to continue a chain. So, what a better way to form an identity, you know?"

As nice as it sounds, Hannah's chain poses a problem. A true "infinity" would seem to diminish an individual link. Relative to so many, the one shrinks in significance. But Hannah claimed that the Hannah joined to others, roped into Adam and Noah and her husband and all seven children, was more present to herself than the unlinked Hannah—it made her who she was.

But how can you find your identity by giving up independence? Esther, less talkative than Hannah throughout, offered one of the pithiest answers we heard: "It gives us structure and allows us to grow and feel connected to something higher than ourselves. At the same time, allowing room for each individual person's contribution and experience."

Hannah and Esther seemed to be getting at a team analogy. Any one player is tied in to the team, makes commitments, loses some freedom, and accepts being one among the others. But the team makes you who you are. Without the team you can't be good at your sport. The catcher can't be a catcher without a pitcher, nor the quarterback a quarterback without a receiver. Personal growth is built in. If you do what the team requires—practices, drills, evaluations—you become better, more yourself. You might even come to say that you found yourself by belonging to the team because you accomplished what you could not have achieved without it.

There were certain assumptions behind this idea about personal identity. First, that growth into something better, or someone better, is possible. Second, that the better self, not the current one, is the true self. Third, that growth into the true self depends on being stretched by one's role, or position, to help the group achieve the goal. As athletic excellence might be the purpose of a team, the women we met often took childbearing to be what their families were *for*. The role they played was mother. Lauren had said, "My identity is totally changed. I'm a mom. Like that's who I am. That's what I do." Leah, whom we'll get to know in chapter 18, said motherhood becomes "a really big tenet of who you are." So, tied in to the chain of family life, stretching to become better mothers, they could say that they found themselves.

Childbearing as a purpose of family life implied a set of norms about how to live, including openness to children and trust in God's providence. These in turn required that definite roles be filled: mothers towards children, fathers toward supporting the family, children towards each other. Taken together, these roles gave their marriages and families more the character of an institution than a set of relationships. This understanding suggested that what we call "family structure" might be defined by the shared highest good of the persons who establish a family—the reason for their coming together, and the basis for the roles that challenge them to become more of who they can be.

For what purpose did Hannah and Esther's marriages begin? Hannah said, of the time in Israel when she traded transcendental meditation for her Jewish faith, and her husband traded dreadlocks for a beard, "We were both very clear and very focused that one of our main goals of getting married was to begin a family right away and wanted to have a large family." Their goal was to have children, and a large family at that. Hannah doesn't feel diminished by her chain because the normative structure of her family life has propelled her to become more herself. Her personality and capacities have grown. "Things are possible," Hannah said, "like possibilities of expansion in your life." She also said, "Your love grows."

Esther remarked, "Women are so strong; I wish that women knew how strong we can be."

### "Marriage as a Mission"

Hannah and Esther's view of childbearing as a goal that gives rise to personal growth mapped almost perfectly onto their views about marriage. When I mentioned to them that some people think kids are bad for your marriage, Hannah exclaimed, "I have such a strong thought on that." She continued:

> People go to school to become doctors for how many years? They go to school to become lawyers and scientists for how many years? Marriage and raising children is a full-time job, 24/7, the rest of your life. Does anybody go to school for that? No.
>
> We're lucky we have a few classes that we've taken with a few mentors and a few living examples. But even that I find is not enough unless you have ongoing mediation, even marital therapy, self-knowledge like reading about it, and information from teachers that you trust that you're committed to practicing.
>
> What do you know about it? You've got to put work in. You've got to put work into this.

Both women believe that love and endurance in marriage come from the effort people put into their marriages. If things are going bad, they argued, it isn't the kids, but the ordinary stresses of life and domestic living. And it would be easy to blame the kids for that. Hannah said,

> A lot of that just has to do with the way you run your household. I mean, this could be one aspect of it.
>
> It's just stress. It's just planning. Me and my husband are both really ADHD. I'm diagnosed, maybe he got a diagnosis. We have a really hard time with basic functioning and scheduling and structure in general in our lives, on a personal level. And magnified so with our family.
>
> It's hard, like basic living is hard for me in general. That's why I went to Hawaii and lived on the beach and didn't have any possessions. I didn't have any responsibilities for anyone. It's a lot easier to live that way when I didn't have a lot to organize.
>
> So having kids and their schedules and their bedtimes and keeping them clean, keeping their clothes, the laundry, feeding them, I'm not good [at it].

Sometimes it gets especially hard, she said, and she "checks out" for a while. "I'm like, 'I'm done, I give up, I am not doing this anymore,' and I put everything on [my husband]." Hannah continued:

> But he's very understanding when I have my bouts of checking out, but that's how it could be hard because [having kids] makes things more crazy in the house and if you have personal problems with structure and organization, then you get all emotional over these lack of basic functioning [things] and then of course that affects your marriage.... If you don't have children it's going to come in some other area....

Now, if you're going to have a large family, or [even] if you have three kids or five kids, and these stresses happen to come out through this manner, then who gets the blame? The children, or the idea of having children.

But if people understood that this is your allotted degree of stress by who you are and your nature...why not have the best things anyway? Have the children anyway!

She concluded, "If we could somehow highlight that the blessings so far outweigh any of the, 'Are they bad for your marriage?'—nothing could be farther from the truth."

Esther concurred, bringing up again the theme of children as the shared purpose of the marriage in an exchange that went back and forth between them quickly. Esther began, "If you could view marriage as a path to self-fulfillment or enjoyment or having a good time, then yeah, you might not be having as much fun with kids."

Hannah chimed in: "That's not the definition of marriage."

Esther nodded and continued. "But if you view marriage as a mission, and as a long-term thing you grow over time—"

Hannah interrupted again. "It's unification. You become a new entity by bonding with another person."

Finally, Esther finished. "Then the children are a part of that goal. They're a part of that mission. So how could they take away from it?"

And Hannah said at last, "They're an offspring, or a fruit of it."

Both women seemed to think the core of the reason that kids couldn't ruin your marriage is that children *are* your marriage, or at least, children are the point of your marriage. As if playing in competitions could destroy the unity of a sports team. Children, by their account, were often the scapegoat for something else: the ordinary stresses of life. If a sports team lost its unity, it was a failure to put in the work of team building—not a problem with playing in tournaments.

## *"You Start to Love Anybody That You Give To"*

Esther went on to develop the idea of love as a fruit of the work you put into a marriage. She continued:

> A lot of parents probably get hung up on dividing responsibilities and, "Am I doing more than him?" I remember at a premarital class that I took…the teacher said, "It's not 'I put in 50 percent and my husband puts in 50 percent' and that's that, it's you give 100 percent."
>
> What [my husband] does is his business and only I know (and really I don't even know fully, God knows) what is my 100 percent, even if I feel like I'm working so hard and how come my husband has time to sip coffee leisurely? But if I'm capable of putting in this hard work, then I'm not doing extra. That [is] a part of me doing my 100 percent. And I can't judge what someone else's 100 percent is.

Hannah interjected with an expression of genuine humility, and friendship: "[Esther's] a shining example of what she just said and learned. She really is. That gives me inspiration because I didn't come from that and I have had a hard time doing this in my household. It's very hard. I don't feel like I'm giving 100 percent at all."

I began to wonder if their view of marriage was maybe a little bit too rugged. But Hannah closed the circle, connecting all that hard work to the spirit of love in a marriage. She said, "I think it's the difference between giving and getting…. Giving to someone else develops love. You love your kids so much because you're giving to them so much. The more you love your spouse, the more you develop feelings of love for them."

Esther nodded, and added, "Actually in Hebrew, in Aramaic, the word for love shares the same root as the word for giving. The idea being that you start to love anybody that you give to." She concluded, "It's work!... What I feel lucky about is that I have a partner who is willing to put up with me as much as I'm willing to put up with him. And what I'm really saying is that I lucked out by having somebody who has the level of loyalty and commitment to put in the work it takes to get through it. I don't think any marriage is the easy, wonderful, no-problem marriage. Maybe that exists for some people, but most people I know, it's not the case."

Perhaps it was the effect of interviewing them together, or the effect of their strong Jewish community life, but talking with Hannah and Esther felt more like a chat with a mentor or a grandmother. Little wonder that Hannah declared with a grin, "In twenty years? God willing, I hope I'll be a grandparent! I really do. I don't think I want anything more than that."

As we neared the two-hour mark, Hannah let us know she had to go, and the two women shared one more exchange. Hannah mused about what might hold people back from having children. "I don't think people trust themselves."

Esther chimed in. "I think a good place to start if you want to stretch yourself is just to say, 'Maybe I'll have one more kid.' Just be open to having one more kid."

Hannah agreed. "A little bit at a time." And Esther went on: "And then after that, 'Well, maybe just one more.'" They both smiled, and Hannah concluded, "No regrets. Not a one. I mean, like this is way harder now than [where I was in my early twenties] but I have inner peace in my life that I didn't have then. I was searching. I'm not searching now.

"Nothing compares. Not the most ideal career that I wish I had. Like, 'Oh, I wish I had been there, or done that. I wish I had accomplished this or that.' These are so obviously the most unbelievable accomplishments we could ever hope to produce in this world."

Esther concurred but offered a correction. "Do I feel like my children are my accomplishments? I more feel like they are who they are. I think women feel pressured to have it all and do everything, which is also not realistic, and [I'm] okay with making a choice or doing one thing at a time. Maybe I'm not going to have that career that I thought I would, but I can still do other things."

Hannah elaborated on Esther's comment: "I feel accomplished that I got to this point where I had children, but I don't feel like they are my accomplishments." I understood what she was getting at. Having children at all seemed like a miraculous occurrence in her life, given her story. And I tended to agree with her first statement. Her family was an accomplishment! At last, Esther broke in on the awkwardness, getting the final word. "I would like to get one thing on record. I actually recall thinking when we had less than five kids, 'What are we going to do when we don't fit in a minivan?' That seemed like a barrier to moving forward. But life continues when you don't fit into a minivan. You just don't go anywhere all together at once, or whatever."

CHAPTER FOURTEEN

## "Me Doing Something Else"—Danielle, Seven Kids

"I mean, is there less of me? No, it's me doing something
else. It's me like parenting, shepherding, nurturing,
teaching, fostering the growth of these people."

—Danielle, mother of six

W
e met Danielle, barefoot and pregnant, in the early after-
noon on a steamy summer day in the Rocky Mountain
region. Her home was about twenty minutes from a
nationally ranked medical center where her M.D.-Ph.D. husband
worked as a hospitalist and a medical ethicist. They don't wear shoes
in the house owing to her husband's Chinese-American traditions.
"We met on the first day of medical school," she told us, and "we were
in the same study carrel and part of the same campus ministry." They
began dating in the fall of that year and got engaged in March.
Danielle and her husband completed medical school together, and
she went on to finish her medical residency in pediatrics at a major
medical center in Texas.

Danielle is relatively petite in frame, pregnancy notwithstanding, and her medium-brown hair fell around her shoulders in an unfussy way. She loves to talk. Conversation was central to her life at home, she told us:

> We met really as, you know, academic peers, and then with our training and then, you know, he became an attending [physician] and began practicing independently...and I really took this sharp turn [from medicine to staying home full time].... It's really nice for us to have this sphere of our life...like his Ph.D. provides lots of good opportunities for conversation. We talk about...all kinds of things all the time.... He's a very interesting person, and is interested in a lot of things....
>
> So, I find like even with a lot of kids we're still always talking about stuff related to [his interests], related to ethics and things in philosophy. The great thing about...philosophy is that it undergirds everything. So, you're always sort of talking about things that are happening and what undergirds it and why people are the way that they are, why we make decisions the way that we do.... I mean for us that's great.... Maybe our ability to ignore the tasks and talk is helpful.

### "We've Really Had to Pull Together"

"He's a great dad," she continued. "But he's not necessarily someone that when I met him, I thought, 'This guy is going to be like champion dad,' but it turns out that he's a great guy and just kind of shows up for what is going [on]. And in our world, it's been kids and so he's just, he's great. He's super engaged and helpful and I would say pretty like egalitarian in many ways and sort of doing what needs to be done, and sometimes doing the things I hate doing."

Describing her steady partnership with her husband, Danielle said, "I think one of the great gifts" of having a lot of kids is that "you have to sort of be on a mission together. And that's not necessarily true [in some marriages], right?... For us it has been, we've really had to pull together to continue to make the world go round, you know, to make our world go round."

How did two doctors who met and fell in love in medical school end up with so many kids? Danielle and her husband didn't set out to have a big family. She more skidded into full-time motherhood rather than having it as a goal:

> I don't know if you have to do this for other graduate programs, but [in] medical school you have to write these sorts of like "here's how I imagine myself down the road" [statements]. And my forecasting was always sort of two kids, city, you know.... And I never planned to have a lot of kids.
>
> I really loved medical school [but] when I did residency, I thought it was fairly devastating. I really developed horrible anxiety and hated it. And so, when I finished, I was so thankful to be done. It was right before my son was born. So, I finished like the very end of June. He was born at the beginning of August. So, in some ways I feel like I entered motherhood in this hard state because those years had been so difficult. But it was such a mercy too... to feel like I didn't have to still do the same [thing] that had been so hard for three years.
>
> I just went from this really intense lifestyle of working a ton into [being a mom]. The plan at that point had been... I

planned to take a year off and then start a fellowship at the children's hospital. So, I had only planned to take a year off with my son.

And then by about December of the year that he was born, I realized it was the first time in my life that I hadn't just sort of gone from one thing to the next. I came up for air and realized, "I don't want to keep doing this."

Mothering her son, Danielle discovered a different type of intensity that she truly loved. At one point she told us, "Maybe for me I just sort of went from one thing that was really consuming to another." But it wasn't merely the intensity that she craved. Having her son gave her the breathing room to figure out that she didn't love medicine.

I really, really didn't want to keep doing it. And so, it wasn't something where I said like, "Oh, I don't want to do the fellowship, but I'd be happy to work in primary care or something." I just really wanted nothing to do with practicing medicine. So, at that point, then, I just became this sort of like "Surprise!" full-time, stay-at-home mom.

And then I just, you know, I enjoyed my son. I enjoyed being his mom, I think in a lot of ways.

Her words resonated with me. When I had my first son early in a doctoral program, I was immersed in another world. And I thought that I would like having him. But I didn't expect to like having him as much as I did. I remember looking around and wondering if other women enjoyed their babies as much as I did. To me it seemed motherhood had been sort of undersold. Danielle explained it in similar terms. She no longer loved her first calling, and had a surprise encounter with a new joy: the enjoyment of her son, and then of her daughter, and then of having more kids and seeing no reason to stop:

> It sort of sounds ridiculous in terms of planning.
>
> We just sort of kept liking the kids that we were having, and liking having kids and enjoying the little years.
>
> I think there was some degree to which we kind of thought, well, the kids are little, so if we're going to have more like this, they should probably be close. And I don't really know when we tipped over from that, sort of having our kids close together when they're young to like, "Oh gosh, there's really kind of a lot." But it certainly was not our [plan], you know, I mean...no romantic candlelight dinner dating and sketching out our life plan with seven kids. We would have been the most shocked, probably.
>
> [Now] I'm sort of like, this is what I'm doing all the time anyway. And so...there was no like impetus not to have more, you know.

Danielle's no "impetus not to have more" language echoes the posture of openness that we heard across our sample—from Kim and Miki, Shaylee and Terry. The moms we met didn't have a grand vision for how many kids they wanted, but the door wasn't closed, even if the next baby wasn't imagined yet, or even wanted yet—as with Hannah. That openness allowed for a reassessment of costs and benefits at later stages of childbearing. "I do think we sort of crossed that point that I'm thinking...like if we're going to have one or two more kids, like is that going to be a game changer for everybody at this point? I don't think so. And so I think I would be open to that. And it, some ways it feels easier to be open to that than at other...inflection points."

She explained that with more children, the lifestyle cost of an additional child becomes a lot smaller. Your life is already rearranged—"one or two more kids" won't "be a game changer."

Danielle's commentary recalled the claim made by demographers that the difference between old and new birth rate trends came from a seemingly tiny change in the childbearing decision tree: whether couples were basically deciding *when to stop* having kids, or *when to start*. In the past, they argued, after having a few children at the beginning of marriage, the "issue was to adopt contraception in order to avoid pregnancies...." But beginning in the 1960s, couples began their marriages postponing children, and "the basic [fertility] decision [was] to stop contraception in order to start a pregnancy."[1] If the opportunity cost of starting a family—of switching fertility "on"—is a lot higher than the cost of additional children down the line, then the regime change from "when to stop" to "when to start" could be monumental. The stories we heard supported this thesis. The women talked about the enormousness of the personal and domestic adjustments called for by having a first. And they insisted that second and third babies were almost as hard. But it didn't keep getting harder. There was a "peak" cost in terms of the personal and lifestyle challenges of having children. Hannah said, "Three is the hardest number of children to have."

The women in our study had a general sense that after two or three, additional children were much easier to have. Danielle, as we saw above, spelled this out more explicitly than anyone else: "If we're going to have one or two more kids, is that going to be a game changer for everybody at this point? I don't think so." It was easier to contemplate one or two more after having six, as she—pregnant with her seventh at the time—explained:

> I mean like we had to buy a bigger car, and all of it, all these sort of places where you might...draw a line in the sand and say like we really can't afford [another one].
>
> I definitely felt it with the sixth, that [it] definitely pushed me into the realm of like...even with four kids...it just gets to be sort of so onerous [to go out to eat] that you're like, "It's easier to do things here."
>
> So, [having our fourth] was the point that I think really reframed a lot of the logistics of life.

Besides eating out, Danielle (like Esther) mentioned the size of her car and the shift to traveling less. "I feel like that ship has sailed." It wasn't wistful, just matter of fact. Since Danielle and her husband had already made those adjustments, having "one or two more" children wouldn't impact their lifestyle. And they expected to enjoy "one or two more" a great deal. Maybe even more than the first ones, since there would be more people to share the joy. So, a peculiar type of cost-benefit reasoning started to tell *in favor* of the additional child for some of our study families after a fourth or fifth child. Fixed costs, such as giving up a career or a second income, or getting a bigger car, had already been borne. The variable costs, personal and lifestyle-related, became smaller. And the expected value to the family in terms of excitement, joy, and love seemed to grow larger with additional children.

If the marginal costs of childbearing diminish with more kids, there is a sober lesson for family policy. Fiscal inducements to have children, such as subsidies, tax credits, and other benefits are likely to be more effective for those who have already opted to bear the substantial fixed costs of a family—especially the opportunity costs related to career, income, and lifestyle. Where do these fixed costs start to give way to smaller variable costs? Based on my interviews, it seemed to be somewhere after the second child and not later than the fourth child. If you want to nudge people into having more kids, it's going to be a lot harder to nudge them into the first or second child than the fourth or fifth.

### "It's a Gift to Have People to Care For"

The way Danielle saw it, the lifestyle cost of starting a family was so great that it had to be seen as an investment, or a down payment, on a certain kind of growth that one had to value for its own sake.

> So, I think the first, the transition from not having kids to having kids is so profound because you go from being responsible for yourself to being ultimately responsible for another helpless person. It really, you know, it's such a, such a dramatic change in your capacity to do the kinds of things that you're used to doing.
>
> And the gear shifts so dramatically there, so I think it's easy to feel like that first one. And even sometimes the second can do this too because you think, 'cause with your first child, you're like, "Okay well my whole world changed." But you also got used to doing everything that you wanted to do for that child.
>
> And the second one is when you have to learn to not be able to do everything that you want to do for everybody. But past that point, I think the dynamic shifts a little, right? 'Cause you've already, you know, we joke about it like, you

know, when you go to three kids, you go from like man-to-man to zone defense.

Danielle's experience was that children, especially the first few, change your world by requiring more than your capacity. When the first kid comes, you can't do everything for yourself that you're used to doing. When the second comes, you can't do everything for the first kid that you've learned to do. Each additional kid challenges you to adapt to a more complicated set of needs. You grow, but as you grow, your own limitations allow others to grow. She continued:

> My experience has been having more kids has [meant] like by definition I cannot make everything [be] the way that I might want to.
>
> But I, I think it's good for them in the sense that it liberates their play, their creativity, their responsibility, all of those things are somewhat elevated because of their circumstances.
>
> And I know that's, that can be hard for older kids…but it's also a privilege to have and execute well your responsibilities.

Danielle explained, as other women in our study had, that when mom can't do everything for everyone anymore, that gives rise to a type of freedom for children, where they can recreate without the strictures of parent-planned "fun." It also gives rise to an opportunity for kids to feel needed and valuable. Older kids ultimately become part of the nexus of caregiving and enjoyment that constitutes the heart of the family. Danielle elaborated: "You do also start to see the dynamic between them evolving… [they may do some] legwork of like cutting grapes or changing diapers but there is like a relational piece [too]. All the language my baby acquires are words that I speak to them [but] also words that they hear from their siblings' discussion."

Building on this point, Danielle rejected the idea that each child is an additional burden: "To say that it's sort of additive the way that [they're] taking more and more and more from you...doesn't take into account the relationship between the children themselves. And it doesn't take into account the way that the wisdom that you glean over time from parenting changes the way that you parent subsequent kids."

The inputs from older children augment your contributions as a mother, and lighten your load. Younger kids aren't left with less of you, because you become more, and your nurturing is extended through your other children. But, she asked, "Does it cost you something?" Danielle answered her own question in the affirmative: "Yes, but the dividends are there too.... I mean, there's a piece of sacrifice too. There's a good thing in that.... It's a gift to have people to care for, to love, [and] to help encourage them to do that for others too.

### *"Other Things Die"*

Danielle stressed that the choice to mother many wasn't so much a loss as a new direction for her talents and time. "Is there less of me in the sense that...things have changed? In terms of interests?" The doctor-turned-full-time-mom continued:

Sure.... You know, if I just woke up tomorrow and it was just me and it was sort of do whatever you would like to do, I'd go to church on time and go to an art museum and eat at a restaurant, you know, so things change.

...and this is a super interesting thing that [my husband] and I have talked a lot about...we talked about this in medicine. Like when you make one decision, other things die. They just do. And when, when we decided to become doctors, other parts of our lives died. And so, anytime you make a decision to do something, particularly something that is somewhat consuming, yes, other things will die.

Like having a big [family], like are there parts of my life before that I don't invest in or engage in like I once did? Sure. But I'm doing something else. It's me parenting, shepherding, nurturing, teaching, fostering the growth of these people.

But that's not [bad], I mean 'cause then you'd look at anyone's vocation and say like, "Oh well, you're no longer sleeping in until noon anymore because now you have a job." You wouldn't say that like, "Oh, you've lost yourself."

Danielle's "other things die" captures the notion of opportunity cost crisply. Mothering full time was more valuable to her than what she was giving up, not a choice against professional work per se. But—her professional work was a good that had died in this instance. Not only that. Also eating at restaurants and going to museums on a Sunday. All goods, but not the goods that had the highest value for her and for her family.

Danielle suggested that the narrative about losing your identity as a full-time mother may come from a culture that doesn't treasure motherhood as highly as other things. She explained:

I think maybe some of that is rooted in like not meriting the work of parenting richly enough. And of course, it turns into a whole minefield because of course there are people who are doing like paid vocational work that is

wonderful and are also mothering. And so, it can get kind
of hard when you talk about it. And certainly, it's culturally
sensitive.

Caregiving . . . there was a book and it talked about how
we would benefit from dignifying the work of caregiving
as adult valuable work. And how it could be across the
board, could be neighboring, could be caring for elderly
adults, could be caring for children.

But the fact that it has sort of become . . . regarded as
anyone could [do it], which you know, okay, but to raise
the value of it I think pushes back against that idea. . . . I
mean if you're saying like I'm developing my skill set as a
parent, you know.

Danielle fumbled around the notion that mothering isn't just a
state of being—it's also a practice, with definite skills, habits, and
expertise. Mothers who dedicate themselves to mothering can grow
as mothers, in the virtues of motherhood. Danielle worried about
the logic of seeing mothering as essentially unskilled labor. It would
follow, she argued, that caregiving isn't worth dedicating your life to.
In contrast, if mothering is more like one of the great pursuits of
human life, like summiting a high peak, then the grueling practice
and hardship of preparation would be undertaken with a view to the
worthiness of the goal. It costs you something, but "the dividends are
there too."

Danielle was humble about the costs she had borne personally.
Regarding pregnancy and childbirth, she said she'd "been fortunate
to have had . . . essentially no complications. Pretty smooth pregnancies." Socially, she said, "I don't think we've gotten very much vocal
pushback. Yeah, we've been fortunate. I know a lot of people who can
receive some pretty cruel comments and we have not received that.

I also would not say we have had like a lot of overly enthusiastic [reactions]." She observed that attitudes toward sizable family commitments seemed cooler, compared to attitudes toward being in a demanding medical residency:

> Maybe it's unfair to accuse people, but I feel like there is sort of an implicit notion [when you have a lot of kids] of like, well, "If things are busy you kind of asked for it." Which is a really interesting contrast to the years of residency, which I also asked for and also made decisions surrounding.
>
> But it was always like I felt the overarching vibe was empathy or just more affirmation, like yeah, [medicine] is worthwhile work…a worthy choice. It's consuming but worthy. [With kids] it's sort of like, "Well it's your life."

### "The Story of Growing Up Female in America"

Danielle believes that such soft denigration of motherhood as a life choice is part of the story of why women rarely choose to dedicate their lives to having children. But she doesn't think that's the whole story. She also blames ignorance about the life course, evidenced by a social patterning of a woman's life plan on the model of a male life plan: first secure a professional income, then secure a family. She pointed out that the path of schooling for women leads inexorably through the years when it would be easiest and most favorable to have children:

> I think there's a piece of the story of growing up female in America that's like, you can be and do anything. And when you've accomplished all of the goals that are time sensitive,

then you can do these other things. And for some people that's true....

[But] many people can't have children without medical assistance, you know, well into [their]... late thirties, forties.... I feel like a lot of people never even think about it though, until they're starting to get to the point that they [are worried], 'cause there's so much like hit the ground running—like high school, college, grad school, build your careers and professions and your track.

It's hard not to see Danielle's commentary as partly autobiographical. Earlier she had said about her maternity leave, "I realized it was the first time in my life that I hadn't just sort of gone from one thing to the next. I came up for air and realized, 'I don't want to keep doing this.'" She continued:

I know this is so controversial, but, truthfully, I would not want to go back and do my training now. I'm like, oh my gosh. I'm too tired, you know. So, there is a sense in which there are some things just best done young. Um, but I also think that sometimes having kids is one of those. Like it's easier. It seems to be easier. It seems to be.

You know, I don't know if this is horrible to say, but I think there's some ways too that when you're younger [the transition to kids is easier]. I think that shift for my friends who've been older can be so hard because... you've put all this effort in and then you're used to like, there've been dividends from that in terms of control. And the transition to parenthood at that point I think can be really, really, really hard.

And so, I want to sort of be cautious there, but I do think that there's a sense in which... there's very little thought early on and I've had lots of conversations with professional women kind of into their late twenties, thirties that are like all of a sudden sort of taking stock of like, "Hey, what do I, what do I even want familywise? What is going to be possible?"

And I just feel like that question is not even on the table, and it would feel, antithetical and sometimes there's a strong sense of betrayal of people who've invested in their career.

It's complicated, I think. I certainly don't want to say like, "Oh, these women shouldn't do anything interesting academically." I don't believe that at all.

But I do think that we [should ask the question] when we look at the progress of like feminism in general, right?

Danielle's monologue needs little interpretation. She raised the problem of the new calculus. Women's professional education and work crowd out time for having children in myriad ways—even when women want and expect to have families. It begins with the long march of formal schooling undifferentiated from a male timeline. It continues through college, graduate training, residencies, and assistantships. None of these programs is normed for part-time progress, even if some renegades pull it off. Where part-time options do exist, women often pass them up for fear of being relegated to "second class" status. Establishing oneself in a profession on part-time terms is difficult.

The "sense of betrayal" that Danielle mentions is real. Women who have been encouraged to look at career-building single-mindedly suddenly find themselves up against a gut-wrenching quandary they don't remember opting into—their desire for a home and children on the one hand, and the fruition of years of training on the other. Most of the time women split the difference, leaving neither incredibly fulfilled nor fulfilling. Mothering small children while working makes mother-hood less enjoyable. And working while juggling family responsibilities taints the natural satisfactions of throwing oneself into a career. Danielle continued:

> You know, like I mean like there's no option for a part-time residency. You can't say, you know, "I'm going to do this over six years instead of over three because I have young children and I want to be around for them. I feel like these are important formative years."
>
> There are some places that are changing. Some fellowships I think are a little bit part-time. Certainly. There are some academic programs that are more or less accommodating, but some of it's just so arbitrary.
>
> And part of that probably, I mean, I'm speculating here, but part of that's probably because a lot of these things in formation were formed for men who had different biological [reality], I don't know.... It always feels hard to comment on.

Danielle tried to avoid pouring salt on the wounds of the mommy wars. Every time she came to a place where her remarks might imply judgment or criticism, she held back or qualified her speech. But she's conscious of the problem, and spelled it out:

> We're always in a weird place when it comes to family size. Because it's like if you make too big a thing of it, then you're being pretty ungracious to people who for whatever reason don't [have kids].
>
> And if you make too little of it, then you start to feed this idea of like who would want to really do that and is this even really valuable work for someone's life?

## *"People Are Good for the World"*

Danielle had a way of turning things on their heads: We don't want to judge family size, so we don't laud childbearing. But when we don't laud childbearing, people conclude that it's not worth doing. And that has implications for the value of children themselves.

The Presbyterian mother of five advanced a counter-thesis about the merit of childbearing, based on the value of children:

> They're good for the world. I don't know, like, in general, I think people are good for the world.
>
> That overall notion of like, this is a good thing. These children, they are good. It is good. It is good.
>
> Like the idea of a tapestry in generation and the handing down of wisdom from one generation to the next, and faith and like looking back and looking forward and seeing, like through Scripture, the tapestries of family, even some of the hard places, but the places that you see, you know, I mean it can be so profound.
>
> And so, I think that sort of informed my [view], sort of seeing myself as a part of it, a tapestry of this thing, like you don't know where these kids are going to, you know, fall out and things.
>
> But also...a strong thing has been feeling like they're a gift. They really are a gift and it's a privilege to have them and to raise them and to know them.

Danielle's tapestry reminded me of Hannah's chain, and her heart seemed to mirror the heart of the biblical Hannah, with an almost reverential attitude toward the gift of children. As a rule, that attitude wasn't present in my subjects' memories of what got them started.

But it was deeply present in their reasons for continuing to have kids and their descriptions of how it was going. "The dividends are there too," Danielle said.

She turned one other thing around. "So, I think sometimes we're asking the wrong questions," Danielle said. People focus on the logistical problem, how to fit these two conflicting pieces together, work and family. But "some of the questions about how do these things serve one another could be helpful." She continued:

> Lots of times we talk about how working in paid vocations people will say, "Oh, it makes me a better mom. You know, I'm able to have this space, I come back refreshed." But I think more of the conversation [should go] the other way too.
>
> My husband, is he better doing palliative care for his patients because he's used to slowing down and listening to his kids? Maybe. Maybe he is.
>
> So, I think to ask some questions about... our role as parents, as nurturers, how does this grow our character in such a way that we're growing into the people that we want to be?

Danielle was asking one of the biggest questions of all: How does being a mom or a dad affect our outward-facing work? Is a nation having children later and later different from one in which childbearing happens earlier? It's not a question I can answer based on this study. But my subjects believe that raising children results in profoundly altered attitudes, behaviors, and loves. It would be reasonable to expect those alterations to spill over into other areas of life, from work to church, politics, and community. Certainly, red-blue voting patterns reflect some kind of spillover. As Danielle put it, "I think all children are training the affections of their family."

She recalled with consternation that as a young woman she "didn't even think about what would happen if [she] didn't have any children. But I should have," she said:

> There are so many people who have struggled and, in my own family story too, but I think I have been thankful, and it probably has gotten stronger with time because I've realized more and more, like as I've gotten older, I've seen more people struggle.
>
> I've had more older women say, "Oh, I wish I could've had, would've had one more . . . more period."
>
> So, I do think there are little pieces of encouragement that sort of reinforce that idea of like, this is hard, but this is a gift too, right?

She hadn't thought about missing out on children in part because, as she told us, "From the time I was a young child I wanted to be a physician." She had thought that "the practice of medicine" would be the "identifying sort of manifestation" of being "conformed to Christ." But after having kids she found herself "embracing more and more" that motherhood was her way of being transformed into Christ. So much so that when she declared that being a full-time mom was "[her] doing something else," she used the image of a shepherd. "It's me like parenting, shepherding, nurturing, teaching, fostering the growth of these people." She continued: "We teach our children that the Lord delights in them. I also want them to have that borne out in their experience . . . to just have that unwavering sense of like, 'I'm for you. I'm for you.'"

Ultimately, the kids weren't just for her, to make her into something more, or different, or better—even if that happened. Rather, she was for them. She was *for them*. Talk about turning things around. Their goodness didn't mean desiring children for the sake of having them but having them for the sake of desiring them. Stated otherwise: children give love, but they also call forth love, and the latter is the greater gift.

# CHAPTER FIFTEEN

# "May I Ask Why?"—Steph, Six Kids

"Get educated as much as you can. And then you have
your children and whatever works out with you and
your husband. You have as many [kids] as you can and
it's the greatest joy."

—Steph, mother of six

I f Danielle discovered when she had her first kid that she hated
her profession, that certainly wasn't the experience of every
woman we talked to. Not even close. Many worked full or
part-time in their work vocations despite large families. Steph, a
pediatrician with a stay-at-home-husband, was one of them. She
always knew she wanted kids. "I found journals from when I was
younger that I wanted six to eight children," she said, "and *this* is
seven." She gestured toward the wonderfully adorable teacup poodle
in her lap. Her husband came from a family of seven. "He always
was happy with that. He loved that," she told me. "But I came from
a very small family. I came from the exact opposite because I was an

only child. So, I yearned for family my whole life." After getting married, they waited to have kids "longer than [she] would have liked." She continued:

> I wanted to have children right away. I mean it's not just that I came from a small family, but I love children and my mother loved children. You know, like if there was ever a baby, she was right next to that baby and holding it. And I remember babysitting once and the baby was so sad, and I couldn't find a way to calm this little baby down.
>
> And so, I called [my mother], and she came over and I remember being so touched at the way she just picked that baby up and all of a sudden, the baby was calm. And I loved that. And so I love children and that's why I do pediatrics.
>
> But we waited three years because of medical school.... It was hard. But as soon as we could, we just lined things up so that it didn't put a burden on anybody in medical school. I put my vacation from the third year and the fourth year together, did a breastfeeding home study basically for another rotation and got about twelve weeks off—and didn't nobody even know I was gone.

When Mary and I arrived for our interview, Steph led us from her front driveway to the back porch of her home. She sat cradling her tiny puppy lovingly. From where we were seated, we could see into the rear living area of her house through glass doors. It looked like a page out of a *Magnolia Journal* magazine. Looking back to the hopes in her journals, she had gotten her six—the poodle, she kidded, was seven.

Steph and her husband had been married for twenty-eight years at the time of the interview. They had six children aged twenty-four, twenty-one, nineteen, seventeen, fifteen, and thirteen. Her kids were older than those of most of the women we interviewed. They don't go places all together anymore, but she recalled that when they did, "Lots of people [would] say, 'Are these all your children?' and kind of gawk and stare. But most of the time," she said, "people actually [said] nice things.... There was a man who said to my husband, 'Are these all your children?' And he said, 'Yes.' And [the man] said, 'You've got it right.'" But one memory from those days was less blithe. She recounted,

> We took our kids to Disneyland in California, and we were in the, you know, little restaurant eating, Goofy's Kitchen. A woman came up to me, she'd been sitting nearby with her husband there with her one child. And she said, after a while, "Are these all your children?" We were there with five and I was pregnant with our sixth.
>
> And I said, "Yes."
>
> And she said, "May I ask—and you're having *another* one?"
>
> And I said, "Yes."
>
> And she said, "May I ask why?"
>
> And I was so taken back. I didn't even know how to respond. I don't even remember what I said, I was just so stunned that that's what she said.

### *"He Understands Both Sides Too"*

Steph was born in New York City, but her parents moved west when she was eight. She told me she had "studied botany in college and was premed," and her lush backyard proved she still loved plants. "[I] went to medical school at the University of Utah. And did residency in pediatrics in Tucson, Arizona. And I practice pediatrics today." Her husband? "He's home with our children," she told me.

Of the fifty-five women we interviewed, Steph was the only one with a stay-at-home husband. I asked her to tell me more.

> So, he's two years younger than I am. And so, he finished college when I finished medical school and then we went to do residency. He stayed home with our one child. We had a second in residency. [After that we came back to Utah to] take care of my father. My mother had passed away just a week after we got married, and so, we came back to take care of my dad who had some special needs.
>
> [The plan was] that I would work part-time and he would work part-time. So, we did that for the first few years. And then had more children. And after the fourth my dad was failing; his health was failing and somebody needed to be with him all the time. So, we thought about it and made the decision to have [my husband] stay home all the time. And he's done that ever since. He really fell in love with it.

When I asked her how it worked, and whether having a large family had diminished her professional life, she was quick to credit her husband: "My husband and I do this together, so there's no way for it to take it away from me because we're a team. We did this together.

"So, I provide the ability for him to do things that he enjoys, and he provides the ability for me to, you know, fulfill what I believe is my gift and my calling, to be a physician. So, I don't see it that way."

Steph went on to describe some of the pros and cons of their nontraditional arrangement. There were more pros than I might have imagined:

I don't work full-time as a pediatrician. I work part-time. Because we started with my husband doing part-time and me doing part-time. And we remained like that we— because we realized that I could earn enough to support our family part-time and we enjoyed so much the days that we were together. So that we could tag team and be a team together on those other days.

And yeah, um, it ended up [that] I pick up a little bit, it's not exactly half, I pick up some night calls [and] I do some extra you know, some weekends and things like that. But the children, they know what to expect because it's pretty consistent. Tuesdays and Thursdays, I'm just gone.

If they need something suddenly, they need to go to Dad for it. I'm here the other days to fulfill all of the mothering that, the things that dads can never do, you know. I mean, my husband loves it, and he tries his very best, but there are things that they wait for Mom, period, and that's okay. But we've enjoyed so much being together, and I think the attitude of teamwork maybe provides that.

Because he experiences what a mother does when they stay home all the time, he doesn't ever, you know, like there's never an attitude of, "Well, why wasn't this done or that done?" Or, "How come you did this and didn't do that?" Or, you know, [with him] it's much more, "How can I get you out to do what you'd like to do?" Or, "How can we make it happen?" That, you know, and we do that for each other because I understand what it's like to stay home. I understand what it's like to be at work all day. And he understands both sides too. And so that's great.

*"When We Just Get to Hang Around Together"*

Steph thought the hardest part of big family life was managing "the details of the day-to-day, the 'How do you get to this game and that game at the same time?' And, 'How do you balance all that needs to be balanced?' and you know, but you figure that out. And we, we've learned to tell our kids, 'You play one sport at a time. You know, you just can't do everything at the same time.'" She quickly added, "But it's okay, because like kids these days do too much. They need downtime." When I asked what she liked best about her family life, she didn't hesitate:

> Oh, my goodness. There's just never a dull moment. It's that there's just so much joy. I guess if I had to answer that lady [at Disneyland] again, I would just say, "Because this is where the joy in life comes from."
>
> You know, those relationships and watching them grow at every stage, and accomplishments, and watching them become their own independent person and you just can't replace that with anything else. It's remarkable. It's precious. It's life's greatest gift, right?

She expanded on that point, bringing up her delight in everyday family meals, movie nights, and staying up late with teenagers:

> Sitting around with your family around the dinner table. It's so great.
>
> And everybody just chitchatting and yeah. Teasing each other and enjoying the meal and, yeah. And just sitting around watching a movie together or playing games or just being together. And just enjoying each other. And not

having any, I mean it's, you know, we do have other constraints and places to be.

But when we don't have those things, that's my favorite
time, when we just get to hang around together. That's
sometimes when you have the best conversations with kids
too. When it's not preplanned and you're just sitting there
and all of a sudden out it comes, "Hey mom, what do you
think about this?" Or, "So-and-so did this, and am I going
to do that?" And you're just kind of together.

And somehow, they open up, especially teenagers after
10:00 p.m. And that's why we've always stayed up because
we have really the best conversations when they come
home. We got a little chair in our room, and they come in
and they sit down, and they sit there and maybe it's just a
minute or two, "Okay goodnight," and sometimes they
unload all sorts of stuff.

But those are great moments, you know, we're doing
great. So that's happiness to me. I think that's, that's very
fulfilling to me. And then someday to have grandchildren
to do the same thing with. That'd be great. That I know,
so exciting.

Steph lamented that there had not been *just one more*. She blamed
the late start from medical school. "I know, I know; we would've had
more. I just didn't start, we didn't start till I was twenty-seven, so you
know, and you're hoping there'd be at least one more that came, but
that was the end, sad."

She's not alone. The median age for a mother to have her first
birth has increased from twenty-seven to thirty since 1990.[1] And
lifetime fertility decreases the older you are when you have your first
baby.[2] Even if women try to "catch up" after starting late, and often

they do try, demographers point to "biological constraints and nor-mative limits" that can "shorten their time to have children." The later you start, the harder it is to have your desired number. The phenom-enon of delayed first births is a big part of the story of the transition to low fertility in the West and worldwide.[3] And the phenomenon of college and graduate school is a big part of that story for women.[4]

But women like Steph and Danielle make the real lesson clear. College, medical school, law school, and the like don't *require* lower fertility, they just eat up childbearing years. If you get married early enough, and have kids right away, you can still have an average-sized family—a big family even. But the biological deck is stacked against you, and the opportunity costs mount as the years of schooling go by. To have children anyway, you have to know what you're about. And find the right spouse on time, and hit all the green lights, so to speak. Higher education and women's entry into professions don't *cause* lower fertility any more than a spike in the cost of inputs *causes* lower output—what causes lower output is a decision to reduce out-put because there is not enough demand at the new (higher) price. Women's time is the biggest input into childbearing; if that input has become more expensive in terms of opportunity costs, only those with an extraordinarily high demand for children will still have children—whether they go to medical school or not. No social wel-fare policy in the world is (or could be) generous enough to change that calculus. What you need is the conviction, captured in Steph's considered answer to the rude lady at Goofy's Kitchen: "Because this is where the joy in life comes from."

## "It's the Best Work There Is"

Steph, a member of the Church of Jesus Christ of Latter-day Saints, credited her faith, and the faith of her mother—a Catholic convert to Mormonism who loved babies—with influencing her view of family. She also said the value of children was proved in the doing of it:

> And that's the, that's the whole thing. And you know, multiply and replenish the earth. So, you can have joy in your posterity. That joy word is not inconsequential. That's, that's a promise. You get joy.
>
> So, yeah, it absolutely has to do with faith because in the [Latter-day Saints] religion we're taught that families are the eternal unit of heaven. It's the most important thing that we have, and those relationships will endure forever.
>
> And so that's where we spend our energies. And once you start doing that, you find that that's, that's true. It's true. There is absolute happiness in this. It's work. But it's good work. It's the best work there is.

She told us, with a laugh, how often she gets taken to be someone she's not, given her standing as a successful pediatrician.

> Yeah, it's, it's fascinating. I have had people that they, like, they come to see me professionally and they expect that I'm a certain way. They have a certain kind of person [in mind]. Yeah. Um, and then when they find out some of my attitudes and then my family, they're shocked because they don't think that that's who I am.
>
> I had one woman that said, "I want to bring my daughter to you because I want her to have a role model, a successful woman." And after a while I think she became a little disillusioned when she realized that I'm not driven by my career. I'm good at it. And I give my heart to it when

I'm there, but I'm not there every day, that I have that family that is so important to me. Because that's not what she wanted for her daughter.

She wanted for her daughter to really not worry about children and family, and you know, [be] driven. Right. Get a career and that's what's most important to you.

Steph continued:

Yeah. I mean she was a little disillusioned when she went, "Huh? Oh, that's funny. I guess you weren't who I was looking for." She still comes, but she knows that, you know, she can't expect that from me.

Because I'll always tell her daughter that, you know, she can be a mother and have a career too and you should get educated as much as you can. And then you have your children and whatever works out with you and your husband. You have as many as you can and it's the greatest joy.

### *"Love Is What It Takes"*

When I asked Steph why she thinks others don't make the choices she has made, she talked about various issues, beginning with women and work.

So, our situation, granted, is unique in that my husband's willing to put his career off and just say, it's okay. Yeah, this is where I'm going to take my fulfillment in life.

I don't need to have promotions and other people pat me on the back. It's this that gives me joy. And that brings me satisfaction. So, but that's not true for lots of people.

So, I think if women had more flex-time opportunities that would be helpful. Absolutely. And not to feel like they're somehow second class because of that or not getting reimbursed as much.

Sometimes I hear this, you know, the research and the studies about how women, how we're not getting paid for the same job. And sometimes I think you're not looking at the numbers exactly. Because most of us are choosing that.

So yeah. If you, if I went full time, I'd get compensated the exact same. It's that I choose not to. Yeah. And that's okay. Yeah. And we need to stop looking at that as a negative. Right. That's all right.

As long as we have the opportunity to do what we would like to do and get fairly compensated for what we are doing.

I'm not sure what Steph has been reading, but she's exactly right about the best labor research on women's pay. Harvard University economist Claudia Goldin demonstrates that today's remaining gender pay gap results from the reduced hours that women choose to work. Many jobs reward work on a nonlinear scale, because two part-time workers aren't worth as much as one full-time employee. Goldin sees the future of pay equity coming from making work responsibilities more "stackable" across employees—opening up part-time options for proportionally similar pay.[5] Whether these changes can occur, and whether they can enable women to have the families they want, remains to be seen. Either way, Steph isn't wrong about the role of labor opportunities competing with childbearing.

She didn't stop there, however. In answer to why others have fewer kids these days, she also raised the problem of "just general attitudes." Steph speculated, "I don't know how much abortion and stuff plays into it, but I feel like the whole idea of that whole concept that a child is a negative thing on a woman. I just, I don't know. And I—there's situations where it's difficult and it can't be managed and all sorts of things, but the culture that's developed because of that, the thoughts that [we] are putting in people's minds, the whole attitude, I think has something to do with it too."

She wasn't the first in our study to mention abortion as a possible driver of the momentum of falling birth rates. Kim with twelve kids at the Harris Park Bible Church had said the same. Steph wondered about the habits of mind fostered by legal abortion, Kim about the coldness of our hearts. Both women seemed to be asking, If babies are disposable, how valuable can they be? And if we can sacrifice our living offspring for the sake of school, income, or a profession, why not sacrifice merely potential offspring for the same? Few ask such questions.

### "You Can Do It"

Steph moved on to a final concern—that people are mistaken about what it takes to have kids:

> Plus, I think it's, I don't know, the world is so selfish these days and I don't know if that's why people are choosing not to have so many children because of selfishness or because they feel like they don't have the means. That just kind of reinforces itself and I [think], yeah, it's going to continue to go down.
>
> I think people need to be awakened to what they know in their hearts is true. And that is that families are really wonderful. And that it's okay and you can do it.

If you ever thought you wanted to have more children, you can do it. And you know, you don't have to have a ton of means. I know a lot of people—there's a couple...who have, are having their tenth child and you know, they don't have a lot of means, but they're making it work. Um, he's actually a tattoo artist. Isn't that funny?

I laughed and joked that I would like to interview them. She went on:

Um, but they're wonderful and they do it because they love children. And she loves children. I mean, she just, you know, one of her last ones was Down syndrome, and she loves that baby. She just said, "This is my angel. I love this child. Why would you ever be sad about this baby?"

And then she's having another one. And I just think that, you know, people need to be awakened to that because you don't have to have a lot of means to do it. They don't have a lot of means and they're making it work. Love is what it takes.

Ironically, Steph might have been talking about herself. In the world of opportunity costs, she may face a higher price for her kids. Sure, the tattoo artist's wife probably has less cash to buy groceries, but women like Steph are squeezed in other ways. I can't judge, because the personal value of giving up one thing or another is ultimately subjective. And I surely don't want to minimize the challenges of paying for a large family. I merely note that economic logic is not all on the side of childbearing's being more affordable for professional women. Quite the reverse. Steph is right, however, that whatever costs you face, love for something higher is what overcomes them.

# CHAPTER SIXTEEN

# "Plans to Prosper You"—Jenn, Six Kids

"So, there was this time when we were kind of in limbo,
not sure where the money was going to come from. . . .
But it was just amazing how God provided for that, for
all our needs during that time."

—Jenn, mother of six

We met Jenn in an open common space at a large Baptist church in the South. She was soft-spoken with an almost melodic voice and smiled warmly and frequently during our interview. Some of her six children were there at the church too, and I met them when our interview was over. Jenn had studied pre-med and Chinese language at U.C.–Berkeley. She recalled that she had encountered a fiercely anti-child mentality in her first weeks of college: "When I went to college and I took my freshman year classes, one of them was geography. And it was required for most freshmen. And on the first day of class, the teacher was talking about how the world is overpopulated and our earth is not able to sustain that many people and gave all these statistics and said that it was irresponsible to have any more than one or two children, or any children at all."

Jenn believes that this sort of messaging at elite colleges and in the media is part of the story of falling birth rates. She continued:

> In the movies and TV shows, it seems to constantly be saying that human beings are the worst thing for our world because we are draining the earth of resources and being so irresponsible, killing off all these animals and taking up their habitats.
>
> From a philosophical point of view, it seems like the world feels like human life is a detriment to the world. And then from a personal point of view, there is a very strong push in our society for following your dreams and doing what pleases yourself. And having children and parenting is all about living for someone else, not yourself.

Jenn and her husband met in college, though they weren't at the same college. He went to Penn State. She explained how they met: "When we were in college we went to the same study abroad program in Taiwan, so we just happened to be in the same group. It was a pretty large group, about fifteen hundred students. But both of us were Christians already at the time and we were praying that even though it was a secular program that we would be able to find some sort of way to serve the Lord there. So, he decided to start up a Bible study and he came and knocked on my door as he was going around to invite everyone to it and that was how we met."

They didn't get married right away, she told us. "Well, we dated long distance for about four years and then got married after that."

### *"Leave It Up to the Lord"*

Jenn grew up as the eldest in a family of five, the daughter of Bible-believing Chinese Christians in Oakland, California. She knew she wanted to have a family, but she never imagined six. "That wasn't my original thought," she said, laughing. But shortly before her wedding the pastor of their large Asian-population Bible church in California influenced the course of her life dramatically:

> I grew up in a large family so I know the challenges and I thought maybe three or four children would be a good size. And I know that there was also a possibility that we might get a surprise. That's what happened to my mother. She was planning on four and got five.
>
> But when I talked to my husband about it, he didn't express any opinions, so I just thought, "I guess he doesn't care," and, "We're going to go with my plan."
>
> And then we found out, well, two weeks before the wedding our pastor actually preached about something related to planning your family and birth control and things. And he is of the persuasion that you should leave it up to the Lord because the Lord will provide and that it is in line with the values that he lays out in Scripture.
>
> My husband, turns out, had been quietly thinking about this. So, I found out two weeks before the wedding that we weren't going to be planning [our family].

Her husband took his faith and study of Scripture very seriously. So seriously that after finishing medical school and a residency in eye surgery, he felt called to religious studies. When she said he was thinking, she really meant it. "[The pastor] had not been preaching anything on that topic up until that point. But he does have six children. At the time, I had never heard of such a thing because of living in California where the cost of living is so high, and there is a very liberal mindset."

"Were other people shocked?" I asked.

"Yes," she laughed, "our whole church."

I followed up by asking if people took it seriously besides her and her husband.

"[At church] nobody voiced to us anything otherwise. I think we were all very, maybe it's part of being Asian, but we are generally very submissive to authority, and we valued what [our pastor] had invested in us so we weren't going to be talking against him."

As Jenn told this story, there was no suggestion of being coerced into having children. It was rather that two weeks before the wedding she saw that there were two plans for her marriage, not one. There was her private plan—"my plan," she had called it, since she and her husband hadn't discussed it when they were engaged. And then there was another plan, new to her, a plan that her pastor and husband now favored, the plan of not-planning: "Leave it up to the Lord because the Lord will provide." She chose to go along with their plan because she trusted in God and loved her husband. Her choice cost her something up front, in giving up another good that she valued—her own plan. But she valued God and her husband even more:

> I was really looking forward to having some time alone with him because having dated long distance pretty much our whole time dating, I kind of wanted to finally be together with him, just the two of us. Also, I knew that having been the oldest of five kids, I knew that when babies come, they really change your life.

So, it was a little bit of a struggle for me. But my husband was fully convinced in his heart that this is what God wanted us to do. And I didn't feel like I could or should change him.

At that point in her marriage, it wasn't so much a child that she was choosing as a way of life that involved openness to children, swapping her plans for those of the "planner of all plans," as Hannah had put it. Sure enough, however, a pregnancy came soon. "[We] married in June and in November I found out I was pregnant," Jenn said. It was a hard and lonely time for her:

Well, my husband was very busy in [medical] training and so I felt like he didn't really have the time or energy to talk about the baby names or any of the things I had been reading. So, I did feel kind of alone. And also, I had very bad morning sickness, so it was difficult because I felt like I was going through it alone.

But then I started having difficulties in the pregnancy. So, in December we found out that the baby wasn't developing. But we were just about to leave on vacation to visit his family so when we came back and had another doctor's appointment, I found out the baby was gone.

So it was during that brief period that I had come to actually want the baby. Up until then, it was a struggle.

Jenn reminded me of what Miki, from chapter 8, had said about the link between infant mortality and having more children. Intuition may suggest the opposite, but among our subjects we found that child loss led to greater openness to life, rather than to fear of death. Mary, who had eleven kids, lost her four-year-old son, her sixth child, to leukemia. She had five children more after he passed, saying, "Life is never as precious as when you realize how brief it is, how fragile it is."

Jenn continued, "I was really thankful, I think, because the Lord took the first one away, I was really able to treasure the second one."

Jenn practiced a kind of "holy imagination" where a person strives to see each happening in life, good or bad, as something God uses for good, even if it doesn't look good at the beginning. Jenn seemed convicted of the sentiment Saint Paul expressed about God's ability to weave together all the events of one's life for the better: "We know that all things work together for good for those who love God, who are called according to his purpose."[1]

### "It Just Felt Like It Was What I Was Designed For"

After all that had happened—the lonely start to her marriage, the sickness and pregnancy loss—the birth of her first living child a year later brought about a sea change for Jenn: "When [my son] came along, I felt like I had somebody with me, and he was precious and perfect, and it just felt like it was what I was designed for. It's hard to describe that feeling of peace and joy and fulfillment, even just in the very beginning of motherhood."

Her happiness and delight in her son, after she let go of her own plans and hopes, seemed to confirm for Jenn the words of Jeremiah which I learned she had adopted as a kind of personal motto: "'For I know the plans I have for you,' declares the LORD, 'plans to prosper you and not to harm you, plans to give you hope and a future.'"[2]

Jenn continued, unfolding her story child by child. When there were problems, needs, or anxieties, God took care of things. For instance, her second surviving child, a girl, was born just thirteen months after her son. Soon after that, she told me, she found she "was pregnant again." She went on. "Then I was scared and depressed because of all the difficulties I had had. But I miscarried, and then I miscarried the next one. And then when my daughter was two years old, two years and two months, I had my third. And by that time, I felt ready to have another one. And everything went fine. Then I had another when he was eighteen months old. And everything went fine with both those pregnancies."

So, when she hadn't felt ready for another baby, the babies hadn't come.

Another thing she felt God had taken care of was their financial situation. When her husband decided on a total career change and money was scarce, things worked out anyway. "At that point, my husband graduated from his medical training, and he was starting to feel that the Lord was redirecting him. So, there was this time when we were kind of in limbo, not sure where the money was going to come from because of, he was going to go back into training again after having already had such an extensive training. But it was just amazing how God provided for that, for all our needs during that time."

Incredibly, after his many years in medical school and residency, her husband embarked on a program of study in a Bible college in Texas—leaving life as a surgeon behind. After that, he began a Ph.D. in theological studies, hardly a lucrative path for a father of four. Jenn told me how during those years of "second college" and "second grad school," she again didn't have children for a while, owing to more miscarriages; there is a five-year gap between her fourth and her fifth. When she was anxious about the delivery, because she hadn't given birth for so long, "The Lord took care of it." The baby was born after an easy labor. "That has just been a pattern," she said. "When things have been scary and difficult and I prayed about it, the Lord just took care of it."

Finally, she told me about her sixth, and how things had taken a frightening turn:

So even though we thought we were probably done after five because I had had so many miscarriages and I was getting older, the Lord gave us the youngest. And during that pregnancy though, I did have more heart issues and I had escalating heart issues. At the end of that pregnancy, I had a heart attack.

And when they went into the cath lab they said, "The arteries are all clear," but they saw that there was an ulterior dissection. So, they told me not to have any more children.

And I knew all along I had been willing to accept whatever the Lord decided for us, and I kind of felt like that was his way of saying, "That's enough for you." But I think the Lord has given me peace about that, the health issues and all that helped me realize I'm at my limit.

[The baby] was fine. And I'm so thankful.

It's hard to overstate the significance of that story. Jenn's account highlights one of the seemingly problematic issues we encountered in our interviews: devoutly religious women who traded comfort and health for another child because of their faith in the supernatural value of a new life. Jenn understood that the heart attack meant she had reached her limit. But we met several women who had children anyway, in the face of severe emotional and physical hardships too personal to mention. They had a high tolerance for threats to quality of life and even health because they weighed those goods as secondary. They saw a good life as more than just an additive bundle of all the secondary goods. They valued something more than health, or even being able-bodied, and they believe that anything great requires real risks.[3] Jenn's persistence in welcoming pregnancies after so many miscarriages seems a testimony to that view.

But another way that Jenn represented women in our sample was her apparent reluctance to let go of having more when she realized the end of childbearing had come. She hadn't wanted the plan of not planning at the start. She hadn't looked forward to having her first. And during her years of having babies, she often felt apprehensive: Would she be ready, would they have enough money, could she handle a delivery? In contrast, when the end of her childbearing came, she talked about "accepting" whatever the Lord decided and needing peace from the Lord about her limits. You don't need peace and acceptance when something is exactly what you want. So after six kids and a heart attack, Jenn had to *let go* of having more—and did so, she says, with God's help.

Across the sample, we heard expressions of sadness at coming to the end of childbearing. Having babies meant something different to these women by the end. Mary, the mother of eleven quoted above about losing her sixth child, told me, "I wasn't planning anything [after the loss], I was just trying to survive." She continued: "But I was *so grateful* [to have another]. I was so grateful because one of the things I learned is that when you're young, you think you're doing God a favor by having the babies. Like you think you're so generous because you inconvenience yourself to have a baby. And it's hard to understand what a gift it is and how precious they are when they are little, and you just don't have that perspective about the lifelong gift that they are."

Mary reminded me of Terry, and of Kim and Esther too. They had started out idealistically, wanting to *do a thing*—to "have" children, to "do the right thing," Esther had said. But by the end, whatever difficulties had been borne, they viewed it more as *receiving something*—having been blessed by children as by a gift. Jenn said simply, "I think [my children] are mostly His gift to me, but I know it's not for me to hold. It's for me to give back."

Jenn herself didn't dwell on this change directly, but she elaborated on the sense of purpose she mentioned when she had said of her first, "It just felt like it was what I was designed for." About all six she said,

> I think the loving part is the easy part because there's just—God made them so perfect for us. I mean, we love the way they look. We love the way they smell. We love the way they feel. And their voices and everything about them is something that pulls on your heartstrings and makes you want to give them whatever you can.
>
> It is difficult because they have so many needs and it's unending, but they also provide their own therapy. They love you to death too. And when you see them grow and you see that what you're doing is making a difference and what you give to them, nobody else can.

Jenn was articulating how the giving and the receiving were bound up together. You receive your children as a blessing—but the blessing is to be able "to give to them, [like] nobody else can."

### *"I Do Feel like a Very Different Person"*

Jenn did dwell on personal changes in another respect: how she felt about herself on the inside, and how she appraised her personal strengths. "I do feel like a very different person," she said. She went on: "During that time before I was married, I was much more in leadership in my church and at my school. I feel like I had a lot of boldness to step out. I don't know if it was foolheartedness or courage."

She laughed and continued:

But I think that time has a way of giving wisdom that makes you not jump out so quickly and it makes you think a little bit. And sometimes I miss the old me, but the thing is, as a woman of faith I can also see that dependence on self is not necessarily a strength. When you're depending on your own abilities, you don't have the full picture always.

As you sense your own limitations, you're actually growing in wisdom, because then you know when to go and seek for help. And you know how to pray and think a little bit more before doing things. So, you don't feel as confident, but actually you can accomplish more and do better, I think.

When I asked if she felt that she had left something behind since she wasn't "using" her Berkeley degree, she said, "I think there are times when I do—but I think part of it is also because of those outside voices and seeing what other people seem to feel is noteworthy and honorable. But I also realize that the experiences that I've had have allowed me to be a better mother because I can use what I've learned to care for my children."

Jenn had come to think that her feelings weren't a reliable guide to the reality of things in her life. She didn't "feel as confident" when she encountered her weaknesses, but nevertheless she was able to "accomplish more and do better." Other voices sowed negative emotion, but she believed in the person she was today, "making a difference" for her children, "[like] nobody else can." The internal change that marked her being "a very different person" seemed to be that she found strength in her faith, which proved a better guide to reality than her feelings.

Her sense of her marriage witnessed to the same distinction. Though her affection for her husband was apparent, her marriage didn't sound like a poster for the modern romance. She told me,

In the beginning I think if I just had my marriage hanging on the romance, it wouldn't have gone far. Because my husband was so busy. He is a very task-oriented person, and we were struggling. But after I had a child, that kind of took the pressure off of that in a way and I was able to find the companionship, and not feeling like I was pouring into something where it was not appreciated.

And as the years have gone on, my husband has grown some and I still wouldn't say that this would be what I had imagined, but my trust in him has deepened a lot because I can see his faithfulness to care for all of us and his wisdom in the decisions that he's made. And I know that he loves us all.

In the beginning I kind of wondered, because just my idea of what love was [differed] from his ability to express it.

Her feelings of doubt in the marriage—"in the beginning I kind of wondered"—stood in relief against what she had come to know about her husband. "I can see his faithfulness to care for all of us.... I know that he loves us all." She continued speaking about her marriage. "I can see how if we didn't have the Bible to guide us that it could really tear our marriage apart because it is so draining. And if you make the children the center of your universe, then it's easy to let your marriage kind of fall apart on the side and barely notice. But because we do have the Scripture that puts that priority in place, that helps us to at least be careful not to let that happen."

Jenn evidently believed that where perceptions could fail, time could reveal the truth, "as the years have gone on," she said, and that Scripture was a guide to the ordering of values, putting "priorit[ies] in place." When I asked her to tell me more, she said,

I think God kind of gives us clues in his word by his terminology because he calls the Church the bride of Christ and he pictured himself as the husband of Israel. He calls himself our Heavenly Father. So that kind of clues us in to his idea of what family is supposed to be like, and he himself is the picture of the husband or the father.

And the way that we relate to him as his Church is how we are supposed to relate to our husbands. And there is great joy. In Psalms it says, "In his presence there is fullness of joy." And that is true, but there is so much more to it than just feelings. There is the fact that God is just there all the time for us, providing for us, protecting us, faithfully taking care of us in ways that we might not even recognize or appreciate as being good, but they are good. Because his wisdom is so far above ours.

And I think that that is how I've come to appreciate my husband, because his decisions are not—at the time, I hadn't felt like they were something I was comfortable with or wanting. But I could see over time that they were the right decision. They have given stability and peace and strength to our family, and safety, provision, you know.

Jenn's understanding was that marriage mirrors God's relationship to the Church chronicled in the Scriptures. But "because his wisdom is so far above ours," what mattered most was the reality of his providence, his protection, and his care over the long run— "there all the time for us," she said. "There is so much more to it than just feelings." She clarified that romance isn't missing from a marriage grounded in Scripture, but it's not the center of attention:

And I think God gives us the sense of romantic joy to draw us in. And we do sense that joy when we are in close fellowship with him still. But it's not all the time. And it's the same with our marriages. We still have those times when we feel romantic but it's just not all that marriage is about, because marriage is not really supposed to be all about us and how we feel.

If God allowed us to focus on [romance] more, it would not be as good for us and our children because a lot of what is good for us doesn't feel good. Making our kids eat their vegetables is not good—I mean, they don't like that.

People think of [marriage] as a way to feel happy and fulfilled and valued by somebody. And all that is included in a biblical marriage, but your feelings aren't always focused on [yourself].

On Jenn's account, marriage also provided its own therapy, like having children, if you were willing to put emotional ups and downs in second place behind the form and function of marriage in salvation history. True romance was the outcome of a biblical marriage, what you got in the long run; it wasn't the foundation.

### "If Everybody Has Only One or Two, the Whole Generation Is Used to Being Spoiled"

I laughed when Jenn misspoke about the kids and the veggies. But she liked the analogy and used it again when we talked about what families mean for the character of the nation.

One more thing that's needed for children to be happy is to understand the concept of authority because nowadays children are taught that you have answers within yourself and to follow your own heart. And that doesn't lead to happiness because feelings in your own heart are so changing and each person doesn't have the wisdom to know the future, to know their own needs in the long run and what's good for them.

So, if kids were to follow their heart in their diet, they'd be eating ice cream and candy every day. So why would you encourage them to follow their own heart when it comes to their life in general?

She rounded out the analogy: "And so, recognizing that there is truth outside of themselves and being willing to submit to that and recognize the value of it is very important."

For Jenn, the "truth outside" started with God, and the whole of reality created by him and redeemed by his Word. The truth included his guidelines that we learn about in Scripture and find grace to accept in faith through prayer.

But the truth outside of ourselves also comes to us through people who make demands on us, who challenge us merely by being other than ourselves. And there is no surer way to be confronted by a *some-one* as a truth outside yourself than by living together. As Jenn put it,

I think one of the things that I hadn't mentioned before about the dynamics between the children is that it really helps people not to be self-centered. Because it is very tempting for us as parents to want to center our lives around our children and when there are just a few of them, then pretty much their world revolves around them. It does tend to make it more difficult for them to function in a society or a community where they have to not put themselves first and think in terms of the whole and work together and adjust for other people.

I mean, the home is training ground for when they go out into the world, and the more people you have, the more

different personalities you deal with, the more group mentality you need to have and the less self-centered or selfish
you can be. So, I feel like it is a good preparation for real
life. I know that I would spoil, probably, my children if I
had only one or two.

So, then you end up with, if everybody only has one or
two, the whole generation is used to being spoiled and
having their own needs and interests being the center of
their world. And it does make it very difficult to build in
the character of them being selfless and giving and serving
and understanding of others in their personalities and
their different ways of seeing things.

Jenn's commentary called to mind the insight of the wise Elder
Zosima in *The Brothers Karamazov*, who recounted an old doctor's
confession: "As soon as someone is there, close to me, his personality
oppresses my self-esteem and restricts my freedom. In twenty-four
hours, I can begin to hate even the best of men: one because he takes
too long eating his dinner, another because he has a cold and keeps
blowing his nose. I become the enemy of people the moment they
touch me."[4] Daily living with just one other person is the hardest
truth there is. Common living leaves no room for illusions about our
virtue. Our faults—pride, vanity, sensuality—are under constant
assault. Living with several others only increases the effect. Jenn
traced out a path from smaller families to an accidental culture of
individualism, because adults who grow up with fewer siblings will
be disadvantaged in the development of other-centered virtues. On
her account, it happens apart from anyone's intention, accidentally,
merely because "everybody only has one or two."

When I asked Jenn why she thought "everybody only has one or
two," she brought up her experience in college, quoted above, when

she was told in geography class that "it was irresponsible to have any more than one or two children, or any children at all." She also blamed arts and media for misinformation: "In the movies and TV shows it seems to constantly be saying that human beings are the worst thing for our world." She asked if I had seen the movie *Zootopia*. I nodded in affirmation. It tells the story of a country bunny from a big family who leaves the farm to go to the city and become a police woman. The bunny family is presented as old-fashioned, prejudiced, and rather dull in comparison with the exciting, open-minded, progressive city culture. Jenn continued: "Okay, that [movie] seems to kind of put in a nutshell the stigma that's out there about families and faith...the way that they portray the bunny family. Because the world portrays faith and family that way, that's another big reason why people don't choose that direction because it's not cool. It also shows that there's such a deep misunderstanding."

Jenn lumped families and faith together, implying that where families were disparaged in the media, faith was also undermined. She sighed and said that negative media about family was "like everywhere you look."

Jenn turned next to characterological explanations for falling birth rates. She said, "From a personal point of view, there is a very strong push in our society for following your dreams and doing what pleases yourself. And having children and parenting is all about living for someone else, not yourself."

She continued, "It's fulfilling to a certain point, but just like having a pet is fulfilling to a certain point. But when it starts to encroach on what people feel is their lifestyle, their pleasures, maybe even what they feel is necessary for their well-being, then that's where they draw the line. And [children] do change your life so very much that I can understand how after one or two you would feel like, 'Well, I just can't handle anymore.'"

Here Jenn seemed to suggest that smaller families may result from adults having a greater focus on self-interest, external accomplishments, and lifestyle preferences. Combined with her earlier remarks about small families giving rise to adults with a greater self-focus, she hinted at a self-reinforcing cycle, with small families spiraling down to smaller ones—a low-fertility trap.

She then addressed the possibility that a concern for providing enough holds people back from having more kids: "And maybe even from a financial standpoint, they would feel like this is such a huge financial burden to care for these children. And in the best way possible. To provide everything for them, all the way through college. And there is definite competition.

"I guess you're always looking around and thinking, 'Am I providing enough for my children?' And so, the fewer you have, the better the chance you have of providing enough."

She obviously didn't concur with that reasoning, but she laid it out plainly, as if she understood perfectly well why it was rational in the eyes of other women to have a small family. I didn't have to ask her why it wasn't compelling to her. She had just filled half of our interview with stories about how God had provided even when it looked humanly impossible.

Finally, she pointed to the notion that women shouldn't forego their opportunities for the sake of children—something she dismissed with a wave of the hand as feminist ideology: "And then of course there's also the sense that a woman can't pursue her own interests if she's pouring [herself out] and giving everything to her children and there's definitely been feminist ideas behind that. So, there are a lot of reasons that people just feel like it doesn't work to have large families. It doesn't fit in with all those ideologies."

Jenn herself seemed a living picture of "pouring [herself out] and giving everything to her children." Did she have regrets about the plan of not-planning?

> There have definitely been times along the way where I questioned it and doubted, but that's kind of like Peter walking on the water and getting distracted by the waves, you know? I felt like when the challenges have come up and as I have waited for God to take care of it, then he has.
>
> And it is hard to say that I would tell somebody else dogmatically that they should do it, because it is not an easy thing. And then I would never want to stand in the place of God and say, "This is how you should live."
>
> I can see though, even how what we would term as negative, that God has fulfilled his promise to make it work together for good. Like all the miscarriages had a way of spacing out the children, of making me appreciate the ones that I have even more, timing things correctly.
>
> And I love every one of my kids. And I know that it was just perfectly planned out, the ones that we have.
>
> And I had wondered whether I was being responsible sometimes because I didn't want to be presumptuous and foolish. But since I did pray over it and leave the decision up to the Lord and consistently seek him, then I had the peace of trusting that he does answer prayer. So even the things that seem hard, it's just part of his plan.

CHAPTER SEVENTEEN

# "People Matter"—Angela, Five Kids

"But since autonomy is not my primary value,
it doesn't matter. People are actually my primary value.
Persons are my primary value, and I have a home rich
with persons."

—Angela, mother of five

We met Angela outside her university office on a sunny, unseasonably warm fall day. Her college had a classic academic feel, with open quadrangles and courtyards, traditional-looking buildings and occasional avant-garde ones, and preppy-looking students pouring across campus in groups of various sizes. Angela greeted us with a warm smile, looking the part of a professor, a few minutes late, wearing glasses and a conservative but rumpled dress. She welcomed us into her bookish office stuffed with shelves, stacks of papers, and a child-sized table with little chairs. Tiny "masterpieces" were taped to the walls. Her remarks were frequently humorous but mixed with a gritty seriousness. Disarmingly, she didn't seem to take herself all that seriously. "I can't exactly say that I'm a paragon of self-care," she joked at one point. And "let's be honest," she quipped, "I don't have a published book. That's not happening. I don't care. But it's not happening, actually. For some it's fine. I'm not that person. Would I be a better scholar if I didn't have children? For sure. For sure. Honestly, I mean, I used to work all the time before I had my children. So, for sure I would."

Angela was forty-four when I interviewed her, balancing five kids and full-time work as a college professor. Married at age twenty-nine after trying out the convent, she had her first baby at thirty-four after starting her academic job. By the time we met, she had tenure and five kids: nine-year-old twins, an eight-year-old, a five-year-old, and a one-year-old. "I did have a longer gap after [my fourth]" she said. "Now partially that's my age, but partially that's also...I just needed a break. I don't think that's the children. I think it's because I work. I honestly think it's work and children. I had four of the five on tenure track. And it's difficult, as you well know. And it's, for me, I think there's so much stress going on here that that's the real delay for us."

Angela is almost a unicorn in the academy. Female, African American, and tenured, she has more than double the children of the typical American mom. Miki, whom we met in chapter 8, also a professor with five kids, had talked about the expectations in the academy surrounding childbearing. At the elite university where she studied, she recalled, having kids "was not a thing.

"People did not have kids. Faculty didn't even really have kids." When Miki had her first kid as a graduate student working on her dissertation, people had said to her, "You're not going to pursue a career anymore?" When Angela talks about the hardship of being on the tenure track while having kids and the stress surrounding her work-life balance, she's not exaggerating.

Nonetheless, like so many others in our sample, she expressed genuine heartache that she's probably not going to have another kid. "Well, you know, I'm actually sad. Believe it or not, it's ridiculous. I know I'm forty-four and the average forty-four-year-old is not having another child. But nothing has wound down yet. *I love children.*

"And [my youngest] won't have a sibling close in age. So, I'd love to have one more, just so he could have a little friend. I would. So, I'm not going to lie, I would enjoy that immensely."

### *"Wait, Do You Want Children?"*

Like Steph in chapter 15, Angela blamed it on getting married late. With her characteristic humor, she went on:

It does feel sad to me.

I am so blessed, and so lucky, that I don't have a right to feel sad. I mean, I have lots of friends who have serious medical issues whose medicine cannot tolerate children.

And they would love to have more, but they can't. So, you know, and they have less than I do. I also wish that I had gotten married younger. But then that would have been illegal, because my husband is ten years older than me.

Angela always knew she wanted a big family—so much so that that desire punctuated her engagement in an amusing way. "My husband proposed to me—and it was funny, it was right outside of Carnegie Hall, and he proposed to me, and I didn't say yes right away. I was actually turning green and getting sick. I had to pause for a minute, and I was like, 'Wait, do you want children?'

"He's like, 'Yes.'"

She laughed and continued. "You know I didn't want to commit without it, because we didn't have that talk or anything. There's a lot of reasons [we didn't talk about kids], but it has to do with [having been in the convent]. But it never occurred to me to bring it up. I didn't really realize I was dating my husband until pretty far into this. 'No, we're just hanging out' . . . 'oh, we're getting married!' So, it was kind of a funny thing."

She wanted kids so much that she didn't want to commit to her husband unless he was on board. "I mean I think [having kids] is what marriage is for," she reflected. "For me, that's really just coming from religious belief," she said. "I mean, I'm a cradle Catholic. It's just normative. But positively normative."

Although Angela describes wanting kids as a natural consequence of her Catholic faith, most Catholics aren't like her in that respect. Rather, her view of marriage and childbearing—"it's just normative"— is a key marker of what makes the women in my sample different in kind from other Americans, and from other Americans with kids, whatever their religion. Like the Baptists, Jews, Evangelicals, and Latter-day Saints that I talked to, Angela's life contrasts starkly with the lives of the typical women in her church. She has much more in common with the other women in my study of other faiths. Long ago, American Catholics did have higher fertility than the general population, thanks to the larger families of immigrants. As Catholic immigration diminished, Catholic fertility converged to the general American norm. By 1979, the convergence was so pronounced that scholars declared the end of "Catholic" fertility.[1] What made Angela different was the belief that children were the purpose of her marriage—"Wait, do you want children?"—valuable enough to give up other things for. In her case she had given up, at the very least, a published book, and greater professional success: "Would I be a better scholar? . . . For sure."

Angela also credited her family background with fostering her attitude towards children:

> I had one sister, and that was not the choice of my parents. So, my one sister...passed away actually, but she was eight years older than me, and there was an eight-year gap between my sister and I, and that was also a source of sadness for my parents.
>
> They would have loved a large family, but fertility is what it is. So, it was just two of us. But I always knew that I wanted more siblings, because eight years apart, that's hard. You can't play with somebody.
>
> I always remember my sister leaving, and she was like a second mother. Which is sweet, but you know, I knew I wanted a big family. But I take it for granted. I can't say this was highly thematic. It's just, I'm Catholic, marriages produce children. And this is a positive thing. So, I didn't overthink it.

Among the ways that women in my sample got started, Angela was more like Shaylee and Terry and Esther—women who grew up practicing religion, in homes where children were welcomed and valued. They attached profound significance to children and made costly sacrifices to put children above other goods. They thought their own attitudes were ordinary. In Angela's words, "I wanted a big family.... I take it for granted.... I didn't overthink it." But they were anything but ordinary. Describing how they were different in kind is the task of this project. Understanding where the kernel of difference ultimately comes from will be the task of future work.

## "Probably the Most Overwhelming Thing That Ever Happened to Me"

Angela recalled that starting out with twins at age thirty-four was almost crushing. She's not alone. Mid-career professional women, home for the first time with a baby, often lament the frustration that arises as they go from feeling highly skilled at work to feeling nearly incompetent at home with a newborn. Worse, the change happens almost overnight. One day you're nine months pregnant, and good at everything. The next, you're trapped at home with a baby, fumbling to complete simple tasks like a diaper change or a feeding. You don't know if you're doing it right. Your baby doesn't affirm your efforts yet—that comes later when they finally lock eyes with you and smile. The early weeks can be devastating to the sense of self. Angela put it this way:

> Oh my gosh, it was utterly overwhelming. I think it was probably the most overwhelming thing that ever happened to me. I mean because I think, you know, again, I didn't grow up around children. I have no family. I have my parents and my sister has died.
>
> So, I never grew up around children. I didn't babysit, I didn't play with babies. I just had no knowledge of them. So, it was all kind of a shock. I remember driving home from the hospital like, "They're really letting me out of here with these two infants. *But who am I?* And what am I supposed to do with these kids?"
>
> And then I got home, I remember the fourth day I had a breakdown, because no one ever told me, this is the most idiotic thing ever, this is truly idiotic, but...I had literally no idea that babies did not go to sleep at night, and that they don't [sleep through and] wake up in the morning and then eat.

It never, no one ever told me that you're going to feed this child every two hours for who knows how long. And I just literally was clueless. And I was old. I was probably thirty-four or thirty-five. I was like, *old*.

She might as well have said she was too old to feel clueless and too accomplished to be so idiotic. That frustration might have done her in for having more children—as it does for many women. But it didn't. She recalled that by "three months" the twins "just calmed down," and "around the fifth month, by the grace of God, they actually started sleeping for a stretch. I mean, this required almost circus-level acrobatics. But they did it."

Her second arrived two years after the twins. "Like, [only] one baby?" she quipped. "No baby has ever been hard after the twins. It's just not hard." She described her approach to family planning as somewhere between being open to another and not being closed. She said, "So, for us it's never—with the exception of the twins—we don't ever really try. We just are open. There's a difference I think between open and trying. So, in other words we're not *not trying*." She laughed. "So, we sort of discern on a monthly basis. Are we ready to be open? Or are we not?...And then when we think that we are, honest to God, it feels like 'boom,' we already have a baby."

But having babies was all done now, she thought. And she was grieving that. "Well, you know, I'm actually sad." Carrying another baby at her age was unlikely, she thought. "I mean, I'm forty-four, so what are the chances I would still have one?" And in any case, her risk factors were too high. "I ended up with postpartum preeclampsia which I didn't even know was a thing.... I could have stroked out and died." So Angela and her husband were avoiding having another child, and she was beginning to reflect on that reality.

It's just such a beautiful gift, I just never could have imagined. I said I did not grow up a baby person. I did not grow
up around children. So, it never occurred to me, while I
wanted to have them...it wasn't ever a felt need. You know
"I would love to have a baby."

Well, not really. It [was] just, I'm going to [have kids],
but you know.

But it's such a joy. Oh my gosh. Having children is such
a joy. That I do feel like it's something that God is doing for
me. It seems like such a tremendous gift, and I can't believe
that I get to have [them].

While Angela never had the anxiety about children that Jenn
experienced at the beginning, they shared a degree of sadness at the
prospect of the end. Angela too had come to see her children mostly
as a blessing and a joy, God's gifts to her. "I can't believe that I get to
have [them]." She explained how the tensions surrounding her identity at the beginning, questioning who she was, feeling insecure, idiotic, and overwhelmed, were resolved by clarifying what mattered
most to her. She reflected:

I often wonder if I don't have a problem with [my identity]
because I'm African American. I mean, I'm obviously
Western. But I wonder if it's not a little bit of a cultural
difference, because I often think that...we're sort of over-
run with a misbegotten sense of autonomy. And I don't
necessarily think of—autonomy is not the first thing I
would think of as the characteristic of the self.

If it were, then I imagine that [my life] would look
absolutely dreadful. Because I don't have any time for

myself. I can't exactly say that I'm a paragon of self-care. That is not happening right now. It can when you have a kid who's three. But it can't when you have a one-year-old. That's just reality. But since autonomy is not my primary value, it doesn't matter. People are actually my primary value.... And I have a home rich with persons.

## *"A Connection between the Culture of Hospitality and the Children"*

As she elaborated, it was clear that Angela was rejecting autonomy not in the sense of personal agency, but rather as a type of individualism—something like Hannah's description of her pre-conversion self in chapter 2: "Where I was just doing my own thing for wherever I was at that point in my life." Sociologist Andrew Cherlin, whom I quoted in chapter 3, has described expressive indi-vidualism as "people [looking] inward to see how they are doing."[2] From that perspective, the self isn't realized in and through the hap-piness of other people, but on its own terms.

Angela went on. "I don't want to randomly throw out the race card there, because—but I sort of am anyway—because I'm completely, fully Western. It's not like I grew up any place cool, or interesting. I grew up in the suburbs of [city]. I mean, seriously, with no black people. But I do think that deeply embedded in black culture is a sense of other people, a sense of interdependence. I do think that." I recalled Ann's story, in chapter 6, about the Nigerian workers who said Ann's big family was the first thing they had seen in America that they wanted.

Angela continued:

There's no shame in sharing yourself with people, and reli-ance on other people. The best example I can give is it's really normal to stop by somebody's house without calling first. No one would do this now. I grew up like this, and I miss it actually. I just had a friend who moved to the South, but—"It's Sunday, stop by. Put another plate on the table. Let's have some dinner." You know what I mean?

Everyone I know who is not black would be utterly horrified if you showed up on their doorstep, because they would feel judged, because of course their house is not perfect, you know, whatever.

She laughed and finished her thought:

People matter. People *matter*. And they also—my sense of identity is sort of co-related to all those other people. So, my identity is not in contradistinction to other people, I don't have to pull back and have my time. I mean, everybody needs some time. I could talk about that in terms of [prayer]. But I wouldn't talk about it in terms of the cultural value of individualism and autonomy.

I don't have to pull back to be myself. I have found that I'm most myself with my family—more than I ever even knew I could be, with my family, than I would be apart from them.

Angela offered a vision of identity in motherhood different from but complementary to the ones we've read already. Where Danielle spoke about a redirection of herself—"me doing something else"—and Jenn of the difference between feelings and reality, and where Hannah and Esther had focused on growth in capacity—"possibilities of expansion in your life"—Angela posited that her "self" was co-related with the others in her life. Her identity is a being in relation. Relation, as she described it, means "sharing yourself with people," and "reliance on people." The fact of being in relation doesn't diminish the self but augments it, because each self takes joy in the other. The mother enjoys the child and depends upon the child as much as the child depends upon the mother and enjoys her presence. Being in relation with more people means a richer you, since the essence of the relation is joy. "Persons are my primary value," she had said, "and I have a home rich with persons." And "people matter." She saw a healthy type of dependence as the opposite of the autonomy she rejected.

Returning to the notion of Sunday drop-ins, I asked if her mom practiced that. "Yeah, yeah," she said, "everybody [I grew up with]." She continued. "I grew up in a predominantly Catholic area. Almost everyone I grew up with is Irish or Italian. And they were Catholic Irish and Italians. So, I don't know what to tell you about that, there was one other black family, and they were Protestant."

She laughed and went on. "It just is what it is. But I think Italians are a lot like this in my view, and I don't know if I can talk about Italians, being black, the Italians I know are similar to black people this way, that there's a sense of hospitality and a sense of openness."

She clarified that she didn't think she was "thematizing this as a child anyway." She was "just excited to go to so-and-so's house for dinner.... I would most definitely make a connection between the culture of hospitality and the children. If you have an openness to the other, you have an openness to the other. And you don't fear the loss of yourself in the openness to the other. I think that's my fundamental point—that I'm most myself in the openness to the other."

Angela's imagery suggests a family table crowded with children, and a mother and father seeing an open door for Sunday visitors as the moral equivalent of welcoming another child to that table. Looking back, I wish I had asked her whether openness to immigrants might also be connected to welcoming children—but perhaps she answered it already: "Almost everyone I grew up with is Irish or Italian."

### *"What Do You Mean by Planned?"*

Angela brought up religious reasons for her confidence that identity isn't diminished by others, that you can become more yourself by losing yourself.

> I mean really, I guess it's just Pope John Paul II's self-gift, the whole personalism thing.[3] You know, love is the gift of oneself to the other, for the good of the other, and it really just comes down to that. I mean, I think you are most yourself in that act of gift.
>
> We are most ourselves when we give ourselves away— it's the paradox of the Cross though. That is Christianity, I mean, that really is the Cross. That's just the paradox of the Cross. So, I do think that's a mystery.

The intuition behind the thought that Angela was expressing here seems roughly analogous to Hannah's chain—that you can find yourself irrevocably tied to others. I asked Angela to tell me more. Did you have to be religious to view yourself in the way that she did, I wondered, as a shelter, or a safe house, for people yet to be conceived? She hedged a little, but eventually settled on yes. "I think it's accessible to human experience, but I don't think it's fully comprehensible apart from the religious element. I think that's what I'd say.

"I think most people really understand food. You know people just understand food, and they understand the sharing of food as an important thing. If you ever watch YouTube—apparently, I watch too much YouTube...if you watch vegan YouTube, I'm obviously not a vegan....

She laughed and continued, "But if you watch vegan YouTube, it's very interesting how their entire life is centered around their veganism, and vegan eating, and the sharing of food amongst themselves.

"I don't care what you are. I think food is understandable and shared food is understandable. So yes, I think you can have a secular conception of hospitality being openness to another and what that means in gift. But I don't think you can really penetrate to the heart of it without the Cross. I think that's the bottom line."

It might seem as if Angela's appeal to faith means that she is punting on making the value determinations that I highlighted in chapter 12. But I don't think that's what she was saying. Her reliance on convictions embedded in her Catholic faith led to an explicit ranking of goods. Children mattered, above other things, even above personal pursuits, career interests, and comfort, because children—and people in general—are part of the divine plan to "prosper you and not to harm you," as Jenn put it, quoting the Bible. Jesus laid down his life for us first. Following him, we can play a part in the salvation of the world through our own oblation for others.

### *"I Did Not Make the Rules of Engagement"*

As Angela delved into religion, our discussion of identity and openness to others led me to inquire about freedom and choice. How could she know, I asked, that her decision to have children was "free" when she had aligned herself with a value structure proposed by Scripture—God's will, and not hers. Her response, lengthy but worth quoting in full, reflected what others in our study had said, from

Hannah and Esther to Miki and Jenn. It also reflected that she was practiced in giving an impromptu lecture.

She began in her characteristically witty way. "I've got to say, that question doesn't actually have value for me. I will still answer it." She went on:

> How do I know I made this choice freely? I don't know that I have to be convicted to know that I made the choice freely. Because that goes back to that thing that I was saying about autonomy not being my first and foremost value. So, I think there's that. I don't have to feel like "I decided this for myself." I'm just not that person who has to decide it for myself for it to be valid. I mean, I don't want it forced upon me. Obviously, I don't want an arranged marriage. But I don't have that inner sense of "If I didn't pick it"—and I have a son like that, my pugnacious one—"If I didn't pick it, then it's not valid." I just don't have that temperament. There's that.
>
> I guess it depends on whether you believe your faith or not. Is this a human institution or a divine institution? Is it a divine institution with human elements that act according to secondary causality? I'm going to go with that one. In that divine institution, are these norms in the colloquial sense of it, as customs, rules, baseless rules even, or is it a matter of revelation? I take them to be a matter of revelation, actually.
>
> Which is why it doesn't actually matter whether the pope says it or not, because it's a matter of revelation. [Which means] God said it. God says these things. And for our own good.

She smiled, paused, and then continued:

So, first, I take very seriously that it's a matter of revelation, and second, I don't believe that God reveals things for our detriment, but only towards our good. I'm only going to live a better life if my life is conformed to God's vision of my life. I'm only going to live a more diminished life if I'm separated from God's vision for my life. So why would I do that?

I do think that it requires a basic recognition of our own contingency. I did not put myself here. I am not taking myself out of here. I did not make the rules of engagement. So, you can either kick against the goad, and be upset about that, or you could surrender to it, in all of its beauty and pain. Honestly.

She continued:

I didn't freely bring myself into existence. There are things that are beyond my choice. I do have free will. Absolutely. And that's an element of the image of God in us. So, I'm not trying to say, "Just be an automaton." But I am saying that you've got to have a healthy sense of contingency.

You know, this is not your show, as some Protestant preacher said in a book sometime, I can't tell you the name of the book, but I thought it was hilarious. Because it's not your show. It's not your show. You know you're in it, but this is not your show. You know.

She laughed and continued:

Our choice should be free because that is what it is to be a person. A person needs freedom. But I think we often mistake freedom with free choice. We often mistake freedom with license, freedom with the ability to choose anything from an infinite possibility of choices and I don't think that conforms to reality at all.

There's always limits in our choices. And the first limit in our choice should be morality, actually. So, any choice outside of a moral choice is not free. That's slavery. At least that's what Christianity says, right?

So, an immoral choice is already bondage. That's not freedom. So, I do think the human person is called to freedom, but freedom is conformity to God, not conformity to my own whims and desires.

Angela didn't reject personal agency or free human action. She seemed to think, rather, that freedom was realized not so much in the choosing as in getting the value determinations right and acting accordingly. She also thought that because we're limited, we need help getting the values right. As Jenn put it, "Each person doesn't have the wisdom to know the future, to know their own needs in the long run and what's good for them." For both women, God's word and Christian tradition were indispensable guides to the right ordering of values.

I asked Angela whether her view of freedom and choice applied to the language of children being planned or unplanned, wanted or unwanted, since women in our study had chafed at the terms—and I heard them. Most of us with children have faced the dreaded questionnaire checkbox in a doctor's office: Is this pregnancy intended or unintended?

Oh my gosh, it's so irritating, and I don't even know how to answer the question. Well, of course they're wanted. Well, was this all planned? What do you mean by planned?— planned by God.

I think the conventional planning, wanting, and choosing is just a smoke screen. I think it's an illusion. I think the illusion is "I'm in control of things."

You're not in control of things. You do have free will. But you're not in control of things. I really think it comes back to the contingency thing. We just think that we have Nietzschean power over the world around us, and we do not. Or over ourselves, we do not.

By contingency, Angela seemed to mean that our own existence isn't a guarantee, or a fixture. We did not always exist, we might not have ever existed, and we could go out of existence. The truth of our being is a mystery to ourselves. We were called into life apart from our choosing.

So, it just seems like toddlers to me. It seems like a toddler. "Mine, mine." "I picked it." "I want what I picked." It's like, you know, you get to that point with your first child or children, where you finally figure out, "Oh, maybe I shouldn't give them only the things they want to eat."

I mean, did you hear about the poor kid that died from the French fries—not died, he went blind—from the French fries and the potato chips? You've heard this story?[4] Because now I'm like, "You're eating your vegetables." Seriously, we're not doing any of this.

I feel like our culture is so infantile. I mean, I hate to be that negative, but it is.

### *"Children Are the Scapegoat of This Culture"*

We laughed. Angela was not the first woman in our study to use the food analogy. But her humor gave way to peak gritty seriousness.

I don't get it, though. I'm a bad person to answer the question [about the wantedness of children] because I genuinely don't get it. I don't understand why our culture has such a negative viewpoint on children.

I mean, seriously, children are the scapegoat of this culture. We put all of our anxiety and evil on something, and how twisted is it that the scapegoat our culture has chosen is an innocent child.

We don't choose an actual person in prison, mind you. That person is innocent, actually, in common discourse.

But an actual child is the scapegoat of our culture, the axis of evil, the destroyer of marriages, and individuality, and freedom, the suppressor of women—a child. That's irrational. I mean, that's irrational.

Even from a scientific point of view, that's irrational. Obviously, you need to continue your species. That's irrational.

Hearing all of this, I hardly needed to ask Angela why she thought her peers didn't have as many children as she did. If children are bearing all the negative emotion of the culture, how could they possibly be an object of desire, something you would make sacrifices to obtain? Nevertheless, I did ask her. And Angela did want to add something:

I think it's feminism. I honestly think it's feminism. I just do. I mean, Second Wave–feminist presuppositions are now our standard view. It's just that women cannot thrive, unless they're in the workforce, living their passions, literally. And children will inhibit you, maybe, [from] working at the capacity that you would otherwise.

Let's be honest. I don't have a published book. That's not happening. I don't care. But it's not happening, actually. For some it's fine. I'm not that person. Would I be a better scholar if I didn't have children? For sure. For sure. Honestly, I mean, I used to work all the time before I had my children. So, for sure I would.

Am I following all my passions? I literally hate that word. Whatever happened to apatheia? Passions with a capital *P*.

She laughed. "No, I'm not. Okay. I can live with that. My hobby right now is sitting and watching soccer."

She went on. "If you make a choice, you're giving up one thing for another. But five-year-olds understand that if you make a choice, you're giving up one thing for another. If you can only make a choice between the chocolate and the Skittles, you're not having chocolate AND Skittles. I'm not going to give my kids Skittles, I'm just saying, why can't we grasp that? You can't have everything. Only spoiled people think they can."

Angela's discourse called to mind a memorable quip by economist Tom Sowell, another African-American academic who combines humor and gritty seriousness: "There are no solutions. There are only trade-offs."[5] Angela might have said the same thing about the calculus of choosing between work and family: There's no solving this thing. Decide what you're willing to give up. She continued:

> If you think that career and passions are the only way that a woman can fully flourish, then obviously you're going to think children are an impediment. Because your career will be diminished unless you rely on an army of other

people. Which, if you have the capacity, more power to you. But most people do not have those economic means. I mean, what's her name, Sheryl Sandberg got slammed for that.

And you probably won't follow all of your passions, or possibly any, until you retire. And then you might be dead…or too tired. So, but that's okay.

It's just, what do you value? So, I just think that our values are more for individual self-fulfillment than they are for anything collective.

When I asked her to say more, she added, "I think that we value, we definitely value money and the means for making it over persons. Because we value money more than persons, we value economies and systems and these abstract things, but we don't value persons.

"I mean if you just look at porn in this country. Porn is—we value the pornographer's right to make money more than we value the innocence of children."

She paused, and then reflected, "I don't have a clue. We're so far gone. People literally shouting their abortions. That is such a low moment that I don't think this is the moment where we're going to see a renewal, personally. But you know, God is the God of surprises. We've heard. So, there you go."

Angela seemed content with her trade-offs. She knew what she valued. Her home was "rich with persons," and as a result, her hobby was "sitting and watching soccer." Good thing, too. When I asked her what children needed for a happy childhood, she answered without skipping a beat: "I think they need their mothers. I think they need their mothers. More than anything. I don't think they need a giant institutionalized day-care system. I don't think they need a preschool. I think they need their mothers. That's it."

# CHAPTER EIGHTEEN

## "Goodness and Light"—Leah, Five Kids

"I think our culture really values the sort of very
rigid perception of success and work and has started
to devalue a mother's contribution to society. And
it's almost like radical and feminist to say that my
contribution is healthy, well-balanced children and that
is a contribution. Like it's not just about my music career
or how much money we make or any of that, really.
Those are all secondary to what you contribute to the
world, which is the future of humanity."

—Leah, mother of five

Early morning on a quiet summer Sunday, Mary and I met
Leah at her suburban home. Petite in stature, wearing a
maternity jumper and a wrap in her hair, she settled into her
living room sofa and offered us chairs across from her. She was very
pregnant with her fifth. Her sweet, melodic voice alerted us to one of
the great loves of her life. "I have a bachelor of arts degree in music

performance and composition," she told me. "In the past years since graduating I have recorded two full-length CDs; I've performed internationally and nationally. I sing and I play instruments, so I play flute, guitar, and percussion. And I currently lead a women's music group, so that meets about once every six weeks."

Music had played a major role in meeting her husband, too. As she recounted, "So, we met either the end of my first week or the beginning of my second week in college. Somebody that I had met and become friends with said, 'Oh, I have this friend. He's a musician. You need to come and play music with us.' So, we met playing music and we hit it off right away. And we developed a relationship while in college, but we also began a religious journey while in college."

Another love of Leah's is helping women bring their children into the world. She attends a couple of births per year as a doula (certified birth attendant) "typically for pay," she says. "Basically because of my other work obligations, my children, and my husband's work obligations, I have kept it at a minimum until maybe the next stage of my life." Her passion for healing doesn't end there. She "did a two-year apprenticeship program" in herbal medicine. Combined, her vocations provide a window into the serenity that radiates from her countenance. I'd want to call her myself if I needed a doula.

But her main work these days? She works from home as a schedule manager for a green cleaning company. It isn't related to what she loves, but it provides for their needs. "Instead of doing my music, I'm now working 9:00–1:00 p.m. every day to help support our family. So that's been really hard, feeling like I care a lot about being able to provide for my family. And I think I've had to sacrifice some of my own interests and pursuits at this time. I don't think they're on hold forever. But I also think that creatively, there's only so much that a person has at any given time. I think as a mother of a large family, you have to understand sometimes things are on a back burner. It doesn't mean the burner is off. It means you're rotating priorities as needed, and I've done a lot of that."

## *"This Journey Together"*

Leah recounted how she and her husband had "met in college" and "kind of went on this journey together of building a life based on religious values."

> I think I always knew that I wanted to have children, but I never had a preconceived notion of, "I want to have x amount of kids." I just knew that I wanted to be a mom and I knew that I wanted to have a family. But I didn't grow up with a lot of siblings and I didn't have that experience and I didn't grow up super religious.
>
> Like I grew up in a Reformed congregation which is basically completely secular except you do token Jewish things. And now, we've chosen a different life where we are much more intentionally practicing religion and the traditional.

In college Leah and her future husband adopted Jewish practices uncommon for college students at secular schools, like keeping kosher and observing Shavuot. These "things are not easy and straightforward," she said. "They take effort, and they take commitment . . . outward actions that commit you to a godly life." At their liberal arts college, "It was really swimming upstream," she recalled. "It was really challenging." After graduating, they parted company to immerse themselves in learning more about the life they had chosen. She spent eight months, he eighteen months, in full-time programs of religious study. In a yeshiva, "You carve out the time to really devote yourself to prayer and growing your knowledge."

> It was hard, but it was exciting at the same time. Because we knew we were committed and when you—I mean, somebody said to him when he was in yeshiva, like you already have your bread in your basket. So, there's something very comforting about that compared to the unknown, when you're in that. A lot of people go to those programs not engaged.
>
> Our situation was atypical because we met in college, and we already fell in love and knew we wanted to be together, and we were waiting.
>
> And we got married. I knew going into marriage that our intention was to start a family right away. Like we weren't getting married to wait. Part of why we waited so long, and we were engaged so long is because I knew that when I got married, I wanted to start a family. So, we waited to get married for a while because I knew I wasn't ready to drop out of college and have a baby.
>
> And I was in a very intentional mindset when I got married. I was really dedicated to prayer and [Jewish] practice, and I was surrounded by like-minded people. So, I lived in a community that was very conducive to that—a lot of other young people that were getting married and having families. And older people that were still having children and/or just there as support and mentors in my life. And [my son] was born ten months after we got married basically.

She laughed. "Not like instant, but very close."

For Leah and her husband, having children was a part of marriage; children linked them together through a sense of purpose in relation to God's plan for them. She told me,

> I was living in Brooklyn; I had a lot of friends in my community at the time. And so, then I had him, I gave birth. And it was definitely very hard. And as much as anyone can ever be prepared for birth, I was. I did a lot of educating. I read a lot. I felt prepared, as much as a person can be prepared.
>
> But I think the experience itself was challenging. And new motherhood was really hard. He didn't sleep. I didn't get lucky with newborns. My kids are not good sleepers, like for the first stage. I remember the five-week mark and I think I had slept an hour at a time for five weeks. It was *really* hard. But people brought us food, and I didn't feel like alone, but I felt a little shell-shocked by the difficulty and the challenge of it all.
>
> So, my experience of giving birth definitely influenced me to want to help other women in that process. And I just feel like I've really been able to do that. I've really been able to ease the experience for a lot of people and help educate people. And help make educated choices about their birth and their care.

I asked her when things got better with her son. She laughed. "Well, I had another kid like really soon."

> So, he was fourteen months old when I conceived my daughter. They were twenty-three months apart. It wasn't much of a break in that time. I was really young, and I had

my son—I was in labor on my twenty-fifth birthday. And I had the energy and the stamina even though it was really hard and exhausting for sure. But I just did it. And I learned a lot.

So yeah, my daughter was born. He was twenty-three months. And we were just in full-on baby mode. I was a stay-at-home mom at that time so I was still trying to pursue my musical passions and my herbal studies and things like that but I was still like a full-time mom. So, I wasn't doing any sort of hourly paid job outside of the home, which allowed me to be present for that.

Leah recalled that it was incredibly hard "to go through another pregnancy and everything and not having really slept through the night very much," but she told me, "I mean, I just really saw it as divine providence and God's will for me. And I really felt like it was a blessing."

She added,

So, I don't know that I felt ready, but it was kind of like, "Ready or not." But I'm very grateful that I did that when I did it. And I'm really grateful that I had them so close together. They're really close. It was really hard. It was psychologically challenging because I hadn't fully bounced back after my first. I mean, for sure not.

I think that mental health really is important for women. And postpartum health is really critical, and I think that with every kid I've had, it's been more challenging. And I actually had a miscarriage in between my second and third, so that was really hard. And then I had my third kid—I conceived just months after having had the miscarriage.

So, there wasn't much of a break there either, but I think it was a little more intentionally spaced after that. So, my fourth is four years after my third.

Her fifth was due the summer I interviewed her, about four years after her fourth. She told me that her other kids were "super excited. I mean, I was really worried about telling my older two kids because they know how hard it is. Like they're old enough to know like, 'This is hard.'"

She laughed and continued, explaining what it meant to her older kids that she was expecting:

My daughter who is thirteen was like squealing. I have not seen her that excited about very much. So, she's like super, super, super, super, super excited.

My fifteen-year-old son, he's kind of more aloof. I think he's excited at the level to which he gets excited, which isn't like—he's finishing up ninth grade and he's in a different phase. And he's kind of focused on school and friends. He's still very involved with our family and everything but he's happy. I don't think he has negative feelings about it.

My eight-year-old is excited. She's such a kind-hearted kid. I think she's just going to be excited to be able to be a big sister in a way that she wasn't able to last time. Like last time she was jealous because my older daughter could hold the baby and take care of the baby and she was four. Like you can't hold the baby. You can sit and I'll watch you hold the baby—so she's going to be my big helper this time.

And my three-year-old is—at first, I don't think he quite got what was happening. But he has become super excited and tuned into the baby and he feels the baby every day. We talk about it and now he learned about the baby being upside down and I have these little dollies and I showed him how the baby is and where the feet are. He's super, super excited. I feel like he's transitioning in his own identity of him feeling like a big brother and we're already referring to him that way, and he just transitioned out of his crib into a big boy bed. He's excited and ready.

In the course of our conversation, Leah told me about an exchange with a neighbor who paid her a compliment that softened certain feelings about herself as an "older" mom: "I was feeling like, 'Okay, here I am. I just turned forty. I'm pregnant with my fifth child.' You kind of feel sad like you're not the young mom anymore. But she was walking by and she's like, 'Oh, you're such a young mom. It reminds me of when I was in that stage.' And it was just very heart-warming that she saw me, and it brought something positive up for her. So, that was really nice because a lot of the time I feel very self-conscious in this culture about having a large family."

### "A Shift"

But she wasn't self-conscious with me. Or didn't appear so. She bared her soul generously, reaching for the right words. Value featured heavily in her narrative. That part was not hard to explain. What evaded simple description was the unintended consequence: that motherhood had become part of who she was. Moreover, as a creative person, motherhood was part of what she understood herself to be offering to others:

How do I maintain my own kind of self-preservation, my own identity, within the context of being a mother of a large family? That's really challenging. That's definitely really challenging. And I think it has evolved over time. Like I think that when I had my first two, I was hyper-committed to my goals. I still was recording full-length CDs and playing in concerts and having rehearsals late at night. I had more energy and stamina, and the will, and the drive. I think that has definitely been affected by having a large family, and I think that after having the third and fourth, I think there are identity challenges.

It's not as easy to pursue personal dreams and pursuits right now as it once was. It's a sacrifice that I've made because I value having a large family, and I value every child as a gift. But I wouldn't be honest if I said it wasn't a struggle.

Also, there are times when I'll be supporting my husband, for example, when he was getting his graduate degree, I was pregnant with my fourth. So that kind of had to take priority during that time. So, we kind of support each other. There have been times where he really supported me with my music and things like that. So, we kind of work hand in hand.

And I think that part of your identity just evolves into motherhood being a really big tenet of who you are and what you're giving to the world, like a shift.

She seemed to be describing a process whereby motherhood becomes more *who you are* than *what you're doing*. At first it might be added into a mix of identities: I'm an artist, an athlete, and a mom. A lawyer, a writer, and a mom. At this stage, the mom identity is balanced with the others, inside and out, requiring a high level of "energy and stamina," as Leah put it. Perhaps this is where most moms are—or even where most moms stay.

But according to Leah, add a couple of *more* kids into the mix, and some worthy pursuits are likely to be set aside to make time, demoted for a while—to "a back burner." And in that "rotating of priorities" motherhood becomes a primary identity rather than one identity among many. The "shift," as Leah had called it, resolves the tension between two realities. No more balancing. The mom-self and the old self become one self, herself, for whom motherhood is who she is and what she gives. She continued.

> I think our culture really values the sort of very rigid perception of success and work and has started to devalue a mother's contribution to society. And it's almost like radical and feminist to say that my contribution is healthy, well-balanced children and that is a contribution. Like it's not just about my music career or how much money we make or any of that, really. Those are all secondary to what you contribute to the world, which is the future of humanity.

Are children more a consumption good, something you can enjoy *because of* your work and your contribution? Or are they more something supplied for others to enjoy, a vital good, a contribution of themselves? Well, both, of course—and Leah drew this out more plainly than anyone with whom we spoke. To the extent that children can be considered as goods, they are *private* goods, "bought and paid for" by households alone. But children simultaneously have the character of a most critical public good—"the future of humanity." And yet society can't "demand" that good in the way that it demands other public goods. Only mothers and fathers can demand children, when they value them above other things, assigning to childbearing enough worth to counterbalance the weighty personal costs—the putting things "on a back burner," as Leah said, "rotating priorities as needed, and I've done a lot of that." Leah concluded this thought by saying,

> Which—literally—the future is about good people being in the world. People that will go on to raise their own, healthy, happy families and contribute positively. And yeah, coming from a divorced family, that was a big motivation for me in choosing this life, I think. *Like valuing children first.* The family unit being the priority above career and personal identity.

Can society redistribute Leah's burden? Not in her estimation. It might be able to honor it, or reward it, but not carry it. Only Leah can suffer the loss of her career aspirations and the disruptions in her personal identity. It must be worth it *to her* before the benefit spills over to society. If you need more babies, you need more people like Leah. Because women are both the demanders and suppliers of the same good. They bear the incommensurable costs; they alone assess the balance of the merits against the costs.

Leah described a down-to-earth approach for getting through until her personal interests can be on the front burner again:

> I still care about finding myself and recalibrating and continuing to pursue things that are important to me and that feed myself creatively. I care about that a lot. I just have to be realistic that I can't have that all the time. So, I hope that going forward, I will find more opportunity for that.

I think working [for pay] has been more challenging, regarding that than my kids. You know, filling that space with work takes that time away from creativity.

But yeah, I think I've also found ways to integrate my kids into my interests like gardening. My kids enjoy that. Different things that I enjoy, I'll integrate with them, and try to share my interests. Like I love nature, so we spend a lot of time outdoors. Things like that. Trying to just adjust and bring children into those experiences that are meaningful and important to you because that's what teaches them who you are and what you value.

I told Leah that I understood her. "There was a point in graduate school," I recalled, "where I was like, '[Graduate school] is pointless. I should quit this. This is ridiculous.' But then at some point I kind of got woken up and I was like, 'This is a lot of what I love to do.' Not as a mother, but as a person. And I thought, 'If I finish this out, it's something I can bring to my children.' It somehow seemed like a thing that was a realization to me. I had thought of my studies as something I was doing for me. And then I realized, if I can be true to who I am in this, it's something I'm giving them. Because that's who their mother is. That's who their mother *is*."

Agreeing, Leah responded,

That's huge. Absolutely. I think that trying to hang on to those things that we care about definitely enriches their lives in a real way. My youngest son is extremely musical. Like he's just been really musical from a young age. I mean, all of my kids are musical but he's like really, really pronounced. Like his teachers at school are always talking about it and stuff. I think it's part of who we are so it's a part of who he is. You know? And some of my kids are really into art, and when my older two were little, I spent a lot of time doing art projects with them because I love art too. You know, I think you find ways to integrate—it's so important and it's so challenging. Like it's not easy. But I really do think it's important.

It seems that the identity shift Leah had described wasn't as simple as the old self becoming a new self. In her words, "Motherhood [becomes] a really big tenet of who you are and what you're giving to the world." But you don't lose who you were before. Rather, threads of your old self are woven into the type of mom that you become—what you bring to your children uniquely from the way that you see the world. The old self may die in some respects, but as Danielle in chapter 14 pointed out, the old self was going to die in some respects no matter what choices you made. You can't take every path. But on Leah's reckoning, the new self *as a mother* brings her old self to fruition, planting the seeds of herself in her children—giving new life to the old self: an immortality of sorts. Or perhaps an infinity, to borrow from Hannah: "Children are this key to infinity."

### *"It's about Sharing in That Purpose"*

When I asked Leah about her marriage, she reinforced what we heard from other women about how kids make marriages better:

So, I think that we built our marriage around family. So, we weren't building our marriage around romantic dinners for two at fancy restaurants. And I think that that is very superficial. To think that that will bring you happiness ultimately in life is silly. I mean, it's a meal. We do enjoy those

rare and special occasions like for our anniversary or
Mother's Day or something like that. And it's always a challenge I think carving out that quality time for one-on-one
time, and that's an evolving process always. But I think that
that is less important to both of us than what we're doing
as a unit.

I think children bring a lot of meaning and depth and
purpose to a person's life that—there just would be a really
big void. We all know that when you engage in selfless acts,
it brings you joy, even though it's counterintuitive. But parenting is a selfless act in many ways. I mean, yes, [you] are
propagating your spawn, your offspring. But beyond that,
so much of the actual workload of parenting, which is
huge, is selfless.

And it's not based on, "What am I getting out of it in
this moment?" And it's finding those hidden treasures of
beauty and joy that children bring to the world and to your
life. It's the little things that enrich our lives the most, like
something cute they said while eating their cereal in the
morning, or one little precious fleeting moment. And life
is so fleeting and so short and so precious. And I almost
feel like it's funny, do we really have time to waste on all
these fripperies? Parenting is the meat and potatoes, basically. I feel like we won't be in the childbearing years forever. And this may be my last baby.

I didn't miss her last line there. As with Angela, Jenn, and so many
others, contemplating the likely end of her childbearing called forth
a lamentation of sorts: "This may be my last baby." And the lamentation called forth a more refined statement of her life's purpose:

I feel like it has gone by way too fast honestly, even though it is hard and there are times that I feel really overwhelmed and like this is a really big responsibility I am bringing on my shoulders, bringing another child, starting from square one at age forty. I could be doing this another eighteen years. I could be on the beach drinking margaritas. But that's just not what my life is about. And I just didn't build my life around sitting back and relaxing. I built my life around working really, really, really hard and bringing goodness and light into the world.

If anything, children are light. Every child brings a divine gift into the world that nobody else can bring. Nobody else can do what that person is here to do. And yes, it takes so much self-sacrifice, but I ultimately feel like my husband and I are really happy. We are really, really happy and fulfilled even though we have had to work really, really, really hard, to the breaking point at times.

For sure, I mean, sleepless nights, endlessly. Both of us working. Both of us parenting. Putting aside some of our personal pursuits. But ultimately yeah, we went out for our sixteen-year anniversary this past March and those moments are really, really special. We appreciate them more, I think, because they're rare.

Leah made the personal accounting of cost and choice as plain as could be. "Sleepless nights, endlessly," working "really hard, to the breaking point at times," and "so much self-sacrifice"—all counted as worth it for the sake of bringing "goodness and light into the world" and a "divine gift" that "nobody else can bring" except for that specific human being who will be welcomed into the world next. These were her incentives. Because the cost was worth it to her, she had become a *self for another self*. "Like valuing children first," she said, "the family unit being the priority above career and personal identity." She defined her purpose and meaning by other persons—not things, not goals, not accomplishments. And not persons in general, "mankind in general," as Dostoyevsky said,[1] but specific people: her own children. They were the meaning of her self.

At last Leah got around to telling me more about her marriage. It wasn't just that she, Leah, was for her children. It was that she and her husband as a couple were for their children. It was their shared purpose, the meaning of their life together, the highest good of their domestic community—their family structure. Children couldn't ruin her marriage since children were the meaning of her marriage.

> I feel like our marriage is better than ever now, even though I'm pregnant and I'm forty and this is my fifth kid. I feel like the passion is still there. The love is still there. I think we're definitely in it together forever. There's no doubt in my mind at all. I see us—and it's through thick and thin. I'm not saying we've never had our arguments or disagreements or had problems or challenges, but on the whole, we are very happy.
>
> Because [if] it's all about self-gratification. That always is going to go away at some point. Like if it's all about self-fulfillment, there's going to be that point in any relationship where it's not fulfilling for you. It's literally not. It's not—and that's the difference. Marriage isn't about me being fulfilled all the time and me getting my needs gratified all the time. It's about sharing in that purpose.

Not only that, she said, but having so many children had made them better people, more capable, with more to give. She continued:

> It's really interesting to think about that. What creates tenacity in a relationship ultimately really? Because yeah, we have so many household duties. It really is overwhelming. The dishes and the laundry and the parenting.
>
> And yet you grow so much as a person. Your capacity grows. What I was capable of with one kid almost seems like probably looking back at a vacation when you have five. And it seemed really hard at the time.
>
> Because my capacity as a person has grown so tremendously. And my tolerance and my ability to field stressful experiences and manage them differently. So, I think we grow a lot. We have a lot to give because we've learned how to manage a very full life.

Leah envisions the job of raising five kids as a thirty plus–year mission that she and her husband are committed to carrying through together: "I see us—and it's through thick and thin." Her oldest is fifteen, and it will be at least another eighteen years until her baby is launched. For her, motherhood has become a way of life, not a limited phase of life. Leah will have had a kid under age five for more than twenty years of her adult life. For some of the mothers we met, that span stretched to thirty years.

### "A Lot of Value in Being Raised in a Large Family"

If Leah believes that her marriage is better for having children as a shared purpose, she thinks her children are better too. Better how?

Like Jenn, Leah believes that growing up with many siblings works against selfishness and individualism in favor of maturity. She said,

> I think it's interesting to think about, "How will this influ-
> ence the future?" I think there's a lot of value in being
> raised in a large family in that children that are raised in
> large families have what those that are not don't have.
>
> My older kids are really learning about independence
> and responsibility and how to contribute and they already
> at thirteen and fifteen know that life isn't all about them
> and their self-fulfillment. They understand that life is about
> responsibility, give and take, giving back basically. It's not
> just take, take, take.
>
> And I feel like a lot of kids that grow up in a smaller
> family end up with the message that, "It is about me and
> what I want, and I get it." They don't learn how to give back
> in the same ways.

Leah's frank speech about smaller families—"They don't learn how to give back in the same ways"—was sharper than most. But we heard a version of this from many women we met. In general, it was expressed more as large families having a definite advantage in foster-ing pro-social virtues.

Our subjects held first that the character of children is not immune to family form. It mattered, they said, whether you grew up with one sibling or ten. Variously, they talked about children who learned how to share space (like bedrooms), time, and goods with others; about how they learned to take responsibility for each other from a young age; about children who had to tolerate differences of opinion, per-sonality, and interest; and about how their children learned to under-stand themselves as deeply connected to, and loved by, many others.

Second, our subjects connected the character of their children with the future character of the society they would inhabit. They believe that children from larger families are less likely to understand freedom as license, and more likely to understand liberty as a form of responsibility. If my purpose is you—then my freedom, the only thing that is fully mine, finds its meaning in your good.

Many of the women, and Leah was no exception, pointed out that their teens seemed happier—and better to live with—than cultural expectations would predict:

> Oh, it's so good. I think it really tempers their experience of the natural separation that takes place as a teenager. And I can say for my son, he's having a radically different experience than I had at his age. He's living a much more wholesome life. He's spending Friday nights at home with a family meal and Saturdays in the synagogue with the community praying during prayer service.
>
> But family comes first. And also, that there's a community looking after him. He knows that he's accountable, whereas I think a lot of teenagers live in their own world and they're not accountable to a community. So, it's definitely good. And just the experience of contributing with the care of younger siblings is huge, learning how to be a caretaker. Not like a parent, just someone who is looked up to and influences.
>
> I mean, I feel that my teenagers have never been easier, more independent, and self-sufficient. I mean, if anything, they've become so much easier with age. Of course, they say, "Bigger kids, bigger problems." The stuff on their minds is big, but who they are as people, how they behave is exemplary.

Leah is genuinely enjoying raising her teenagers. Not only that, relying on them, even. We heard the same from women across our sample. I couldn't help but wonder if one of the unseen human costs of the birth dearth has been the warping of the teenage years into a muddled state of insecurity, anxiety, depression, and self-centeredness. What if none of that is biologically determined?

Assume an average of two years between births in a typical household. In a family with four children, when the eldest is thirteen, the youngest will be seven. In such a household, half of the children will have a sibling under ten during the early teenage years. Not an incredible ratio, but better than none. In a family with two children, by contrast, not even one of them will have a sibling under ten by the teenage years. And neither will even have a memory of a baby in the house. In families with five or more children, however, like those of the women in my study, things get more interesting. My own mom, for instance, gave birth twice when I was in high school—once my freshman year and once again, when I was a senior. Those arrivals were the happiest times of my high school years. I cradled and cherished those tiny people—loving them and pouring myself into them. Was I a perfect teenager? Far from it. But those babies kept me at home far more than I might have been, and expanded my interests beyond clothes, boys, the length of my phone cord, and my own problems.

Leah identified various culprits when she talked about our tendency not to give priority to having children. "Our culture literally abandons new moms, and I think that it's really traumatic for people. And if you go through trauma, why would you want to do that so many times?" She continued:

We are in these little individual boxes and it's completely unnatural to be alone with a newborn for twelve hours a day. It's psychologically torturous to not have the support. And I would say the vast majority of women that give birth in America don't have adequate support, physically, emotionally, psychologically, and medically.

No one's coming for you.

You're literally alone. And it's not normal, it's not healthy. It's not—that is not what we're programmed for, psychologically. The human is not prepared for that. Nobody can be.

Leah said that "in religious circles there's more support." Friends had brought her meals for two weeks after each kid, for instance, and, she noted, "Childbirth is celebrated for us as a community." But she didn't think that was the whole answer. It's the loss of "the village mentality" she emphasized, where the day's burdens, however heavy, might have been shared with other women over your backyard fence, or on the front stoop, without leaving your home. And it's the loss of being valued when you leave the working culture. She said, "Women don't feel valuable when they have a baby in the secular world. You become invisible. Now you are no longer this productive member of our working culture. So, you're not valuable anymore." She continued. "People want to feel valuable. People want to feel like they're contributing something important. And when the culture makes them feel that that's not what they're doing, it's very painful."

## *"I Feel Like I'm Doing This Work for God"*

But like other moms, Leah's discussion of structural roadblocks gave way to characterological ones. "I think that work ethic is a big problem," she said. "I think that people have the expectation of instant gratification and self-fulfillment, and that's not what parenting is about. It's like long-term gratification, long-term self-fulfillment, through a lot of hard work. So, I think people are afraid of the level of self-sacrifice and hard work and tenacity that it takes to bear the responsibility."

And their fears are stoked by overestimates of what it will take. Leah drew an analogy between marginal financial costs and marginal personal costs, both of which decline with more kids. She explained, "[People think] raising a child is going to be expensive. But they don't realize that you don't buy everything for every kid. You know what I mean?"

She laughed and went on. "It's funny. All that up-front investment for nothing. And same thing with the learning curve with parenting. It's such a shame to only have one or two kids because you've put in so much effort, so much blood, sweat, and tears to learn how to be a good parent and by the time you get to kid three, four, and five, you're a different person. You're good at this now."

She laughed again, before turning to a more serious thought. Ultimately, she believed, not having children came down to the competition between the self and self-sacrifice.

> Our culture has influenced women in the direction of not choosing to have children at an early age and prioritizing our own personal fulfillment, careers, financial success, and free time. Time to "enjoy" life, over selfless acts of giving back to the world and raising children.
>
> And I think that's reflected in my experience of my peers. When I had my son, I was the first person by far to have children of anyone that I went to college with and had three kids before they all started having their first.
>
> So, I highly doubt that it's [biological] fertility rates declining. I think it's cultural attitudes shifting and economic

trends shifting. And I think it's hard to come to the conclusion of, "I'm going to devote my life to something that takes a lot of self-sacrifice," when there are a lot of other options available and easier ways out. More theoretically self-fulfilling roles that women could play in society.

Leah described the value determination problem, the new calculus, and the opportunity cost framework. The choice to have a child is always, *Compared to what?*

But choosing self-sacrifice required a supernatural perspective, she said. "I definitely think having a large family is very much tied in with my faith. Because again, I think you could live your life pursuing self-fulfillment, vacations to Florida. But having five kids is," she laughed, "I'm not even going to be kicking my feet up that often." She continued, elaborating on the role of faith:

So yeah, I feel that having children is definitely intentional. Definitely something that I feel is a divine blessing, just like wealth and health. And it is a partnership between us and God for sure. I feel like I'm doing this work for God, the work of raising children that will be bringing light and holiness and goodness to the world, to the best that I can.

There's no guarantees about your children's choices but all you can do is try to raise them in a certain environment and do your best. I think that bringing children into the world is like bringing holiness into the world. Like every soul has a mission that can only be fulfilled by that individual and we don't know what that individual's mission is and even what our own mission is. We're all figuring it out as we go. And I think, yes, it is something that I do for God in a sense of the work component.

Leah paused and continued,

> But I think that children are a blessing from God as well. So, it goes both ways, I think. It's not just one way or the other. It's like we create a vessel for blessing by living our lives with intention.
>
> And sometimes those are things that are beyond our understanding, really, why some people would be blessed, and others wouldn't. It's not even necessarily that that's the reality. I think challenges can be for our best interest as well. We don't have the full picture of why things happen.
>
> But on a revealed level, I think that children are a divine blessing. If my life was all about me and what's good for me and what's convenient, then I wouldn't have a large family.

In the race between self and sacrifice, it was the belief Leah shared with the biblical Hannah that picked the winner. Hannah praised God mightily for Samuel: "There is no Holy One like the LORD; no one besides you; there is no Rock like our God."[2] And we are told that "the LORD took note of Hannah; she conceived and bore three [more] sons and two daughters" after Samuel.[3] Faith in the God of Abraham, Isaac, and Jacob was the catalyst for Leah's births, as it had been for Hannah's children long before her.

# CHAPTER NINETEEN

"*The Lord Repays*"—*Self and Sacrifice*

"I think really the bottom line is they don't want to
sacrifice, and they don't realize how great it is if they
do sacrifice."

—June, mother of eight

"Give to the Most High as he has given to you, and as
generously as you can afford. For the Lord is the one
who repays, and he will repay you sevenfold."

—Sirach 35:12–13

T his is not a book about why people are having so few children. Rather, I set out to learn why people who want so many
children want them, and what their choices mean to them.
The narratives in the second part of this book complete the answers
suggested in the first part. A child is not purchased at market. The

cost of a child is the weight of the personal sacrifices that a woman takes on in order to have and raise a child. The women in my sample had children because the costs were worth it to them: they judged the value of childbearing greater than the value of what they missed out on. The meaning of their choice was ultimately a self-offering. They "paid" for their children—bodily, emotionally, and spiritually—with their own selves. Mysteriously, they received themselves back in return, as other selves, more virtuous selves, more joyful selves—selves gained through loss. Dying to self, they believed they had been restored to life through a divine repayment.

Having a child is "like a pound of flesh," Amanda, with five kids, had said. Our subjects told of sleepless nights, losing their figures, and putting cherished pursuits on the back burner. Some (but not all) had given up full-time careers, foregoing income and status. Some had downgraded their lifestyles—fewer vacations and unsightly cars. Some talked about trouble with family and friends. And most of our subjects described a difficult rebirth of their own person into someone new—someone who lived for others as a way of life. But for all that, the moms reported a repayment they had not expected. None of them had wanted kids in order to find fulfillment. But they got it anyway. Maggie, a Catholic mom of Lebanese descent with six children, told us,

> There's a lot of growth that has to happen, from your first baby or as a new mother. And I think that's maybe why people stop having kids, because you really go through a time of losing yourself and giving so much to this family.
>
> And that's kind of scary, and it doesn't feel good. And it's a lot of self-sacrifice, a lot of self-denial, whether it's your career or your body image or just yourself, your time to yourself, your ability to think a few thoughts all at once.

I'm not saying I have completely [overcome that], but I think not embracing that would have stopped me from having more children because I wanted to preserve that sense of self rather than opening myself up to all these other little lives that, ironically, fulfilled me more than my own interests would have.

Eileen in Los Angeles, also with six kids, styled repayment as the "paradox of motherhood but also of the human journey." She said, "I remember feeling conflicted and thinking, 'Gosh, I could be going to law school' or doing a whole host of things, and it felt like, you know, all the things that moms say: 'I'm not getting any applause, I'm doing all these things and nobody's seeing what I'm doing.' I sunk into self-pity several times." Eileen continued. "But I think ultimately, you become more yourself the more you grow in virtue. We become who we're supposed to be by giving ourselves away. I think that ultimately is what I would rest on—a confidence that you gain in that."

Eileen hit the nail on the head when she talked about how she could have gone to law school. Downstream from the big reproductive technologies of the mid-century was a world of amplified opportunities made possible by postponing children without sacrificing partnership.[1] The more valuable the opportunities in terms of interest, satisfaction, income, and status, the greater the cost borne in foregoing them. Having a child doesn't cost only so many diapers and so much baby food—it costs the gap between what a mom will earn working part-time and what she might have earned with uninterrupted work and an advanced degree. It costs the missing reputation from not being "seen as valuable" as Leah put it. And it costs the missed enjoyments of personal professional interests. As the average family size dives lower, another child also costs the social alienation of defying the norm.

*"We Are Most Ourselves When We Give Ourselves Away"*

The costs are borne disproportionately by moms. Mothers of large families look weird to their peers, they stand out in a crowd, they give up professional status, they (may) lose their figures—and they (mostly) do the getting up at all hours of the night. Maggie said, "There's so much dying to self in that self-sacrifice, like serving these little masters. They are the boss. If they're hungry you nurse them. If they wake up, if they're tired, you take care of them. Not to the detriment of yourself, of course. But coming to not just accept that, but to really embrace that with motherhood, it took me a while." She finished:

> And I will always say, zero to one child was the hardest transition for me. Having six is nothing compared to that. But it all goes back to that mental state, where you go from being a single woman to a married woman, where you still get to do everything that you really want within reason, to, now you're caring for somebody else twenty-four hours a day.
>
> And that shift is so dramatic that I think without a proper perspective of this precious, beautiful, adorable little life, we can very easily spin ourselves into, "What did I get myself into?" and, "I can't, I can't, I can't whatever." And then you blame this little person.

June, a soft-spoken older mom with eight kids—her last born when she was age forty-eight—put it this way: "I think really the bottom line is [people] don't want to sacrifice, and they don't realize how great it is if they do sacrifice. You get so much in return." The women defying the birth dearth had found a way to make sense out of the shock of dying to self that came from having kids. Relying on models of sacrifice drawn from faith and pushing through the hardships, they reported getting "so much in return."

The language the women in the study used varied widely. Hannah and Esther, chapter 13, talked about the way "your love grows," and seeing "amazing miracles," and big blessings that "so far outweigh" the difficulties. Danielle, chapter 14, insisted that "the dividends are there too." Steph, chapter 15, wanted to answer the rude lady in Goofy's Kitchen by saying, "This is where the joy is." For Jenn, chapter 16, God had fulfilled his promise of "plans to prosper her," and "it was just perfectly planned out, the ones that we have." She also said, "They provide their own therapy. They love you to death too." And Leah, chapter 18, testified that "my husband and I are really happy. We are really, really happy and fulfilled."

But Angela, chapter 17, used the language closest to what we heard most frequently. "We are most ourselves when we give ourselves away," she said. "That's just the paradox of the Cross. So, I do think that's a mystery." While women all across the sample spoke of things given up, and of gut-wrenching personal sacrifices, they spoke not of losing themselves but of finding themselves. June said, "You get so much in return," and it was *yourself* that she and the other women seemed to think you got in return—not the self that had died, but a better self. Or a self that was found, as if for the first time—a self no longer searching for itself. Hannah said, "I have inner peace in my life that I didn't have then. *I was searching. I'm not searching now.*"

Amanda, the Latter-day Saint mom and nonprofit entrepreneur with five kids, emphasized the biblical promise made in all four[2] of the Gospels:

When the Savior said, "Give your life to me and you will find it," it's incredibly counterintuitive. Think about his time when he came. And that's why he is who he is. It's super counterintuitive.

Like what I think is, "I need to think about me and my goals."

Jesus Christ said, "No, you need to go outward, give your life to me and serve others and you'll find your life."

And that principle is 100 percent true because I've lived it and it's true.

It is not just because you're this altruistic person giving yourself. It's that by giving of yourself, you find who you are. And that's parenthood, too.

Amanda went on, referring to her baby, three months old:

I've never felt more connected to my body in a good way. To describe the fleshy baby, it's so real. Like the baby is real, my resume is not real. Instagram is not real. Facebook is not real. Is happiness really found there? This is life and joy in its purest form.

Anything in life worthwhile, it's hard and it's sacrifice and you get something in return for that sacrifice. Like, this joy, this connection, my life's work, this eternal relationship where I think I do more good than anything.

I also think having children helps you figure out who you are.

Mary, the mom of eleven who had lost one to leukemia, had worked as a CPA in one of the Big Four accounting firms before she got married. She offered this observation: "The more that we love the more that we discover who we really are."

Monica, a former corporate lawyer with six kids, related a dramatic account of self-discovery:

> When I first became a mother, I was sort of lost because I had previously identified as a successful, high-achieving young professional. I graduated college with honors, and I went on to law review in law school. I wanted to check the boxes and I had a very bright promising career as a young litigator. I had won quite a bit of mention at my firm and all that. So that was really my identity.
>
> And so, when I became a mother, I didn't understand, I quickly realized that everything had shifted. My whole world had turned on the axis. And what did it mean? I just had no idea. It really was for so many years just about getting through the days. It was like, "We'll get through this time, and I'll go back to being that person," and that was sort of how I saw it. I had that person, not just that career but that person, on a hold.
>
> So, it was terrible, right? I was not allowing myself to be me. This [mom] wasn't me and that [lawyer] was.
>
> I feel like after my second one I kind of came into the beginning of an awakening of myself and who I was as a daughter of God. As a person inside—a Christian, a wife, a mother.
>
> All of those things coalescing to an understanding, and when I say "me and who I am"—I really mean why I'm here. So those things are so closely connected.
>
> But for me, the self-discovery was in this total upheaval of everything I thought and knew and this completely different path of opening my life and my heart to all these little people who have taught me a ton about life.

But thank God I didn't stay doing that [law] because I don't know if I would have found that same self-realization there.

Monica felt that she had been repaid for her sacrifices. She gave up herself but received herself. She found her identity and purpose—"who I am" and "why I'm here." Monica tied herself down and freed herself up. "It's wonderfully freeing, it's the opposite of what the culture would tell you, I think, which is that [this] is a cage. Choosing to have a large family which necessarily in most women's situations does restrict her career choices and appears to kind of limit you because of your finances. There's a lot more limitations and need of planning. But it's the opposite. It's freeing."

Hannah's chain all over again—and again.

### *"I Will Not . . . Offer Burnt Offerings That Cost Me Nothing"*

In the first book of Chronicles there is a remarkable story about King David, who is sent by an angel to build an altar on a certain threshing floor—a place where wheat is processed into grain. The altar is for King David to offer sacrifices to win favor from God and save his people from the plague. The threshing floor he is commanded by God to use for the altar belongs to a man named Ornan. When the servant of the king tells Ornan that King David would like to take the threshing floor to make sacrifices, the chronicler recounts, Ornan is eager to be of use:

> Then Ornan said to David, "Take it; and let my lord the king do what seems good to him; see, I present the oxen for burnt offerings, and the threshing sledges for the wood, and the wheat for a grain offering. I give it all."

But King David said to Ornan, "No; I will buy them for the full price. I will not take for the LORD what is yours, nor offer burnt offerings that cost me nothing." So, David paid Ornan six hundred shekels of gold by weight for the site.[3]

Ornan, a good servant, is eager to make a gift of what is his to the king, for the Lord's purpose. But King David insists, "I will not take for the LORD what is yours." So the king, on behalf of God, pays Ornan handsomely—indeed, "full price"—for his willingness to part with what is his. The lesson seems to be that although God is God and can demand any sacrifice from his people, the Lord repays us for giving up what is ours. And he pays its worth—not some token payment. He deals with us more as equals than as sovereign to servant.

But what, ultimately, is ours to give up, to be repaid? It may not be much, but surely at least our freedom is ours. We don't own ourselves, but we are responsible for choosing, for making determinations about what we will do and what we will pursue. The women quietly defying the birth dearth believe that childbearing is worth doing, not as a limited phase of life but as a way of life. Motherhood requires self-sacrifice, they say, "to the breaking point at times." But they also believe that God has blessed them by their children, in ways that evade human design and expectation.

When we live "with intention," as Leah, chapter 18, put it—offering what is ours to God—he stands ready to bless us. "God's not out to trick us, and send us trouble," Esther, chapter 13 said. "He really wants to send us blessings and we should ask for that." But if God is God, and he wants to bless us, why should we have to ask him? Because God respects the one thing that is ours, the one thing that separates us from him—our freedom. He wants us to want what he wants. "'I don't want'—but I want to want, you know?" Hannah, chapter 13, said. And how, in practice, do we want what He wants? We choose what

He wants even when it's costly. Especially when it's costly. King David said, "I will not . . . offer burnt offerings that cost me nothing." Even if it should cost us our life, even if it means "dying to self," the Lord repays even that.

The view of Leah, and Hannah and Esther, and Angela and Jenn, and Danielle and Steph, and Maggie and Monica, and Terry and Shaylee, and Miki and Kim is that childbearing is good—and part of God's plan to prosper us. Against the norm, they chose to have children at considerable personal cost. But the expenses they bore, the investments they made, were compensated in full. "The dividends are there too," as Danielle said. That is their testimony. They were repaid in multiple ways, but at last with their own selves. They understood their meaning and purpose. If having children was mostly work and effort when they were younger women, something they did for God, by the end it seemed to them all bounty and gift. When their childbearing was over, they often hoped for *just one more*. "I'm adjusting, there are good things for sure," said Lynn, ten kids, mourning the end of her fertility. "But I just know all the beauty and the fruits that come with having that baby in the family and just each personality brings so much."

The biblical Hannah was also repaid. Though she had wept, and ached, and implored God for a child, she nevertheless gave Samuel back to the Lord. "For this child I prayed; and the LORD has granted me the petition that I made to him. Therefore, I have lent him to the LORD; as long as he lives, he is given to the LORD."[4] Only a mother can imagine what it cost Hannah to leave the small boy at the Temple. We are told she visited him once a year, bringing him little robes to wear. But we are also told that "Eli would bless Elkanah and his wife, and say, "May the LORD repay you with children by this woman for the gift that she made to the LORD."[5] The Hannah who was barren received five more children. The Lord of Hosts redeems his debts, not only "in full," but "sevenfold," according to the Book of Sirach. Sevenfold implies the perfection of God—without end. So there is no repayment like the Lord's repayment.

PART FOUR

*The Character of the Nation—Conclusion*

CHAPTER TWENTY

# "He Didn't Know He Needed It"—Saving Our Lives

"And, so, that was supposed to be the worst time in his life—you lost your big job and you lost your dad. It was where God pulled the sheet from under him and said, 'Wake up.' And he did. He did. Like I said, it can go two ways, and he went the right way. So, he got closer to God and, you know, connected with the baby."

—Kyra, mother of five

This is a chapter about new beginnings. Not "the birth of new men," but "the action they are capable of by virtue of being born."[1] Apart from the drama of self-sacrifice and reward, my subjects thought that the value of children proved itself over time. Babies better lives and love disinterestedly. They bring healing that no one else can bring. The mothers in my sample, reasoning from their own experiences, believe that the character of the nation has suffered from its dearth of children. The narratives in this chapter present some of these stories.

We met Kyra in a church building on the premises of a Catholic parish in the Northeast where a large homeschool group meets for a cooperative. Kyra described herself loosely as a Baptist. She was in her mid-forties, dressed like an urban fashion influencer, wearing joggers and a cute fedora with dark hair braided underneath. "I had my first son when I was twenty, and, um, I did love being a young mom. I enjoyed that because I was in [a town that] is like pretty inner-city, it is pretty hip." She described how she had had her first son at twenty before she met her husband. He had a daughter from another relationship. She and her husband met, married, and had a son right away after marriage.

## "We Don't Need Any More"

Kyra talked with keen self-reflection about the feeling of accomplishment and satisfaction they had at that time:

> As long as you keep your shape and you still look nice and you're working and you own your own business and you've got two kids—like wow, that's amazing. You know, nobody can say anything about it. No, I didn't see myself being here but I did always know that I wanted more.
>
> And my husband and I do an exercise a lot, like every several years, like, what's your goal? It always comes back to, um, getting closer to God, walking closer to Jesus, trying to live a life that Jesus would be proud of. You know, realistically that's all we were looking for. So no, I wouldn't say that we stepped into our marriage saying, "Let's have a big family and it's going to be beautiful."

Kyra and her husband had met at a Home Depot, working there together. But he got a great new job, and they moved to an apartment in New Jersey closer to the city.

And I had a one-year-old, so—he had a girl, I had a boy. And we always remember this day, we were in New Jersey at the time, and he had just gotten a new job and we were just newly married, and we sat at a café and had our fancy lattes and we said, "You have a girl, I have a boy, we don't need any more." Like, this is life, this is wonderful, this is great. We had [a] brand-new Mercedes, like, you have a great job, we were living on the Holland Tunnel, what more do you need? You bike into Hoboken, what more do you need? Like this is wonderful. So, we always go back to that story because that was where we were.

Continuing, Kyra explained that their backgrounds had not prepared them to want a life with one income, or many kids:

His mom was a lobbyist in D.C., big job, all the time. Big job. Dad was D.E.A., and a business owner, so, he's an only child. So, he grew up in a home that he was always, you know, that's what he was born to do, grow up, be successful and, you know, get those diplomas on the wall and get that job.

That was hard for me as well because of my background. My parents were—they went to church all the time but didn't behave—I don't want to go too deep, but anyway, they didn't come to my wedding because my husband's black. So, they didn't support me that way, so that made me want to be anything *but* my mom. And so, you know, that's my personal struggle that I was like, "I'm not going to be a stay-at-home mom because of the ignorance that comes with that." That was my thought and at the time, you know, it was very immature to not be able to separate her from everything else, but—so I decided I'm going to become a go-getter, I'm going to go out, I'm going to run the world.

So, um, I did start my own business, and we had our first child together and I was doing that. I was a business owner, I was taking care of a little one and I still had my other son and then we had his daughter. So, um, I would say that the shift really occurred for me—it's not only getting closer to God but, um, my son ended up to be more special needs, so he needed my time, he needed my attention. That was kind of the pivoting point, I had to make a decision there: I could either trust everybody else to help with that or I could do it.

So, um, I'm going to do it. You know, I sold my business, I gave everything up, and that was where I had to make the adjustment that I'm telling you that I completely understand that being a mom is enough. It's very hard. Very, very hard. And especially when you're conditioned to believe that it's not—"Oh, you don't work? Well, what do you do? What do you do all day? I wish I could stay home all day."

That's probably the biggest thing I get, is more of the stay-at-home mom thing, not just the big family. Like, even if I just had two kids, I would still get that, because I did only have two kids at the time.

Kyra described how at that point, when she settled into staying home, wanting another child was on her heart—but her husband didn't share that.

So, um, that was the backlash I feel like I got hit the hardest with, is staying home. And I knew that I was needed at home, and so that's what I did. So, we went through that and then I knew that I wanted another child, and so then enter my husband, who's done, I mean we have a girl and two boys at this point—like, never. We don't need any more. So, that was really—and he has a very successful job, and he works a lot.

I understand what it's like to have someone who comes from the home that's achievement, achievement, achievement.

So I had to deal with that, and it's, you know, with me personally connecting with God, I felt like that was, um, I didn't want to do any birth control—birth control is, you know, it's toxic. So, I said I'm not going to do anything, I'm not going to go get my tubes tied or anything because I'm not going to play God. I just said we'll be careful a little bit and see what happens. But really my [hope] was the accident.

And so eventually I did get pregnant, and, um, I was very happy but I felt like I couldn't share that excitement. And I couldn't share the excitement with his parents or anything, so, um, I ended up losing the baby.

But, um, we did it again, we went through the whole process again, and I was pregnant again and, um, he was not—it wasn't his thing. But he's just like, "Look, it is what it is. This is what we gotta do, we gotta do it. We've got to figure some stuff out."

But their world changed forever during that pregnancy—her third, and their second together. It marked the line between the old them and the new them.

So, um, at eight months pregnant, his dad died. And it was soul-crushing to him. And because, I think—I mean it was just right in line: his dad died and then his job was like, "Yeah, we're done." Like, he wasn't there enough at work.

So his dad died, he lost his job. I mean, that's life-changing. You can either go two different ways there. And then here I am, eight months pregnant and knowing that he wasn't 100 percent supportive.

So, um, I had the baby and I mean, that was his world. This little baby comes out—and this was the brown baby that looks just like him. Brown baby, brown hair, just all this dark hair and, um, I truly describe it as I birthed her and then I put her in his arms, and he never put her down. Like, never. That was it.

I mean, he would come down in the middle of the night when she'd fuss, and he'd never come back. He would just cuddle up with her and he needed it. And I don't think he knew he needed it. Obviously, he didn't know he needed it.

So that was, um, such a beautiful moment and a time in his life that was healing and changed him and soul-changing and so I watched that shift happen. And, so, that was supposed to be the worst time in his life—you lost your big job, and you lost your dad. It was where God pulled the sheet from under him and said, "Wake up." And he did. He did. Like I said, it can go two ways, and he went the right way. So, he got closer to God and, you know, connected with the baby.

We met Kyra early in our project, and her story seemed remarkable. But it resonated with me personally. Twenty-five years ago, as a young graduate student, I married a widower with six grieving children at home. My firstborn was a salve for them in a way that I would never have guessed. One of our girls—like Kyra's husband—took the baby in her arms and never put him down. She cuddled up with him on a beat-up old sofa in the front living room for weeks, it seemed, absorbing love from him that she couldn't take from me yet. Imagine my surprise, then, to hear Kyra's story, two decades after an experience I thought was just ours. "I know what you mean," I muttered in reply, fighting back tears. "It happened to me, once," I said.

### *"Almost like a Sunlamp"*

But still—I didn't see it as a pattern, a phenomenon, until I hit the road to do more interviews. As I said in chapter 1, I embarked on this project to know my own reasons for the first time. But I didn't expect to hear about an experience so similar to mine.

Jackie, a mother of twelve in the Northeast, who (after having twelve biological children) adopted a son from foster care, and was now fostering another, had a plethora of tales. "When we had our first who we adopted as a foster child, we were like, 'We could totally do this for a living' because when the baby comes in the house, the charism changes. The joy comes. We would have people coming to our house just to see the baby just because they needed joy." She told us about her older son's twenty-first birthday party, right after their foster baby (now adopted) had arrived: "We had almost like two hundred kids there from college and they spent the entire time taking numbers, like who could hold the baby next. And we were just like, what an amazing group of kids. Like there's just something about babies that just kind of brings you joy. And who doesn't need more joy?"

She continued:

I also have seen, and I could probably do a study on it, my children who are going through adolescence in middle school, their mannerism totally changes if they're holding a baby. One of my sons I think would have probably been categorized with depression or anxiety problems if he hadn't held his sister for like six months straight. I used to say, "Man if I could teach him to breastfeed, I would be all set."

And he would just hold her and his whole mannerism would change, and his demeanor would change. It was almost like the people who have the need to be in sunlight or whatever. It was almost like a sunlamp. He would just hold that baby and I could just watch his body language, his facial expressions, and he would be better. And then it was time for him to go off and he could pass the baby on to the next sibling.

I cannot express enough, and I would tell my friends who don't have babies, "Like come over, and hold mine," because it is a huge, there's just something, when you look at a baby, they look at you like they're staring at God. They look at you like you are amazing. They are enamored with you. The eye-to-eye contact. They just look at you like you are the best thing in the whole world and who doesn't need to hear that?

Especially a teenager who wakes up in the morning a different person every day. I'm ugly. I'm fat. I'm too tall. I'm too short. My hair is oily. I got pimples on my face. My friend likes me today, tomorrow they hate me. This boy likes me, this boy hates me.

It's just to have that constancy with holding a child. Even a mom fails [to provide affirmation]—"Do the dishes, clean your room, do your homework"—they were getting that from my children, and I have seen nothing but positive things.

Jackie had a final tale to tell. "One of my favorite experiences is I had just delivered my eleventh and I just got home from the birthing center. And so, he wasn't even twenty-four hours old." She went on:

I was laying in my bed, it was August sixteenth, and I have a bedroom on the first floor so the windows are open and the curtains are open and I see these two boys on their bicycles biking over. And my son who was thirteen at the time is like, "Mom, my buddies just called from the pool and they wanted to come see the baby. And then I'm like, "Oh my gosh, this is so beautiful." They walked in like it was Christmas and they were like, "I've never seen a baby one day old," and I'm like, "Do you want to hold him?" They're like, "I'm allowed to hold him???"

Now one of them is getting married, like they all say this one thing, "I'll never forget when you let me hold [the baby]," who's now eleven. Holding this baby and looking at these eleven-year-old boys who stopped playing basketball at the pool down the street so they could see their buddy's new baby sibling.

I'm like, I could package this and sell tickets or something for people who do this. But to watch these teenagers stare at this baby, they had never seen a baby and had never been invited to hold one. And what a gift! And like they still talk about this.

And those are the same boys that when we got a foster baby seven years ago, like everyone in town, all their buddies, my kids were away in college, they're like, "...can I come by?" Texting me like, "Can I stop by and see your baby boy?" And even though my kids weren't there, they were all away at college, all their friends who were in town, and at Thanksgiving and Christmas, they're like, "We want to stop by and see the new edition," or, "We heard you had to hire one out [by fostering] because you couldn't have any more"—to watch these kids drive into town, they're home for Christmas break and they're running upstairs to see the new baby. So, I was just like. This. Is. Great.

After Jackie, I updated my expectations. It wasn't just Kyra and me. Interview after interview, we heard stories about babies who had fixed a family problem, cured a health issue, or comforted a suffering person. We weren't even probing for this. It wasn't in the interview guide.

One of our moms spoke about a different aspect of the phenomenon in a roundabout way. Betsy, expecting her fifth, was a social worker in the Rocky Mountain region who had struggled with depression and eating disorders. She volunteered the following story when we asked about whether she thought that babies take a lot out of you:

> One more thing, about that question. I think it's a strange question, because it's a question where you think all at once, "Why is it even a question?"—and on the other hand you see why it needs to be asked.
>
> I have struggled with depression my whole life, and my lowest point, I was living on my own by myself doing things the way I wanted, everything was about me and my brokenness, and I was very lost, and I couldn't find out why

the more focused I was on healing myself the more broken I seemed to become.

A strange situation literally threw me into volunteering at . . . a home for the elderly run by Little Sisters of the Poor. I went once against my will, and then I couldn't stop going, and I went every week. To be around these humans who have been basically given away by society totally left, because they also take in a lot of elderly off the street, just totally, literally abandoned. You see how much love they receive at this home but they're still alone.

It took me years to understand that that's what saved my life, because I had had suicide attempts, I had been in a very dark place. It was when I stopped looking in myself and started looking at these humans and started loving these people so much, and them and their suffering, and worrying about what they were going through, I started healing.

I think that's a strange thing in modernity. We have the luxury to worry about our own internal suffering and we don't always have the opportunity to see suffering around us.

The analogy between babies and the elderly isn't perfect, but Betsy highlighted the curative experience of being with those who need us. It reminded me of Kim, twelve kids, in chapter 7, who said that children who contribute at home "feel much more positive." She said, "They feel useful. You see suicides around in people who don't feel useful. And so it's funny because our culture wants to not have kids do [hard] stuff so that 'they can have a childhood' but then when they don't feel useful then they don't know what to do. They feel depressed."

*"He Could Love on That Baby. It Was Healing for Him"*

On the other side of the Rockies from Kim, we heard a more intense version of Jackie's story. Lisa had six kids when we met her at her suburban home in the Utah Valley. Her husband was a college professor. They had struggled through long years when he had to spend his time writing or doing research. After her first two babies who were close together, she then had twins, born early, who stayed in the NICU for five weeks. "We thought we were done with kids," after that, she told me. But they felt more optimistic about having another when they finally arrived in Utah.

> Once we moved here and we were settled and his career was, like, off and running and we found ourselves in this fabulous place, just geographically the people we are among and the opportunities that we had here and the lifestyle, we just felt like, we're in a really good place and this is a great place to raise kids. I think we can do this. Like we can do more and really give more children this awesome life. This is great.
>
> And so that fifth baby was really deliberate...but it took me six and a half years to get there. [So then I felt like] I'm done, that's all there is. I feel complete. Totally complete. And then I was totally blindsided by number six.
>
> I was just saying, like, "Heavenly Father, why can't you see?"—like my husband at this point was like writing his book, trying to get tenure, up against all these deadlines, right, in the office 'til 2:00 a.m., just coming home, helping to put the kids to bed and then going back and working all night and I was like, "I can't have it, why are you sending

me a baby? I just can't handle this. Can't you see I'm like way beyond what I can handle?" And not realizing that it was this baby that was going to turn everything over.

She continued:

> One of my twins, the boy, had a really bad bout with depression and anxiety when he was about eight or nine. And it was this sixth baby that turned him around—just having this little person that loved him unconditionally and that he could love unconditionally. And it was, the baby was the turning point.
>
> It was a scary, dark, dark place. And we'd been working with counselors and trying to get his meds right and trying to figure things out and he'd really not made much progress for months and months and months.
>
> And when we brought this baby [home], I mean, I just, I can see clearly just him even coming to the hospital and cradling that baby in his arms and just feeling that peace right for the first time—just for me as a mom, watching this boy, with my own anxiety about how are we going to help him get through this, to just see that peace come over him, and holding that baby.
>
> And they've been really close, really sweet buddies from the very beginning. The baby he, I mean, he loves [my older son]. They have a special bond and just to have someone that [my older son] could love and that would love him back with no judgment at all, and not care what his behavior had been.
>
> It just didn't matter. He could love on that baby. It was healing for him.

Twenty-five hundred miles away from each other, Lisa and Jackie offered strikingly comparable narratives about how their babies had rescued their children from depression.

### "The Siblings Did It All"

Rosalie, a Filipino mom of nine on the West Coast, first quoted in chapter 7, had a different type of testimony. It involved her special needs son.

> Number seven is our special needs one. He was born with a chromosome addition and a deletion. I've researched him, but there's no one that matches him, that has the same similarities as him. So, it has been a very difficult time when he was born, because we lived in the hospital, myself and my son.
>
> So the kids at home literally had to take care of one another. Not because anyone told them to, but they just knew that was the norm of what they needed to do, and they just stepped up to cooking more, and laundry more. Because Dad had to go to work. Mom had to be at the hospital.
>
> And I think having the seventh one was very difficult in terms of not having that mom all the time at home. But because you have a large family you don't feel like someone took anything away from you. If anything, they were excited to have that other sibling to come home to, to see how he was, and they learned so much with this sibling. They had to come with me to every appointment after he was released to come home with us.

And so I would take everyone to cardiology and they would do an EKG. And they would stand against the wall, and I'd have the cardiologist explain everything that was on that EKG. And I would tell him, this is my kids' field trip. Explain what you're doing and walk through it. It was the same thing when we'd do an X-ray. It would be the same thing, I mean, we were constantly living in a hospital with everybody, so to speak. So, they all learned and built the relationship to take care of their brother. He was on a G-tube so they all learned how to be part of that, to help him, to change his feedings, to be more like a doctor, like a nurse per se.

There were many times that I was asked to have a nurse live with us to help take care of him, but I didn't see a need for it because the siblings all did it. And therapists to our home. He did therapy at our home, but it was more…the kids. The doctors and the specialists would say, "He's probably improving, not necessarily from the therapists who [come] once or twice a week, but the kids. What do your kids do??" I go, "Well, I ask them whatever the homework it is from the therapist, I put it up, and if it's to flip him, whoever is passing by, flip your brother, flip your brother again, flip him again." Because he needed to build that upper body strength. Everyone would pick a task to do to help the brother. So, if anything, number seven was that best gift to bring our family even tighter together, to grow in charity.

As if this weren't enough, Rosalie, voice breaking a little, told us about the next baby:

Then I got pregnant with number eight. And I remember people slandering me for getting pregnant again, because they figured, "You have a special needs child, why would you have another child after him?" And that was a big one, because I remember thinking, "I don't think God would have given me this trial, if there wasn't a purpose."

And when she was born, because of her, he learned how to crawl. Number seven learned how to crawl because of number eight. Because he wanted to get to that baby that was crying on the other side. So he actually would move. And people were astounded, because he never moved. He never made a sound. He couldn't speak yet. Nothing.

And because of her, he wanted to eat. He never put anything in his mouth, but she was eating, so he learned how to eat. So, number eight helped number seven.

Number nine comes along, same thing. He still wasn't walking—he still couldn't stand. He couldn't do any of that. Now number nine comes along. It just motivated him more and more to get to that other baby.

So, if anything I see our family, if I could look back on it now, they have helped each other the whole way through. I think when you're in it, maybe it's not as organized as we want it to be, or anything like that. You're growing in the chaos. But I can step back, and I look at it, and I'm like, "This is an amazing gift, that everybody has been able to help each other in some simple way."

Rosalie's older children helped her youngest baby get through his therapy with flying colors. But her subsequent babies gave him what no one else could give: the will to move, the will to eat, the will to stand and walk. "I'm not the only one who teaches someone how to read," she says reflectively. "You know, just for them to sit next to each other and read, they've taught each other. I don't really feel like I teach them as much as they teach each other." As we saw in chapter 7, Rosalie said, "You have each other, and that overfills the cup, so to speak."

### "I Was Just So Afraid for Our Marriage"

Kyra told us what happened after her husband "got closer to God and, you know, connected with the baby":

And then I would say that that—to bring it all back around—I would say that that's where the shift happened when it wasn't that big of a deal at that point if you had another baby. Yeah, okay, they're nothing but love. It's so beautiful.

And then, um, when I got pregnant [with our third], I was still jaded from [the two pregnancies where] he wasn't as happy. You don't verbalize these things but in hindsight you see it. So, I was so scared, I didn't tell him for a while. Like, you know, two months, which is a long time to keep something like that secret.

And when I told him I just cried my eyes out and I was just so afraid for our marriage. And he's just like, "Why are you crying? A baby means more love. This is more to love. This is a beautiful thing, don't cry." So, um, that was huge. So, this is probably the first pregnancy I'm like, "Okay. This is my baby; I get to do this." And get to do all that and enjoy it.

So, as we continue to have more children, it's funny the way it happens because, you know, the salary went down, and the children started coming up. So, you know, we went through the entire shift. We've gone through all of it.

[That baby came] when we were out here, it's almost like what's the big deal? Like, when you're around like-minded people and everyone else has it and you're juggling it then you don't really think about it.

Her husband's change of heart was sincere. After their third (and her fourth) child, the one after the one that changed his world, they went on to have yet another:

And then that's when [my fifth] came and we, um—that's the two-year-old—and that was great. I mean, that was—he still, I mean gosh, makes the world go 'round is the way we describe him. His nickname, we call him Magic. He's just magical.

So, um, that's my story in a nutshell, so I can understand all of that. I can understand the feminism, I can understand the husband pressure, I can understand wanting more. We came from a brand-new Mercedes to I have a 2006 Odyssey with two hundred thousand miles on it. I wouldn't even let you ride in it—it's that bad. So, um, being able to do that took a lot. It took a lot of connection with God and having solid faith in your life to know that I don't need anything from anybody around me, I pull my confidence from him. So, um, that's why I do understand these things. So, um, I lived through them.

"You don't want to go back?" I asked her. "Oh, no, never," she insisted.

We had a dinner party and it was kind of a joke because we had a vegan dinner party but everybody's like, "Oh, you guys eat so dreadful." But we really do eat good food. And so we had everybody over and my husband starts telling these hilarious stories of the people we were and he's like, "My wife, she wrecks her Mercedes and she takes the extra money and she's at [the big mall] and she's buying these brand-new boots," and he's laughing about these $100,000 cars that I ripped the front-ends off of.

And so it's comical, it's a joke. And people that know me today were like, "This can't be a true story."

And it wasn't who I was—I know that there was a joy missing there that I have now, so, no, definitely.

And we had a good laugh at the thought of Kyra's younger self with outrageously expensive boots and a smoking, wrecked Benz.

■       ■       ■

As I pieced together the data from this project, I counted at least 20 percent of my subjects who talked about a baby bringing healing or reprieve to a sibling or parent who had been going through a difficult time. I couldn't help but wonder what that means for a two-child nation trending to a one-child nation. Birth rates are lower than they have ever been.[2] Rising depression, anxiety, and other disorders threaten adults and adolescents alike.[3] One-fifth of U.S. adults experience a major depressive disorder in their lifetime;[4] at least 15 percent of adults suffer symptoms of generalized anxiety disorder.[5] A third of adolescents aged ten to nineteen are estimated to be at risk for clinical depression,[6] and suicide rates have risen 60 percent for teens since 2007.[7] Life expectancy for both men and women has started to decline,[8] tied to substance abuse and addiction.[9]

Incredibly, adults with one or two children will spend no more than 5 percent of their adult lives with an infant under one year old, and no more than 20 percent with a child under age five. Today's typical middle school, high school, or college student, will never have lived in the same house with a human infant, and if so, will not remember it.[10] In contrast, the mothers and fathers in my sample are spending twenty or thirty years with a child under age five, and their children are growing up with babies in the house as a norm. Jackie said, "It was almost like a sunlamp.... I could package [the effect of a baby] and sell tickets or something." Lisa's son had "not made much progress [overcoming depression] for months and months and months" with therapists and meds until his little brother was born. And Kyra's grieving husband "never put [the baby] down. Like, never. That was it." "He needed it," she told us, but "obviously, he didn't know he needed it."

Is there a cure for our tsunami of depression, anxiety, and deaths of despair? The women quietly defying the birth dearth seem to have an answer, but it may be hard to accept for a nation so accustomed to seeing a baby as an impairment that more than 60 million babies have been aborted since 1970. What effect do babies have on the well-being of children and adults? It's a hard question to begin to answer, especially given the difficulties of establishing causality in health and social sciences. There is no randomized controlled trial we can run. Still, while many will point to our broken economy, divided politics, declining religion, or social media as causes of our mental health calamity, it is well worth examining a cause that nobody seems to have considered: Is the absence of babies in our midst partly to blame? I can attest that there are no teams of elite researchers scrambling to learn whether there is a correlation between lower birth rates and depression, anxiety, and despair. Let the testimonies reported here be the first to raise the awkward question. We've already tried everything else—exercise, therapy, new diets, and fancy medicines. The women I interviewed for this study thought we should try children.

# CHAPTER TWENTY-ONE

## "He Carries the Baby"—Saving Our Souls

"And for me, it wasn't a big deal. He carries the baby all the time. He changes her diapers. He puts her down for a nap. That's just kind of a way of life."

—Maggie, mother of six

This is a chapter of small stories, not big ones, comments and incidentals that bear on a larger argument about the character of the nation. Polls tell us we are less focused on God, family, community, and the common good.[1] We are less connected to each other.[2] More individualistic.[3] More polarized.[4] Looking for reasons, progressives and conservatives alike increasingly blame our political order and the ideas that give it life. Critics interrogate everything from race and religion to capitalism, liberalism, and the American founding. It is claimed that our system can no longer foster the virtues needed to sustain itself. Virtue has been freedom's victim.[5]

The testimonies in this volume offer a revision to this thesis. The proposition they represent is that virtue is most deeply fashioned by the way we live at home, as children and adults. Aristotle said that "our character traits, whether good or bad, come from like actions."[6] And character is constituted by our habitual actions—what we do repeatedly. "What we must learn to do, we must do to learn," Aristotle also said, pithily.[7] And nothing shapes our doings more than the domestic society: the first society we inhabit as children, and the family form to which we give ourselves as adults. The habits we learn in those circumstances in turn animate the political order and provide its character. Individualism and destructive forms of liberalism are personal habits before they are ideologies. In sum: it's not our political order that erodes our virtue, but our lack of virtue that warps the political order. As Aristotle put it, "The sources and springs of political rule come from the family."[8]

### "Tons of Opportunities for Them to Be Self-Sacrificing and Patient and Charitable"

The moms we interviewed likened families with many children to a type of rich soil for the soul, in which habits of right living—the virtues—are germinated. Monica, the former "promising" young litigator with six kids quoted in chapter 19, said,

> I see a lot of kids that don't have the qualities, the virtues that will serve them well as adults. Badly formed young adults. Because I think, not just the small family, but the philosophy, the approach that comes with it. And the focus on the wrong things, in particular material things. And

selfish ambition and the training of young people to be very lost. They're lost in themselves, in a way.

They're overly focused on themselves because of the way they've been taught, which is that they are of the most importance. And they're oddly disconnected from others. They're lacking the ability to relate to others well and also the problem solving, critical thinking, self-sacrificing, all those wonderful virtues and I just, I think that leads to either no marriage vocation or to a serious challenge if they do get married because those qualities of being able to serve others and to sacrifice for stuff, to work around problems, to get through things together, to understand an individual person's different qualities and temperaments and work with it—all those wonderful skills that are learned in a large family.

With those things being missing, when things aren't right for you and your dream and your plan, then what, right? And why would you sacrifice and change and try and be uncomfortable and all that, if you don't have the what for and the why?

So, both the lack of actual training and formation in virtue and the lack of the why, which is the faith part of it. So, it's not that just having a bunch of kids is some kind of solution to society's problems, but both things together, the why we're doing it, and the formation and constant underpinning of everything with all of that.

Monica didn't blame John Locke, or any other liberal baddie. In fact, not a single mom cited any political ideology, unless feminism counts as one. They were unsparing in their descriptions of a self-centered, individualistic America, but they didn't fault theories about rights or freedom, race, or creed. Instead, they blamed the way we grow up. Contrasting her own upbringing with her children's, Monica continued:

> There are tons of opportunities for them to be self-sacrificing and patient and charitable. Everybody has to share a room. That isn't their desired situation although some of them do love it and are afraid to be alone because they have never known otherwise.
>
> Especially with teenagers now, I see so many opportunities for them to have to not say what they want to say or be patient with the other or sharing the space, or who's claiming one or what not. There [are] just endless opportunities for conflict and resolution so that is what I didn't have.
>
> I had one brother, and I had my room, and he had his room, and he did his things, and I had my things, and our parents shuttled us around with those things. There were just not as many opportunities for [compromise] to happen, and maybe that's part of why we aren't as close, because we didn't have to hash it out and be close and work it out.

She went on, shifting her focus to virtues of empathy and toleration:

> The other important lesson . . . is about people in general. My understanding and appreciation of anyone in the world has truly deepened through parenting a larger family because you see so many different personalities amongst

your children and you realize how innate that is; that their God-given character and temperament is not put there by you or by your parenting or by the school you paid for them to get into—the soccer, the dance.

They're born who they are and how you learn to parent the different children with their different temperaments and needs and all that, and the way they interact with each other also, has so many important lessons for me as a person and also I think for them.

There is a lot to be learned for them in how they relate to the different members of the family based on each one's temperament and personality and strengths and weaknesses and needs and special needs.

## *"That Could Be My Baby"*

Monica's observation reminded me of something one of our older moms had said. Donna, with eight kids ranging from ages twenty-eight to ten, explained,

> Having children, even my first baby, opened my eyes to something I hope I can express well. Ever since then if I see somebody who is handicapped in some way, somebody with Down syndrome, somebody who is in a wheelchair, somebody who is poor, I think, "That could be my baby." It makes it more immediate to me. That is somebody's baby. That could be my baby. You can't just dismiss somebody or try not to think about them or marginalize them in a way, because you realize that's, well, if you're open to life you realize that could literally happen where I could have a baby that has this or that condition.

The logic of Donna's realization—"That could be my baby"—could be extended also to her children: That could be my brother or sister. Maggie, the Catholic mom of six who talked about self-sacrifice in chapter 19, made that inference explicit. She told us,

> Being formed and shaped by the people we're trying to form and shape has hopefully made us better people, more compassionate, more loving, more service-minded. Because if you don't get those things in a big family, sometimes you just don't ever learn them. For the kids, but for the mom and dad too.
>
> One of the things actually our parish priest pointed out, is one day we were picking kids up from school, and my oldest son grabbed the baby and was just walking around with the baby, and our priest said, "Look at that! Look at him! That's what we want." That's what we want around here, is big brothers knowing how to carry a baby and being proud of introducing his younger sister to his friends, and basically just young kids appreciating that young life, or that family life. Or something.
>
> And for me, it wasn't a big deal. *He carries the baby all the time.* He changes her diapers. He puts her down for a nap. That's just kind of a way of life. But from [that priest's] perspective, he doesn't see a lot of big families, or a lot of big brothers kind of loving on this little sister, and for him it was kind of a moment, which I thought was interesting.

Maggie believes that carrying the baby wasn't anything special. It's a way of life for her son, a habit, picked up from daily living. And it would shape the man that he would become.

## *"He Ain't Heavy. He's My Brother"*

Maggie's story recalled the iconic photo and caption from Father Flanagan's home for orphans in Nebraska, called Boys Town. As the story goes, in 1918 a little boy named Howard Loomis was abandoned at Boys Town. Polio had left him crippled, wearing leg braces. Older boys at the home began carrying Howard around. In 1921, a well-known Omaha photographer, Louis Bostwick, captured the common sight: little Howard, grinning, on the back of a bigger boy named Reuben Granger. To this iconic photo Father Flanagan later affixed the phrase that became the unofficial motto of Boys Town: "He ain't heavy, Father, he's my brother."[9] Of course, Howard wasn't the boy's biological brother. He was an unwanted orphan with warped legs. But in helping Howard, the young men found out the meaning of their strength. And the bond between strong and weak took on a brotherly character in which the strong received more than they gave.

In the business of diagnosing what ails America, it's easy enough to name the symptoms: isolation, separation, loneliness, division, and self-centeredness. Perhaps the way to sum it up is the lack of a "brother." Another self. Someone you put before you. Someone you carry. Someone who loves you simply because you're theirs. That doesn't necessarily have to be a biological brother; it could be a brother like Howard had a brother. But the most natural candidate for an "other self" is a brother if you're a boy, a sister if you're a girl. Notably, to have at least two boys and two girls in a family, you're going to have to have about five or six kids. Four, plus extras in case you get more of one or the other first. I would know. It took me seven kids to get two of each, though it wasn't my goal. I ended up with six boys and two girls—not too many boys, but I sure would have liked another few girls. My girls would have liked more too. But an unintended consequence of having a large family is that your kids of both sexes are vastly more likely to have at least one human being of their own sex they can call brother, or sister. The testimonies in this volume suggest that a lack of fraternity and sorority—the state of growing up without a brother or a sister—matters more for the character of the nation than ideas left to us in dusty books. But there isn't even a word in our language for that.

### *"Everything Is for the Me, Me, Me"*

Our interviews were saturated with commentary about the virtues that moms described as emerging in themselves, in their spouses, and in their children. *Emerging* is the best word for what they described. The beneficent changes in character, they insisted, were at least somewhat passively acquired. Virtues were gained without working at them directly—indeed, without even intending them. It went something like this: If you get up twice a night to feed a baby, your intention is to feed that baby. You don't feed the baby to become a better person. But in fact for those months, you did put another's good ahead of your own. Do this for a year and at the end you may slide back into being your old self, thinking, "Gosh, I'm glad that's over." But do this for eight, ten, or twenty years on end, and you may become a person who repeatedly puts the other's good ahead of your own—whatever kind of mess you were at the start. A boot camp may change you temporarily, but if you signed up for boot camp every year for a decade, the habits of boot camp might become part of your character. Just so—the basic contention of the moms in our sample seemed to be that large families have an advantage generating pro-social virtues because of the prolongation of the treatment. That treatment is exposure to the neediest members of the family: infants, toddlers, and young children, for a total of eight, ten, or twenty years of opportunities to practice putting others before yourself.

In the last chapter, I highlighted the way that Rosalie's eighth and ninth babies had unexpectedly saved her seventh baby from aspects of his chromosomal abnormality. But baby number seven, with all his needs, saved her older children from disabilities of the soul. Therapists could only flip him so many times per week. But his siblings could flip him all day long, morning and night, every time they passed. Without knowing it or intending it, Rosalie's kids became habituated to doing things for each other—as a character trait and not a performance. Just as it was true for her children, Rosalie argued, it was also true of herself. She said, "It was gradual, I think if you planted a seed in me, I think now you can see that it's grown little by little. And maybe I grow out this way sometimes, and not directly up, but I'm learning, and I'm asking so many people for help." She continued:

> We're learning, no matter what age we are; they're giving us something back, and we're giving them something back.
>
> Sacrifice is such a big thing to grow as a person, whether it's something so small, or something so big. Being able to just say, "No, I don't deserve that, let me offer it to someone."
>
> I feel like we're in a society that is very selfish now. And everything is for the me, me, me. Because they don't want to have kids, because they want more time for themselves, because they want that peace just for them, they're not willing to sacrifice.

It might sound like Rosalie, nine kids, and Monica, six kids, who opened this chapter, are needlessly harsh on smaller families. However, in our sample, it was the ones who had grown up with fewer siblings who more openly criticized the way of life they had rejected. Monica and Rosalie each grew up with one sibling. They didn't like it, and they didn't like who they became. They were making comparisons from their own experiences. "If I look back on it," Rosalie said, "I think I would have liked for my parents to have been there. That physical presence." She went on: "I didn't need them to work for the money to buy whatever latest thing it was. Because I see my kids growing up, with how I grew up—night and day. So, I see their joy is just different. I don't think I had that joy. Because they were too busy working. You don't really need much when you have a big family, because you have each other, and that overfills the cup, so to speak. That's what I'm thinking when I look back on everything, and with the joy, the childhood joy."

### "There's Nothing More Romantic Than That as a Wife"

Reflecting on her son who carries the baby, Maggie said, "My oldest would not have that—without the opportunity to love he wouldn't know how to love." Implicit in seeing virtues as emergent from family life was the idea of character as a habit. Our subjects spoke of training, of practice, as if a large family were a sports team complete with drills and exercises. In Maggie's view, her son will spend his formative years putting his little sister on his shoulder, taking pride in her, playing catch, and putting up with her needs. That has to mean he will grow into a better man, a better husband, a better father. It has to mean he will know the purpose of his masculinity. As Rosalie said, it would make a husband or wife different too. And that pays dividends for marriages.

Eileen, six kids, recounted how babies had transformed her Evangelical-Episcopalian-turned-Catholic husband into a rockstar spouse. And not because he started out that way. Because of the practice, the prolonged exposure to a meet-their-needs way of life.

"If you are going to have a lot of babies," she said, "your husband is either going to be a total jerk or he's going to become a hero." She continued:

> There's not much of a middle ground. The way the man has to transform in order to meet the challenging demands of his family requires a level of heroic virtue. And a failure to meet that is a failure for your family. So, it's almost like the call.
>
> And to see your husband transformed into this heroic being is so—there's nothing more romantic than that as a wife because you know that you need him and when he's answering that and meeting that, it's really buoying for your love. It creates and carves out a depth and height that you didn't know you could carve.

Guadalupe, who goes by Lupe, a jovial mom expecting her tenth, agreed. She had met her husband, now an oil rig worker off the Los Angeles shore, in a Rite Aid where he worked when they were both in high school. She had her eye on him for seven months before they started talking. Herself one of nine kids, Lupe knew from high school that she wanted a big family. But he didn't. She says, "We had our first and he said, 'That was it.' Then we had our second and he was like, 'That was it.' We had our third and he said, 'That's it.' And I said, 'Not even close, buddy.'" She went on, "Before we got married, we sort of agreed on four. Because I said, 'Well I want five,' and he said he wanted three, so I said, 'Let's have four then.'"

She laughed and continued:

> But the really beautiful thing about it though is that, actually, after that initial "I'm done" after each of the first three,

after we had number seven, I felt like, "Okay, this is a good size family," I was happy, "I like this size, this is good. If we have seven, I'm happy." I was kind of ready to slow down, if not be done. And he was ready to have more!

He told me, "Let's have another baby." I used to tell people that there is nothing sexier than a man telling you he wants to have a baby with you. So, we had number eight.

And the same thing happened with number nine. And I thought after number eight, "Okay this is good, eight is a good number." And he said, "I'm ready for another one." It's just so beautiful how he's changed. He's open, and he's seen the beauty in having a large family and he is so open to it now. Now we are on number ten. I love it. I love that, to see that change in him.

She chuckled, "Ever since I was in high school, I knew I wanted twelve kids. I'm almost there!"

### "Having Kids . . . Makes You Be a Grown-Up for the First Time in Your Life"

Your character changes when you have children. What you love changes. "All children are training the affections of their family," Danielle had said. The more children, the more your affections change. Lupe and Eileen found their husbands more attractive than ever, after ten and six kids respectively, and that was bound up with the way their husbands had become better men with more kids. This seemed a partial answer to the stranger on the train in chapter 1 who exclaimed, upon hearing I had six kids, "I guess your husband still wants you." Maybe it really does have something to do with having children. Leah had said, "I think we grow a lot. We have a lot to give [each other] because we've learned how to manage a very full life."

The women we interviewed believe that the virtues acquired by having children have made their marriages better. Moira, an Irish-Catholic mom with a sharp wit and five kids, quipped, "Babies are bad for your marriage? I think babies save your marriage."

> Because you know, at some point, you're going to find out that your spouse isn't perfect like you thought they were and then what's going to keep you together? I mean, some people aren't able to have kids or don't have kids and are doing just great, married without kids. But for a lot of us, it would be like, "I don't know, I don't know who I am. Things are different. Now what?" And you have to wait it out and then you find out what love really is. You start—you hit that first point of wanting out, that's where you start to find out what love really is.
>
> Because you're committed to that person and to the life that you've built together. I mean, it's just, I don't know why—I think having babies, getting married—it whittles away at your selfishness and the more you have, not always, I mean, there are exceptions, I have just seen the more kids you have the better people the parents are. It requires it. You can't just watch YouTube all day and have five kids. It doesn't work.

Moira finally got round to the heart of it, for her:

> I think what having kids does is it makes you be a grown-up for the first time in your life, because marriage doesn't

necessarily mean you're going to be a grown-up. It just means you are going to hang out with the person you wanted to hang out with anyway. And then for most people, not always, but for most people the first really hard thing they do is have a baby. And then you find out what you're made of and what your spouse is made of and like where you need to grow.

So, did I tell you that we had a garbage room when we were first married? We had a room just for crap we didn't know what to do with and—okay, so, we had a garbage room, and our house is pretty messy right now, but it was so much worse! And just the stuff like—you just don't know what you're doing and then you have to grow up because someone who's less grown up than you needs you to be a grownup.

Children, in Moira's view, helped purge the proverbial garbage of our souls.

The phenomenon we heard about was roughly the same throughout our interviews. Someone more needy needs you, like little Howard. There's no way out—you have to meet those needs because you brought them into existence. The kids depend on you completely. So, grudgingly or not, you rise to the occasion. It looks like the giving is on your side, but you figure out that you're the receiver after all, not the giver. Because you discover your purpose, the meaning of your strengths. Do you have weaknesses too? Fine—these give purpose to someone else's strengths; someone you will love and adore because "there's nothing more romantic...you know that you need him and...he's answering that." So, it wasn't just the kids who matured by having babies around—it was the moms and dads. They had to become grown-ups for their kids, and if they succeeded, they became more attractive to their spouses. They also became better workers and neighbors, better sons and daughters of God.

All this calls to mind the passage from Luke's Gospel: "Give, and it will be given to you. A good measure, pressed down, shaken together, running over, will be put into your lap; for the measure you give will be the measure you get back."[10] If the women in my study believe the Lord repays them for their gift of self, they believe that emergent virtue is one of the rewards that spills over to their marriages, their communities, and the nation. On their account, virtue wasn't victim to freedom; it was victim to the principled sterilization of our families. Principled because it was chosen for its own sake. It didn't fly under the flag of value neutrality. We wrongly came to believe that smaller family sizes are a positive good: for responsible parenting, a productive economy, and a more fulfilled adulthood.

### "I Just Can't Say Enough about How Much of a Lie Everything I Learned Growing Up . . . How False That All Was"

Eileen said, challengingly,

> It's hard for me to understand family life as being good with an intentionally chosen small family. This is so not generally acceptable to say, but there's a selfishness there that you're not going to burn out of yourself with a small family.
>
> And to have a society that is not only *not* growing in the virtues that a big family demands, but also not doing it as a point of principle. So, it's not even accidental, like we've just fallen into this. It's almost like it has become a cultural principle either because of environmentalism or because it's just not as valued to nurture a big family. So

that shift, it's almost more alarming, the principle change
of what the nature of the human being is and what it is to
love.

And then self-fulfillment is more important than
self-sacrifice, [which] is pathologized as being this martyr
syndrome or this doormat syndrome. And then the thing
that we call love is the opposite of it.

She laughed and continued. "That, to me, is maybe the most
alarming thing—that we don't even understand what the good is
anymore. And it's hard to reach after the good, but it's almost impossible if you don't even know where the good lies."

That smaller families were better for us was just false, they argued.
A mirage. It looks like the real deal, but only on the surface—down
deep it's not fulfilling. Or worse, it prematurely fulfills the part of us
meant to grow up and keeps us in a kind of perpetual adolescence:
The boots and Benz version of Kyra. The litigator Monica trying to
keep her mom self from ruining her lawyer self.

The country got on the wrong track, my subjects believe, when
it bought into a neo-Malthusian paradigm: that more people could
ever be a problem—for a family, an economy, or a nation. It got on
the wrong track when a type of overly planned parenthood, book-
ended by deliberate sterility, became the norm for a marriage. No
longer did we pray, like the biblical Hannah, to be set free from bar-
renness; we rather applied our cleverest schemes to give impotence
the reign.

Monica gushed about her last baby. "My sixth baby, she is like the
bonus baby, because I was in my forties and my husband is in his late
fifties. We just thought we wouldn't have any more children. Then we
got her and it's just all good, and it's hard of course. It's always hard."
She continued,

Having a baby in your forties is no picnic. But she is to us like to our whole family, she isn't just mine and my husband's, she belongs to all of us, and she is like a little treasure, she is just such an incredible gift to us. So much so that I worry about her being spoiled and not learning the things she needs to learn because everybody wants to do [things] for her.

And it's so funny because I believed, and my parents had also believed this and taught me, that it was a deprivation for the first ones [in a family if you] have more children. I don't know at what point it cuts off—who's the right ones to have, and who's the wrong ones or whatever. But they say it's abusive to have more children because of what is being taken from the older children. And it's so much the opposite.

The younger siblings are truly treasured and loved by the older siblings the most, and there is so much to that natural school of virtue thing. There is so much they learn through the nurturing, educating, and caring for the younger siblings and the needs of the home and all of that.

She continued, furrowing her brow:

I just can't say enough about how much of a lie everything I learned growing up in my feminist school—how false that all was—and I'm not saying this with any agenda. It just literally was so eye-opening to see these things. I believed what I was told.

My mom will say things about her sister that has one child or another cousin with one child, "They're just going to have that one and raise them right." I believed what I was told and that's how it's done.

I wanted a sister growing up, I just had the one older brother, we never were close and still aren't. I yearned for a sibling I could have closeness with. I felt that naturally but I was told that that was wrong, that then that would mean that I wouldn't go to college or something that then would be disastrous for my life.

And when I started hearing these big families that we began to meet talk about the virtues of a large family for the children, I remember one telling me when I was pregnant with my fourth, "This is so good for your children." I kept hearing that, but I still wasn't really seeing it yet.

And now I just can't believe that this isn't widely known. It's just so true. It's so good for them. We should have started earlier so we could have more, so there could be even more of that.

### "Definitely a Lot More People Could Do This"

My subjects thought the country should have more of that too. They wanted more of the spirit of fraternity and sorority, to build up a culture of solidarity, informing how we order our life together. They knew it wasn't as simple as saying that everyone should have more kids. But they thought it was an option for more people than realize it. When we asked Lupe if there was anything at all that she wanted to get on record, she said,

I don't know, maybe that it's really not as difficult as people think it is. It is, but anything that is worth it is going to be hard. If it's easy, it's probably—sometimes it's not worth it. Anything that is worth it is going to be hard. I definitely, I say that a lot to people. People think they can't have this many kids because they can't afford it. Yes you can. Yes you can. Yes you can.

I think to my friend who has, she has three kids now, but she had two at the time and she said, "Oh my gosh, Lupe, how do you do this like how do you—you have seven" (or however many I had at the time).

And I said, "You're already doing it. You already have to make dinner. You already have to wash the dishes. You already have to wash the clothes. So, you're just doing it for one more person. So, you're already doing it. So, you can do it for one more person. And one more. And a few more." A lot of people are already doing it.

And I say all that with a little caveat, having a large family is not for everybody, I totally understand and respect that and believe that. But it's for a lot more people than they think. It's not for everybody, but I feel like definitely a lot more people could do this than what they think.

I remembered Hannah's chain, which had called to mind Tocqueville's concern about a free political order breaking the links. Something needs to tie people together. If it isn't going to be title and class, and it isn't going to be abundant families with brothers and sisters, what will it be? Identity? Political party? Commercial interests? Maybe that's right. Maybe what ails us is not our freedom per se, but something we mistake for freedom—being detached from family obligations, which are actually the demands that save us from egoism and despair. We're like loose links jumbled together in a scrap heap. It's not liberty we have too much of. It's disintegration. Without the links, my subjects said, you don't know who you are or what you're for—so how could you even be free? A seed buried in the ground manifests itself by the tender shoot—its offspring, and the meaning of its dying.

Hannah discovered her meaning in her chain, Danielle in her tapestry, Angela in her paradox of the Cross. But finding themselves wasn't the most important thing to these women. Even more important were the new beginnings that opened under their maternity—miracles that saved the world. Just as for the biblical Hannah, the seeds of their own redemption—and redemption for many others—were sown in their motherhood. The child, taken for granted, dismissed as a nothing, holds out the real promise of eternity. "Only the full experience of [natality] can bestow upon human affairs faith and hope, those two essential characteristics of human existence," wrote Hannah Arendt in 1958. "It is this faith in and hope for the world that found perhaps its most glorious and most succinct expression in the few words with which the Gospels announced their 'glad tidings': 'A child has been born unto us.'"[11]

# CHAPTER TWENTY-TWO

# Hannah's Children—The Future of the Nation

"Faith, however, is not a matter of imagination or pious
emotion; but, on the contrary, it is an intellectual recognition (if not a rational permeation) and a voluntary
acceptance by the will; a complete development of faith
is one of the most profound acts of the individual, one in
which all his powers become acute."

—Edith Stein, *Essays on Woman*

A single insight inspired this book: that cratering birth rates across the globe—with attendant problems such as the impending bankruptcy of government pension programs including Social Security and Medicare—could be illuminated by the study of higher birth rates. This insight led me on a journey to meet women around the country whose family sizes defy the birth dearth in number and kind. In number, they had five, six, seven, or more children—as many as fifteen. In kind, like the biblical Hannah, they took childbearing to be the purpose of their lives and the meaning of their marriages. Mostly hidden from popular view, they quietly arranged their affairs to welcome new life. They fit their passions, interests, and professions around childbearing, rather than fitting childbearing around those things. As Kyra pointed out, it was a matter of valuing motherhood. "It's hard to say what's destroying families. But it's not women doing more. It's not women working. It's not women being empowered." The Baptist mother of five continued:

> It's taking all of that and just putting so much on a woman and pulling away from the important things that she was doing, acting like she wasn't doing anything before. And when we've done that, and as we've shifted as a society and said, "I am woman, hear me roar," you have all these women that want to be that, and that's great. That's wonderful. But we have taken away the beauty of just staying home and nurturing and loving and teaching. When you tie all of those things together, it kind of doesn't surprise me that women aren't reproducing the same way. It just doesn't.

At the time of this writing, the total fertility rate in the United States is under 1.7 births per woman and falling.[1] In the European Union it is at 1.53; in Japan, at 1.30; in Korea—a breathtaking 0.81. Even countries that had the highest birth rates a generation ago have plunged below replacement in my lifetime. Mexico had 5.86 births per woman in 1976, but now, at 1.82, barely distinguishes itself from the United States. India had 5.11 births per woman in 1976 but has 2.03 today.[2] Births below the replacement rate (2.1 per woman in her lifetime) spell a future of economic decline and international strife as countries compete for the ultimate resource, children.[3] My thesis is that the secret to solving the puzzle of low birth rates, and reversing it, lies in the stories of those who are noticeably immune from the dominant trend. These are people of faith who take God's first command in the Bible—"Be fruitful and multiply"[4]—to be a living rule and a true blessing, as fresh today as when it was committed to the ancient Scriptures. Such women face the same trade-offs as all other women—but they value children more.

The nascent American family policy debate is premised on two unexamined assumptions about birth rates. First, it assumes that large, religious families do not have reasons that can be understood, generalized, or made relevant for policy. Second, it supposes we can incentivize anything we want. The testimonies in this book challenge both myths. First, upon close inspection, women with large families in America today choose their families for perfectly intelligible motivations. They pursue ends that they value, weighing them against other valuable goods and opportunities. Opportunity cost is the valuation of an alternative given up—the road not taken. The most important cost to having many children, these women explain, is the opportunity cost defined by the goods given up: sleep, comfort, and income, but also career, lifestyle, status, and identity. Nobody reported thinking these things didn't matter. If anything, the costs as these women reported them were big—even life-alteringly big. But the women quietly defying the birth dearth valued having additional children more than they valued other things, leading them to have more children than normal, often many times more. So, when David Brooks argued that "the differences between [natalists] and people on the other side of the cultural or political divide are differences of degree, not kind,"[5] he was only half right: Large families *are* like smaller ones in that they face the same trade-offs. But they are unlike them in that they assign greater value to having children than to the other things they could do with their time and talent.

The second assumption challenged by the testimonies in this book is that we can incentivize childbearing with cash and material benefits. Women with large families reported that self-sacrifice was central to the life they had chosen. They spoke of "dying to self," of "work[ing] really, really, really hard, to the breaking point at times." They were willing to do that because they entrusted their family size to God's design and providence and believed that the Lord would repay their sacrifices in a divine economy overflowing with goodness and joy. They wanted more of that goodness for their families and for the nation, wishing that the hidden rewards of having children would become "more widely known."

While telling her story, Kyra articulated ideas we heard in many interviews: "Everybody says, 'Why do you keep having more kids?' And it's really a matter of—every child I've had has humbled me more, has brought me closer to God. With every child I've had it's softened my heart. And the softer your heart gets, the closer you get to God. You know, like the song goes, 'The things of the world grow strangely dim.' It doesn't matter anymore. The things that mattered to me I would never care about anymore. It's almost like, you know, within my experience—sometimes you just have to let go and experience it."

For a woman in this rare demographic, her children are a blessing upon her marriage, a gift to her other children, and a fulfillment of her desire for the infinite good who is God. These are the "incentives" that have tipped the scales in favor of their choosing to conceive, bear, and raise another child again and again—a path of profound self-denial lasting at least two decades. That such a costly choice could be induced directly through any external benefit seems fantastical. The data we heard help explain why such programs have not worked in the past and will not work in the future.

*Religion: The Only Effective Family Policy*

The new calculus of childbearing, described in chapter 4, that is leading to global below-replacement fertility is the product of two distinct causes, roughly sequential in time order: a decrease in demand for children, followed by an increase in the opportunity cost of having children. The decrease in demand resulted from the erosion of value that children once had for the family economy. Children used to contribute to home production in a variety of ways: helping on farms, participating in trades and family business, and even being hired out for pay. As economic life shifted away from the home, children no longer added to the family's material resources. Compulsory schooling and other Progressive Era changes further alienated children from the economy of the home. Finally, modern old-age programs issued a terminal blow to the economic value of children. With Social Security and Medicare, Hannah's children will still support your old age if you have too few children, or none at all.

This is a classic free-rider problem.

Ordinarily, systems that provide public goods do so by collectivizing the costs and requiring individual contributions through taxation. Without a mandatory tax, people would be tempted to pitch in too little—to free-ride—leaving the collective good underfunded. The engineers of old-age programs seem not to have considered the fact that children—who fund tax revenues in the next generation—are a voluntary contribution that families make toward these programs. Given these conditions, standard economic theory would predict under-provision of children. Modern old-age programs that do not tie benefits to childbearing suppress the economic value of children to the household.

Together, production outside the home, compulsory schooling, and New Deal–style programs worked in concert to nearly zero out the economic value of children to the household. On the heels of these changes came another that vastly increased the opportunity cost of having children: the birth control Pill. Family planning wasn't new, but no earlier form of birth control matched the Pill's effectiveness or its use-convenience. Just five years after its approval in 1960, almost half of married women under age thirty were using the Pill.[6] The Pill enabled American women to pursue college degrees and professions without postponing marriage.[7] The Pill also led to a decrease in marital fertility[8] for two reasons: crowding out time, since women's early adult years were increasingly spent on education and work, postponing childbearing; and increasing the opportunity costs of having kids—greater professional opportunity means higher incomes, status, and work satisfaction foregone in order to have a child.

The pressures that decreased the economic value of children, together with those that increased the opportunity cost of having kids, set the baby bust phenomenon in motion. In the horse race between family and career enabled by the Pill, the family—unless valued *very* highly—loses to the alternative: dividing time between career and family, having children plus income, status, and other goods—but fewer children. In the face of this calculus, assessments of loss and gain based on supernatural values offer the only hope of tipping the scales towards children. Without religious formation that fosters biblical values, low birth rate trends will not be reversed.

The private activities of individuals, households, and firms sometimes provide substantial benefits for others who do not bear the costs of those activities. Economists call these activities positive externalities, or neighborhood effects, or spillovers, or sometimes simply "social benefits." If the social benefits of an activity are very large, society might prefer more of that activity than individuals typically choose, given their assessments of the personal costs and benefits. To get more of the activity, such as childbearing, something has to increase the personal reward to overwhelm the existing value structure, making the activity more attractive to the individual. Enter public policy. Governments typically use subsidies and tax credits to incentivize more of a desirable behavior when the normal "free market" level of that behavior seems too low.

Naturally, policymakers have wanted to find a tax- or subsidy-based solution to the problem of low birth rates. But the testimonies in this volume raise a critical question. If the subjective opportunity costs, not the direct expenses of raising a child after it is born, are most relevant to the choice to have a child, what then? And what, further, if those opportunity costs are substantial enough to be likened to a death to self? For more children to be born, more women have to believe that the next child is worth more to them than a plethora of missed opportunities and a life without the dying to self. The value of childbearing has to be higher for an individual woman and household than the value of the competing goods she may choose. It is easy to see why people wouldn't want more kids when the trade-offs are laid bare.

The testimonies in this book point to the "reasons of the heart" that could make someone want to have a child even once, let alone many times over. These reasons cannot be distributed to people. We know we can incentivize moving away from oil, cigarettes, and junk food. But can we incentivize moving away from careers and interests we've prepared women to fulfill from their earliest school days? The narratives in this book suggest that such a choice has to come from deep within. It has to be wanted for its own sake, counted as worth the costs, which are personal and subjective. Whatever their intentions, policymakers cannot *directly* incentivize childbearing, because the motives for having children depend on assessments of value out-side the reach of even very large subsidies and tax credits.

It may be possible, however, to foster childbearing indirectly by cultivating the conditions in which incentives that are weighty enough to inspire women to have more children arise. The policy lesson is simple: the flourishing of traditional religious institutions breaks the low-marriage-low-fertility cycle. People will lay down their comforts, dreams, and selves for God, not for subsidies. If the state can't save the American family, it can give religion a freer rein to try. Religion is the cardinal family policy.

### Let the Temple Flourish

Unfortunately, even now, central planners are busy constructing national programs to raise birth rates. They will fail. There is no his-torical example of a policy that meaningfully increased birth rates. The nineteenth-century French political economist Jean-Baptiste Say observed that Louis XVI could not induce birth rates as well as he could discourage them.[9] Observers might say the same of China's population program, changed from a One-Child Policy to a Two-Child Policy nearly a decade ago.[10] But, even if the unicorn policy that could theoretically improve birth rates existed, no nation on earth would have the material resources needed to overwhelm the calculus that led to the birth dearth. Can you put a number on becoming "invisible," as Leah described it? Can you provide mone-tary compensation for the loss of identity implicit in giving up a beloved career? These are serious questions, not rhetorical ones. If women could be induced to make such sacrifices, surely the price tag would be extraordinary. But the budget of every Western nation is creaking and straining under massive national debts and near-bankrupt entitlement programs.[11] Global debt reached "a new all-time high of $307 trillion," in the first half of 2023, according to the Institute of International Finance, "a staggering $100 trillion more than it was a decade ago. Over 80% of the debt buildup came from mature markets...with the U.S., Japan, the UK, and France registering the largest increases."[12] The money is simply not there to raise birth rates through tax-and-transfer schemes.

For those nations frugal enough to find the resources, policies that reward those already having families may be pursued as a matter of justice—to honor their sacrifices and contributions. Such programs may boost morale for families. They may boost the popularity of politicians. But they will not boost the birth rate.

Expanded maternity leave and parental leave policies will not raise the birth rate either. These programs help firms compete for top talent and will continue to grow in popularity as men and women continue to see them as inducements to pick one firm over another. But universal leave policies created by federal mandates at the national level will fail to raise birth rates. More likely, they will be counterproductive. Maternity leave suppresses the desirability of motherhood in important ways. First, working while raising a young child makes motherhood less pleasant, not more. It is emotionally draining to delegate the care of your child at the earliest ages, to say nothing of the daily separations that take a toll. And it is logistically draining to coordinate work and school schedules when children are older. Finally, compared with being home full time, the opportunities to bond with your baby are fewer and harder, diminishing the emotional rewards of the early years—rewards that compensate mightily for the sleepless nights and annoyances of daily life. Few people arduously holding down a demanding job at the same time as parenting a young child will want to do that more than once or twice.

All of this stands to reason: the large-scale entry of women into the non-domestic workforce was a major catalyst of low birth rates by raising the opportunity cost of childbearing. Keeping women attached to jobs longer when a child is born through more generous maternity leave will not obviously make it easier for them to give up or imperil those jobs to have subsequent children. There is no reason to think that birth rates will increase if we double or triple the length of maternity leave or make leaves universal through national policy—even if we believe that such programs are due in justice. There is no way to square the circle. Work outside the home has militated against achieving the birth rates desired by women and ideal for nations. It's time to put aside the wishful thinking and face the real problem.

What, then, might help reverse the trend of low birth rates? The testimonies in this volume, offered by women at all levels of engagement with paid work, suggest that we look to the strength and vitality of living religious communities. It is in the temple where we find those reasons of the heart that justify the life-altering personal sacrifices that come with having more than one or two children. Religious liberty *is* family policy—in fact, the only family policy that has a chance to halt and reverse the cratering of the birth rate. But to have that chance it must be thick freedom of religion, not merely "freedom of worship," the bare right to spend one hour of the week at church or synagogue on the weekend. Religion isn't truly free if it can't effectively assist families in passing on faith and tradition to their children. So, by "thick" religious liberty I mean, at a minimum, emancipating religious institutions to collaborate with parents in the work of education. The massive system of "free" public education—a government cartel designed to compete against religious schools—represents a drastic violation of religious liberty. Fewer than 7 percent of American schoolchildren attend religious schools.[13]

Religious education doesn't impact only the children who are already in existence. It changes the orientation of family life in its entirety. There are multiple daily trips to and from the school; extra-curriculars, sports, meetings, and festivals all take place in relation to the temple. The women we met went to their synagogues, wards, and churches several times a week, sometimes every day. Their religious communities educated their children, counseled their marriages, fed their poor, celebrated their births, and buried their dead. Their most important family needs were met in the temple. Just as muscles atrophy with underuse and bones lose their density, religion boxed into a tiny corner of private worship, stripped of all its other traditional functions, is no true religion. Nations that crowd out the sacred functions of the Church will continue to reap a sterile harvest of disappointment.

Religious freedom as family policy would mean the government's taking a step back from providing human services directly, starting with education, and asking churches to become stronger by doing more. Our religious institutions are too weak. And they will remain weak, unable to inspire the heroic sacrifices we need, so long as states and nations do their work. The birth rate will not increase until more women give themselves over to the shift that Leah described, where "motherhood" becomes a "big tenet of who you are." Angela said, "[Children] need their mothers." The nation also needs its mothers. Policymakers and the social scientists who assist them should stop ignoring the role of the spirit and start inquiring where Hannah is. She is in the temple of the Lord of Hosts, where she has found in children and the service of God what she was seeking—the meaning of her everything. For the sake of Hannah's children, who are the future of the nation—set the temple free.

# Acknowledgments

"M y soul magnifies the Lord, and my spirit rejoices in God my Savior, for he has looked with favor on the lowliness of his servant."[1]

My husband, Michael Pakaluk, has been my constant friend and intellectual companion these twenty-five years. The character of my thoughts deeply reflects our years of lively discourse. A great spouse is a silent co-author.

My children, young and old, have borne cheerfully with the added work that this book placed upon me. For their patience withal, for their love and affection, and for their genuine enthusiasm and encouragement, especially in the final months, I thank them most earnestly.

The Catholic University of America has been a nourishing mother—*alma mater*—to me these eight years since 2016, providing the conditions for scholarly creativity and receptivity in a womb of true intellectual freedom, aptly signified by her motto, *Deus Lux Mea Est*. I am abundantly blessed here by brilliant colleagues and loyal friends: Andrew Abela, Jon Askonas, Anthony Cannizzaro, Joseph Capizzi, David Cloutier, Aaron Dominguez, Father Robert Gahl, Russ

Hittinger, Elizabeth Kirk, Melissa Moschella, Michael New, Paul Radich, Frederic Sautet, Rebecca Teti, Max Torres, Brandon Vaidyanathan, Andreas Widmer, and many others. My current and past students, too numerous to name, also have my gratitude. Their goodness calls forth the urgency of seeking truth and beauty with singular devotion.

Some friends deserve particular thanks. Brad Wilcox planted the seed of writing a book in mid-2017. Mark Regnerus showed the way and provided life-giving friendship. Emily Reynolds was the first to believe in this project and an exquisite collaborator. Phil Brach was the second to believe in this project and a treasured champion. Mary Robotham (née Bathon) was my research associate throughout the planning and research phase—my gratitude to her abounds. Sierra Smith (née Breshears) and Shayla Green (née Driggs) collaborated as research assistants to Emily Reynolds. Rebecca Miller and Nicholas Swanson provided invaluable assistance in the preparation and writing of this manuscript.

I am additionally grateful to the following individuals for encouragement and support in various forms: Maria Almeida, Helen Alvare, Erika Bachiochi, Andrew Beauchamp, Kimberly Begg, Sarah Blanchard, Sophie Barrows, Jason Carroll, Samuel Gregg, Lauren Hall, Diana Hackler, Edward Hardy, Joseph Hardy, Rob Hardy, Jack Hardy, Jim Hardy, Mary Rice Hasson, Yoram Hazony, Mary Horan, John Horowitz, David Hunt, Father Dominic Langevin, Rachel Laskin, Dan Klein, Leslie Marsh, Erik Matson, Father Innocent Montgomery, Ilia Murtazashvili, Rob and Berni Neal, Alain Oliver, Marianna Orlandi, Michael Ortner, Elizabeth Pakaluk, Greg and Mary Pakaluk, Joseph Pakaluk, Mark Pakaluk, Nicholas Pakaluk, Valerie C. Pakaluk, Valerie Pakaluk, Clara Piano, Joseph Price, Paul Ray, Richard Reinsch, Jay Richards, Bridget Ritz (née Littleton),

Bruno Salama, Sean Schiavolin, Richard Spady, Kevin Stuart, Theresa Stujenske, Michael and Diana Thomas, Angelika Quitschke, Bridgett Wagner, Andrew Yuengert, and Leonidas Zelmanovitz.

Some institutions also deserve special thanks. During the planning and research phase, the Wheatley Institute at Brigham Young University provided financial support for travel, interviews, and transcriptions. For the writing phase, I gratefully acknowledge grants from the Apgar Foundation and the Ortner Family Foundation.

Additional thanks are due to the following organizations and associations for intellectual support, for providing opportunities to develop and share findings from this research, or for both: Austin Institute for the Study of Family and Culture, Cardus, *Cosmos + Taxis: Studies in Emergent Order and Organization*, the Heritage Foundation, the Institute for Humane Studies at George Mason University (Gender and Emergent Order Workshop, December 2022), Liberty Fund, and the Love and Fidelity Network.

Regnery Publishing has my deep gratitude for bringing these important stories to the public, as does Elizabeth Kantor, my brilliant editor.

Many weeks preparing and writing this manuscript were spent among "the peace of wild things" (see Wendell Berry) in the White Mountains of New Hampshire, within the sturdy walls of a grace-filled cabin. To this place, and to God's goodness in creating and providing for it, I owe most reverent thanks. "Even the sparrow finds a home, and the swallow a nest for herself, where she may lay her young, at your altars, O LORD of hosts, my King and my God."[2]

Finally, I am grateful to my parents—Thomas Hardy, who first shared with me Julian Simon's *Ultimate Resource* and inspired an interest in the big questions, and Janet Hardy, whose love for her babies first awakened in me an attention to the miracle that saves the world.

Whatever is good in this work has God for its source, "For we are what he has made us, created in Christ Jesus for good works, which God prepared beforehand to be our way of life."[3]

# Notes

## Chapter One: "He Still Wants You"—Stranger on a Train

Epigraph:  Harry G. Frankfurt, "Freedom of the Will and the Concept of a Person," *Journal of Philosophy* 68, no. 1 (January 14, 1971): 5–20 at 7.

1. "Guttmacher Statistic on Catholic Women's Contraceptive Use," Guttmacher Institute, February 15, 2012, https://www.guttmacher.org/article/2012/02/guttmacher-statistic-catholic-womens-contraceptive-use.

2. Marie Cecilia Buehrle, *Saint Maria Goretti* (Milwaukee: Bruce Publishing Company, 1950).

3. Philip Pullella, "Pope Says Birth Control Ban Doesn't Mean Breed 'Like Rabbits,'" Reuters, January 19, 2015, https://www.reuters.com/article/us-pope-airplane-idUSKBN0KS1WY20150119.

4. Brady E. Hamilton, Joyce A. Martin, and Michelle J. K. Osterman, "Births: Provisional Data for 2020" (NVSS Vital Statistics Rapid Release Report No. 012), Centers for Disease Control and Prevention, May 5, 2021, https://stacks.cdc.gov/view/cdc/104993.

5. Gary Becker, "An Economic Analysis of Fertility," in *Demographic and Economic Change in Developed Countries*, The National Bureau of Economic Research (New York and London: Columbia University Press, 1960), 209–40.

6. Gary S. Becker, *A Treatise on the Family* (Cambridge, Massachusetts: Harvard University Press, 1981), ix.

7. Michael J. Piore, "Qualitative Research: Does It Fit in Economics?," *European Management Review* 3, no. 1 (Spring 2006): 17–23 at 18, https://onlinelibrary.wiley.com/doi/abs/10.1057/palgrave.emr.1500053.

8. Frankfurt, "Freedom of the Will," 7.

## Chapter Two: Reasons of the Heart—Hannah's Chain

Epigraph:  Blaise Pascal, *Thoughts*, trans. W. F. Trotter, in *Thoughts, Letters, Minor Works*, ed. Charles W. Eliot (1670; New York: P. F. Collier & Son Company, 1910), 98–99, https://play.google.com/books/reader?id=8p_HsNO9IFoC&hl=en&pg=GBS.PA2.

1.  A Chabad House is a type of Jewish community center. For more information, see "The Chabad House," Chabad.Org, 2023, https://www.chabad.org/library/article_cdo/aid/244374/jewish/The-Chabad-House.htm.

2.  Pascal, *Thoughts*, 17.

3.  Alexis de Tocqueville, *Democracy in America*, vol. 2, 3rd ed., trans. Henry Reeve, ed. Francis Bowen (Cambridge, Massachusetts: Sever and Francis, 1863), 119.

4.  Ibid., 121.

5.  Ibid., 119–20.

## Chapter Three: "Red-Diaper Babies"—Political Fault Lines

Epigraph:  Ron J. Lesthaeghe and Johan Surkyn, "When History Moves On: The Foundations and Diffusion of a Second Demographic Transition," in *International Family Change: Ideational Perspectives*, ed. Rukmalie Jayakody, Arland Thornton, and William Axinn (New York: Lawrence Erlbaum Associates, 2008), 81–188 at 83.

1.  David Brooks, "The New Red-Diaper Babies," *New York Times*, December 7, 2004, https://www.nytimes.com/2004/12/07/opinion/the-new-reddiaper-babies.html.

2.  Ibid.

3.  Joel Kotkin and William Frey, "The Parent Trap," *New Republic*, December 2, 2004, quoted in Brooks, "New Red-Diaper Babies."

4.  Ron J. Lesthaeghe and Lisa Neidert, "The Second Demographic Transition in the United States: Exception or Textbook Example?," *Population and Development Review* 32, no. 4 (2006): 669–98.

5.  Specifically, the absolute value of the correlation between voting for Bush and traditional family formation was 0.88 in 2000 and 0.87 in 2004; the absolute value of the correlation between non-Hispanic white fertility in 2002 and voting for Bush in 2004 was 0.78. Ibid., 684–87.

6. Ibid., 684. The authors conducted appropriate statistical tests to check for spurious correlation, introducing a variety of control variables to reduce the zero-order correlation. They report that these attempts failed and argue that "the zero-order correlation between SDT variables and voting for Bush cannot be considered spurious...." They continued, "Since the demographic picture was unfolding well before the 2000 and 2004 elections, we accept the hypothesis that the spatial pattern of the second demographic transition in the United States was a nonredundant co-determinant of the voting outcomes at the state level." They extend their analysis to detailed county-level maps and show that the findings hold for counties as well as states. Ibid., 688–93.

7. Michael Haines, "Fertility and Mortality in the United States," ed. Robert Whaples, EH.Net, March 19, 2008, https://eh.net/encyclopedia/fertility-and -mortality-in-the-united-states/; Centers for Disease Control and Prevention, "Achievements in Public Health, 1900–1999: Family Planning," *Morbidity and Mortality Weekly Report* 48, no. 47 (1999): 1073–80, https://www.cdc.gov/mmwr /preview/mmwrhtml/mm4847a1.htm.

8. Haines, "Fertility and Mortality."

9. Michelle J. K. Osterman et al., "Births: Final Data for 2020," *National Vital Statistics Reports* (Centers for Disease Control) 70, no. 17 (February 7, 2022), https://www.cdc.gov/nchs/data/nvsr/nvsr70/nvsr70-17.pdf.

10. See Ron Lesthaeghe, "The Unfolding Story of the Second Demographic Transition," *Population and Development Review* 36, no. 2 (June 2010): 211–51 and Lesthaeghe and Surkyn, "When History Moves On."

11. Gretchen Livingston, "Fewer than Half of U.S. Kids Today Live in a 'Traditional' Family," Pew Research Center, December 22, 2014, https://www.pewresearch .org/fact-tank/2014/12/22/less-than-half-of-u-s-kids-today-live-in-a-traditional -family/.

12. Lesthaeghe and Surkyn, "When History Moves On," 83.

13. Andrew Cherlin, *The Marriage-Go-Round: The State of Marriage and the Family in America Today* (New York: Vintage Books, 2010), 43.

14. Ibid., 90.

15. Brooks, "New Red-Diaper Babies."

16. Thomas E. Mann, "Reflections on the 2000 U.S. Presidential Election," The Brookings Institution, January 1, 2001, https://www.brookings.edu/articles/reflections-on-the-2000-u-s-presidential-election/.

17. The absolute value of the correlation between traditional family patterns and voting for McCain at the level of the fifty U.S. states was 0.83 (compared to 0.87 and 0.88 respectively in 2004 and 2000). Ron J. Lesthaeghe and Lisa Neidert, "US Presidential Elections and the Spatial Pattern of the American Second Demographic Transition," *Population and Development Review* 35, no. 2 (June 2009): 391–400 at 393 and 396.

18. Correlations have been rendered in absolute value here to avoid confusion for the reader. They are negative in the original but have the same meaning. Ron J. Lesthaeghe and Lisa Neidert, "Spatial Aspects of the American 'Culture War'; The Two Dimensions of US Family Demography and Presidential Elections, 1968–2016," *Population Studies Center Research Reports*, report 17-880, April 2017, 2 and 7.

19. Ibid., 11.

20. Ibid., 13.

21. Ibid., 15.

## Chapter Four: The Future of Humanity—Economic Demography

Epigraph: Jean-Baptiste Say, *A Treatise on Political Economy*, trans. C. R. Prinsep and ed. Clement C. Biddle (Philadelphia: Lippincott, Grambo & Co., 1855), section 1, book 2, chapter 11, https://www.econlib.org/library/Say/sayT.html?chapter_num=35#book-reader.

1. Michelle J. K. Osterman et al., "Births: Final Data for 2020," *National Vital Statistics Reports* (Centers for Disease Control) 70, no. 17 (February 7, 2022), https://www.cdc.gov/nchs/data/nvsr/nvsr70/nvsr70-17.pdf.

2. *Vital Statistics of the United States, 2003*, vol. I, *Natality* (Rockville, Maryland: National Center for Health Statistics, 2004), table 1-1, "Live Births, Birth Rates, and Fertility Rates, by Race: United States, 1909–2003."

3. Osterman et al., "Births," 5.

4. Paul R. Ehrlich, *The Population Bomb* (New York: Ballantine Books, 1968).

5.  Paul R. Ehrlich and Anne H. Ehrlich, "The Population Bomb Revisited," *Electronic Journal of Sustainable Development* 1, no. 3, (2009): 63–71 at 67.

6.  Ehrlich's early work influenced at least two works that in turn helped motivate China's One-Child Policy: first, the Club of Rome's 1972 report for the "Project on the Predicament of Mankind." See Donella H. Meadows et al., *The Limits to Growth: A Report for the Club of Rome's Project on the Predicament of Mankind* (New York: Universe Books, 1972); second, a special edition of the journal *The Ecologist*, also published in 1972: "A Blueprint for Survival." It was subsequently published as a bestselling book: Edward Goldsmith and Robert Allen, *A Blueprint for Survival: The Ecologist* (Harmondsworth: Penguin Books, 1972). For a recent popular treatment of these connections, see Marian L. Tupy and Gale L. Pooley, *Superabundance: The Story of Population Growth, Innovation, and Human Flourishing on an Infinitely Bountiful Planet* (Washington, D.C.: Cato Institute, 2022). For the best scholarly treatment of the influence of population science among elite universities on the fateful China policy, see Susan Greenhalgh, "Science, Modernity, and the Making of China's One-Child Policy," *Population and Development Review* 29, no. 2 (2003): 163–96.

7.  Richard A. Easterlin, "The American Baby Boom in Historical Perspective," *American Economic Review* 60, no. 5 (1961), 869–911. See also the same author's "Towards a Socioeconomic Theory of Fertility: A Survey of Recent Research on Economic Factors in American Fertility," in S. J. Behrman, Leslie Corsa Jr., and Ronald Freedman, eds., *Fertility and Family Planning. A World View* (Ann Arbor: University of Michigan Press, 1969) and also, Paul A. Samuelson, "An Economist's Non-Linear Model of Self-Generated Fertility Waves," *Population Studies* 30, no. 2 (1976): 243–47.

8.  Jonathan Bronitsky, "Prophet of Hope," *National Affairs*, no. 23 (Spring 2015): 163–79 at 173.

9.  Joint Economic Committee, *The Global 2000 Report* (Washington, D.C.: U.S. Government Printing Office, 1980.

10. Bronitsky, "Prophet," 174.

11. Michael S. Teitelbaum and Jay M. Winter, *The Fear of Population Decline* (Orlando: Academic Press, 1985); National Research Council Working Group on Population Growth and Economic Development, *Population Growth and*

*Economic Development: Policy Questions* (Washington, D.C.: National Academy of Sciences, 1986).

12. Bronitsky, "Prophet," 175.

13. Ibid., 173.

14. John Feng, "Japan's Shrinking Population Faces Point of No Return," *Newsweek*, April 30, 2023, https://www.newsweek.com/japan-population-decline-births -deaths-demographics-society-1796496.

15. Jessie Yeung, "China's Population Is Shrinking. The Impact Will Be Felt around the World," CNN, January 19, 2023, https://www.cnn.com/2023/01/18/china /china-population-drop-explainer-intl-hnk/index.html.

16. Max Roser, "Fertility Rate," Our World in Data, December 2, 2017, https:// ourworldindata.org/fertility-rate.

17. Ibid.

18. David Harrison, "Social Security Reserves Projected to Run Out Earlier Than Expected," *Wall Street Journal*, March 31, 2023, https://www.wsj.com/articles /social-security-reserves-projected-to-run-out-earlier-than-previously-forecast -60932de5.

19. The Board of Trustees, Federal Hospital Insurance and Federal Supplementary Medical Insurance Trust Funds, *2022 Annual Report of the Boards of Trustees of the Federal Hospital Insurance and Federal Supplementary Medical Insurance Trust Funds* (Washington, D.C.: The Board of Trustees, Federal Hospital Insurance and Federal Supplementary Medical Insurance Trust Funds, 2022), https://www.cms.gov/files/document/2022-medicare-trustees-report.pdf.

20. Haven Ladd et al., "Assessing the Financial Health of US K–12 Public School Districts," EY-Parthenon, Spring 2017, https://www.google.com/url?sa=t&rct= j&q=&esrc=s&source=web&cd=&ved=2ahUKEwiQkvK8zoWCAxXqKkQIH bgkBJQQFnoECBAQAQ&url=https%3A%2F%2Fassets.ey.com%2Fcontent %2Fdam%2Fey-sites%2Fey-com%2Fen_gl%2Ftopics%2Fstrategy%2Fpdf%2Fey -assessing-financial-health-us-k-12-public-school-districts.pdf%3Fdownload& usg=AOvVaw0XgPe-8JsBL2OcWggy_YGA&opi=89978449.

21. Zoe Caplan, "U.S. Older Population Grew from 2010 to 2020 at Fastest Rate since 1880 to 1890," United States Census Bureau, May 25, 2023, https://www .census.gov/library/stories/2023/05/2020-census-united-states-older

-population-grew.html#:~:text=In%202020%2C%20about%201%20in,million %20(16.8%25)%20in%202020.

22. Alessandro Cigno and Furio C. Rosati, "The Effects of Financial Markets and Social Security on Saving and Fertility Behaviour in Italty," *Journal of Population Economics* 5, no. 4 (November 1992): 319–41. See also Alessandro Cigno, "Given That People Live Longer, Why Should We Worry That Fewer Are Born?" in *Fertility and Public Policy: How to Reverse the Trend of Declining Birth Rates*, ed. Noriyuki Takayama and Martin Werding (Cambridge, Massachusetts: MIT Press, 2011), 261–72 at 265.

23. Ibid., 266.

24. Thomas Malthus, *An Essay on the Principle of Population*, ed. Donald Winch (Cambridge, United Kingdom: Cambridge University Press, 1992), 19.

25. Thomas C. Leonard, "Retrospectives: Eugenics and Economics in the Progressive Era," *Journal of Economic Perspectives* 19, no. 4 (Fall 2005): 207–24.

26. See Robert Zubrin, *Merchants of Despair: Radical Environmentalists, Criminal Pseudo-Scientists, and the Fatal Cult of Antihumanism* (New York: Encounter Books, 2013). See also Matthew Connelly, *Fatal Misconception: The Struggle to Control World Population* (Cambridge, Massachusetts: Harvard University Press, 2010), 84, and Ken McCormick, "Madmen in Authority: Adolf Hitler and the Malthusian Population Thesis," *Journal of Economic Insight* 32, no. 2 (December 2006): 1–8.

27. Adolf Hitler, *Mein Kampf*, trans. James Murphy (Project Gutenberg Australia, 2002).

28. James O'Leary, "Malthus and Keynes," *Journal of Political Economy* 50, no. 6 (December 1942): 901–19.

29. Edward Fuller, "Keynes on Eugenics, Race, and Population Control," November 14, 2019, Mises Institute, https://mises.org/wire/keynes-eugenics-race-and -population-control.

30. O'Leary, "Malthus and Keynes."

31. Fuller, "Keynes on Eugenics."

32. O'Leary, "Malthus and Keynes," 919.

33. Julian L. Simon, *The Ultimate Resource 2* (Princeton, New Jersey: Princeton University Press, 1996), 12.

34. Ibid.

35. Ibid.

36. Max Roser, Hannah Ritchie, and Pablo Rosado, "Food Supply," Our World in Data, March 5, 2013, https://ourworldindata.org/food-supply.

37. National Constitution Center Staff, "Benjamin Franklin's Last Great Quote and the Constitution," National Constitution Center, November 13, 2022, https://constitutioncenter.org/blog/benjamin-franklins-last-great-quote-and-the-constitution.

38. Lyman Stone, "Feminism as the New Natalism: Can Progressive Policies Halt Falling Fertility?," Institute for Family Studies Blog, February 21, 2018, https://ifstudies.org/blog/feminism-as-the-new-natalism-can-progressive-policies-halt-falling-fertility.

39. Andrew Jacobs and Francesca Paris, "Can China Reverse Its Population Decline? Just Ask Sweden," *New York Times*, February 9, 2023, https://www.nytimes.com/2023/02/09/upshot/china-population-decline.html.

40. Ibid.

41. Ibid.

42. "SF2.2: Ideal and Actual Number of Children," Organisation for Economic Co-operation and Development, December 17, 2016, https://www.oecd.org/els/family/SF_2_2-Ideal-actual-number-children.pdf.

43. Claudia Goldin and Lawrence F. Katz, "The Power of the Pill: Oral Contraceptives and Women's Career and Marriage Decisions," *Journal of Political Economy* 110, no. 4 (August 2002): 730–70 at 752.

44. Éva Beaujouan and Caroline Berghammer, "The Gap between Lifetime Fertility Intentions and Completed Fertility in Europe and the United States: A Cohort Approach," *Population Research and Policy Review* 38 (February 2019): 507–35 at 507.

45. Goldin and Katz, "Power of the Pill," 75.

46. The size of the fertility gap varies as calculated by country, education, and income, but it can range from as low as 0.2 more children wanted (on average), to 1.5 or more at the high end. Beaujouan and Berghammer, "Gap between

Lifetime Fertility Intentions and Completed Fertility," 507. See also Lyman Stone, "How Many Kids Do Women Want?" Institute for Family Studies Blog, June 1, 2018, https://ifstudies.org/blog/how-many-kids-do-women-want; Lyman Stone, *Declining Fertility in America* (Washington, D.C.: American Enterprise Institute, December 2018), https://www.aei.org/wp-content/uploads/2018/12/Declining -Fertility-in-America.pdf.

47. Betsey Stevenson and Justin Wolfers, "The Paradox of Declining Female Happiness," *American Economic Journal: Economic Policy* 1, no. 2 (August 2009): 190–225.

48. Ibid., 190.

49. Ibid.

50. Ibid., 194.

51. Hans-Peter Kohler, Jere R. Behrman, and Axel Skytthe, "Partner + Children = Happiness? The Effects of Partnerships and Fertility on Well-Being," *Population and Development Review* 31, no. 3 (September 2005): 407–45 at 435.

52. Claudia Goldin, "A Grand Gender Convergence: Its Last Chapter," *American Economic Review* 104, no. 4 (April 2014): 1091–1119 at 1117. See also, Claudia Goldin, *Career & Family: Women's Century-Long Journey toward Equity* (Princeton, New Jersey: Princeton University Press, 2021).

53. Ron J. Lesthaeghe and Johan Surkyn, "When History Moves On: The Foundations and Diffusion of a Second Demographic Transition," in *International Family Change: Ideational Perspectives*, ed. Rukmalie Jayakody, Arland Thornton, and William Axinn (New York: Lawrence Erlbaum Associates, 2008), 81–188 at 83.

## Chapter Five: The 5 Percent—What We Did

Epigraph:  F. A. Hayek, "The Use of Knowledge in Society," *American Economic Review*, 35, no. 4 (September 1945): 519–30 at 523–24; Edith Stein, *On the Problem of Empathy*, trans. Waltraut Stein (The Hague: Martinus Nijhoff, 1964), 87.

1.  N. J. Willis, "Edward Jenner and the Eradication of Smallpox," *Scottish Medical Journal* 42, no. 4 (August 1997): 118–21.

2. Author's calculations from "Historical Table 2. Distribution of Women Age 40 to 50 by Number of Children Ever Born and Marital Status: Selected Years, 1970–2020," U.S. Census Bureau, February 8, 2023, https://www2.census.gov /programs-surveys/demo/tables/fertility/time-series/his-cps/h2.xlsx.

3. Melissa S. Kearney, Phillip B. Levine, and Luke Pardue, "The Puzzle of Falling US Birth Rates since the Great Recession," *Journal of Economic Perspectives* 36, no. 1 (Winter 2022): 151–76.

4. President Emmanuel Macron: "I always say: 'Present me the woman who decided, being perfectly educated, to have seven, eight, or nine children.'" Marissa Iati, "'Perfectly Educated' Women Don't Have Big Families, Macron Said. Then the Moms Spoke Up," *Washington Post*, October 19, 2018, https:// www.washingtonpost.com/religion/2018/10/19/perfectly-educated-women -dont-have-big-families-macron-said-then-moms-spoke-up/.

5. Teresa Castro Martin, "Women's Education and Fertility: Results from 26 Demographic and Health Surveys," *Studies in Family Planning* 26, no. 4 (July/ August 1995): 187–202; T. J. Matthews and Stephanie J. Ventura, "Birth and Fertility Rates by Educational Attainment: United States, 1994," *Monthly Vital Statistics Report* 45, no. 10 (April 24, 1997), suppl., DHHS publication no. (PHS) 97-112, https://stacks.cdc.gov/view/cdc/113196/cdc_113196_DS1.pdf.

6. Tim B. Heaton, "How Does Religion Influence Fertility?: The Case of Mormons," *Journal for the Scientific Study of Religion* 25, no. 2 (June 1986): 248–58.

7. Arland Thornton, "Religion and Fertility: The Case of Mormonism," *Journal of Marriage and Family* 41, no. 1 (February 1979): 131–42.

8. W. D. Mosher, Linda B. Williams, and David P. Johnson, "Religion and Fertility in the United States: New Patterns," *Demography* 29, no. 2 (May 1992): 199–214.

9. Charles F. Westoff and Elise F. Jones, "The End of "Catholic" Fertility," *Demography* 16, no. 2 (May 1979): 209–17.

10. Jana Reiss, *The Next Mormons: How Millennials Are Changing the LDS Church* (Oxford: Oxford University Press, 2019).

11. Brady Hamilton et al., "Births: Final Data for 2014," *National Vital Statistics Reports* 64, no. 12 (December 23, 2015), https://www.cdc.gov/nchs/data/nvsr /nvsr64/nvsr64_12.pdf.

12. Sarah R. Hayford and S. Philip Morgan, "Religiosity and Fertility in the United States: The Role of Fertility Intentions," *Social Forces* 86, no. 3 (March 2008): 1163–88.

13. (1) Spokane, Washington; Seattle, Washington (2) Los Angeles, California; Long Beach, California; (3) Salt Lake City, Utah; Provo, Utah; (4) Denver-Aurora, Colorado; (5) Houston, Texas; (6) Greenville, South Carolina; (7) Washington, D.C.; Arlington, Virginia; Rockville, Maryland; (8) Philadelphia, Pennsylvania; Wilmington, Delaware; (9) Boston, Massachusetts; Hartford, Connecticut; Providence, Rhode Island; (10) Chicago, Illinois; Milwaukee, Wisconsin; Des Moines, Iowa.

14. Since unintended ("non-purposeful") pregnancies are less common among college-educated women, we do not think this altered our sample appreciably from all college-educated women with five or more children. See Kelly Musick et al., "Education Differences in Intended and Unintended Fertility," *Social Forces* 88, no. 2 (December 2009): 543–72.

15. Institutional Review Board approval was obtained in fall of 2018; recruitment took place in spring of 2019; and interviews were conducted in summer of 2019.

16. Carmen DeNavas-Walt and Bernadette D. Proctor, *Income and Poverty in the United States: 2014: Current Population Reports* (Washington, D.C.: U.S. Census Bureau, September 2015). Also, J. M. Tzeng and R. D. Mare, "Labor Market and Socioeconomic Effects on Marital Stability," *Social Science Research* 24, no. 4 (December 1995): 329–51.

17. Sudhir Venkatesh, *Gang Leader for a Day: A Rogue Sociologist Takes to the Streets* (New York: Penguin Press, 2008).

18. Kathryn Edin and Maria Kefalas, *Promises I Can Keep: Why Poor Women Put Motherhood before Marriage* (Berkeley: University of California Press, 2005).

19. Hannah Arendt, *The Human Condition* (Chicago: University of Chicago Press, 1958), 247.

## Chapter Six: Different in Kind—The Biblical Hannah

Epigraph:  Robert Frost, "The Road Not Taken," in *Collected Poems of Robert Frost*, ed. Edward Connery Lathem, (New York: Henry Holt and Company, 1930), 131.

1. Outcast Motivation, "Kobe Bryant's Greatest Speech | BEST Motivation Ever," YouTube, September 2021, https://www.youtube.com/watch?v=dTRBnHtHeh2.
2. Ibid.
3. Muslim and atheist women were sought but not found for this study.
4. Charles Murray, *Coming Apart: The State of White America, 1960–2000* (New York: Forum Books, 2013).
5. Outcast Motivation, "Kobe Bryant's Greatest Speech."
6. 1 Samuel 1:11, New Revised Standard Version Bible: Catholic Edition (Division of Christian Education of the National Council of the Churches of Christ in the United States of America, 1993). Hereinafter cited as NRSVCE.
7. 1 Samuel 1:20 (NRSVCE).
8. Patrick Hanks and Flavia Hodges, *A Dictionary of First Names* (Oxford: Oxford University Press, 1996), 148.
9. 1 Samuel 2:1, 7–8 (NRSVCE).
10. Luke 1:52–55 (NRSVCE).
11. 1 Samuel 2:20 (NRSVCE).
12. 1 Samuel 2:20–21 (NRSVCE).
13. David Brooks, "The New Red-Diaper Babies," *New York Times*, December 7, 2004, https://www.nytimes.com/2004/12/07/opinion/the-new-reddiaper-babies.html.

## Chapter Seven: "It's Just a Wonderful Life"—Kim, Twelve Kids

1. All names of the interviewees in this book have been changed except for Kim's and Alex's; they asked that we share about them personally.
2. "Our Statement of Faith," Harris Park Bible Church, September 1, 2023, http://www.harrisparkbiblechurch.org/7401.html.
3. The average for our sample was between six and seven children.
4. A return to the faith of one's upbringing that involves a change of life similar to a conversion.
5. Alicia Adsera, "Religion and Changes in Family-Size Norms in Developed Countries," *Review of Religious Research* 47, no. 3 (March 2006): 271–86; See also Tim B. Heaton, "How Does Religion Influence Fertility?: The Case of Mormons," *Journal for the Scientific Study of Religion* 25, no. 2 (June 1986): 248–58.

6. Kim seems to mean the seventy-five-year-old classic *The Country Bunny and the Gold Shoes* by Du Bose Heyward (New York: Clarion Books, 2014).

7. See, for instance, Paul E. Jose and Bee Teng Lim Lim, "Social Connectedness Predicts Lower Loneliness and Depressive Symptoms over Time in Adolescents," *Open Journal of Depression* 3, no. 4 (August 2014): 154–63 and P. J. Wickramaratne et al., "Social Connectedness as a Determinant of Mental Health: A Scoping Review," PLOS One 17, no. 10 (October 13, 2022), https://pubmed.ncbi.nlm.nih.gov/36228007/.

8. John T. Cacioppo and Stephanie Cacioppo, "The Growing Problem of Loneliness," *The Lancet* 391, no. 10119 (February 3, 2018): 426.

## Chapter Eight: "You Believe It's Good"—Miki, Five Kids

1. "Where the Public Stands on Religious Liberty vs. Nondiscrimination," Pew Research Center, September 28, 2016, https://www.pewresearch.org/religion/wp-content/uploads/sites/7/2016/09/Religious-Liberty-full-for-web.pdf.

2. Pope Paul VI praised this as "responsible parenthood" in *Humanae Vitae*. Paul VI, *Humanae Vitae*, July 25, 1968, Vatican website, https://www.vatican.va/content/paul-vi/en/encyclicals/documents/hf_p-vi_enc_25071968_humanae-vitae.html.

3. Marguerite Duane et al., "Fertility Awareness–Based Methods for Women's Health and Family Planning," *Frontiers in Medicine* 9 (May 2022): 1–13.

4. Evidence-based FABMs rely upon observations of fertility biomarkers (such as basal body temperature, cervical fluid, or urinary hormones) to make determinations of fertile days. Non-evidence-based FABMs, such as the rhythm method (from the 1920s), make determinations of fertility on the basis of calendar-cycle-day patterns. Effectiveness varies widely depending on the quality of the rules used. See Rebecca G. Simmons and Victoria Jennings, "Fertility Awareness-Based Methods of Family Planning," *Best Practice & Research Clinical Obstetrics & Gynaecology* 66 (July 2020): 68–82.

5. Duane et al., "Fertility Awareness–Based Methods," 9.

6. Adam Chandler, "Why Do Americans Move So Much More Than Europeans?," *The Atlantic*, October 21, 2016, https://www.theatlantic.com/business/archive/2016/10/us-geographic-mobility/504968/.

7. Max Roser, Hannah Ritchie, and Bernadeta Dadonaite, "Child and Infant Mortality," Our World in Data, November 2019, https://ourworldindata.org/child-mortality.

8. Philippe Ariès, *Centuries of Childhood: A Social History of Family Life*, trans. Robert Baldick (New York: Vintage, 1965), 38.

9. Ibid., 39.

10. Mary Ann Mason, Nicholas H. Wolfinger, and Mark Goulden, *Do Babies Matter? Gender and Family in the Ivory Tower* (New Brunswick: Rutgers University Press, 2013).

11. "Full-Time Instructional Staff, by Faculty and Tenure Status, Academic Rank, Race/Ethnicity, and Gender (Degree-Granting Institutions): Fall 2018," National Center for Education Statistics, February 2021, https://nces.ed.gov/ipeds/datacenter/DataFiles.aspx?year=2018&sid=234e2dfe-b3e8-4a09-8026-316cb4ae52a6&rtid=1.

12. Heather Antecol, Kelly Bedard, and Jenna Stearns, "Equal but Inequitable: Who Benefits from Gender-Neutral Tenure Clock Stopping Policies?," *American Economic Review* 108, no. 9 (September 2018): 2420–41; Derek T. Tharp and Elizabeth J. Parks-Stamm, "Gender Differences in the Intended Use of Parental Leave: Implications for Human Capital Development," *Journal of Family and Economic Issues* 42 (2021): 47–60, https://doi.org/10.1007/s10834-020-09722-8.

## Chapter Nine: "Family Is ... Eternal"—Shaylee, Seven Kids

1. W. D. Mosher, Linda B. Williams, and David P. Johnson, "Religion and Fertility in the United States: New Patterns," *Demography* 29, no. 2 (May 1992): 199–214.

2. Jana Reiss, *The Next Mormons: How Millennials Are Changing the LDS Church* (Oxford: Oxford University Press, 2019), 104.

3. Kaitlyn Pieper et al., "Utah Women and Fertility: Trends and Changes from 1970–2021," Utah Women & Leadership Project, no. 47, April 4, 2023, https://www.usu.edu/uwlp/files/snapshot/47.pdf.

4. The study sample isn't representative, so these percentages can't be generalized to the population of women with five or more kids.

## Chapter Ten: "Strength and Conditioning"—Terry, Ten Kids

1. This quotation has been slightly altered to accurately convey the sentiment of the naming story Terry told without revealing the actual name of her child; Therese is a pseudonym. Dan is also a pseudonym.
2. Nerea M. Casado-Espada et al., "Hormonal Contraceptives, Female Sexual Dysfunction, and Managing Strategies: A Review," *Journal of Clinical Medicine* 8, no. 6 (June 2019): 908; Sarah Hill, *This is Your Brain on Birth Control: The Surprising Science of Women, Hormones and the Law of Unintended Consequences* (New York: Avery Press, 2019); Rikki Schlott, "Why More Women, like Me, Are Abandoning the Pill over Emerging Health Concerns," *New York Post*, January 30, 2023, https://nypost.com/2023/01/30/young-women-abandoning-birth-control-pills-for-mental-health. The percentage of women using the Pill for birth control has dropped by about one third since 2002 (from 31 to 22 percent). "Oral Contraceptive Pills," Kaiser Family Foundation, May 23, 2019, https://www.kff.org/womens-health-policy/fact-sheet/oral-contraceptive-pills.
3. H. Chun and I. Lee, "Why Do Married Men Earn More: Productivity or Marriage Selection?," *Economic Inquiry* 39, no. 2 (April 2001): 307–19.
4. W. Bradford Wilcox and Steven L. Nock, "What's Love Got to Do with It? Equality, Equity, Commitment and Women's Marital Quality," *Social Forces* 84, no. 3, (March 2006): 1321–45; W. Bradford Wilcox and Steven L. Nock, "'Her' Marriage after the Revolutions," *Sociological Forum* 22, no. 1 (March 2007): 103–10.

## Chapter Eleven: "He Wants Nine"—Lauren, Five Kids

1. Karin Hammarberg et al., "Men's Knowledge, Attitudes and Behaviours Relating to Fertility," *Human Reproduction Update* 23, no. 4 (July–August 2017): 458–80.
2. U.S. Census Burea, "Census Bureau Releases First Ever Report on Men's Fertility," press release, June 13, 2019, https://www.census.gov/newsroom/press-releases/2019/mens-fertility.html.
3. Lindsay M. Monte and Brian Knop, *Men's Fertility and Fatherhood: 2014* (report number P70-162) (Washington, D.C.: U.S. Census Bureau, June 13, 2019), https://www.census.gov/library/publications/2019/demo/p70-162.html;

"Table 6. Completed Fertility for Women 40 to 50 Years Old by Selected Characteristics: June 2020," in "Fertility of Women in the United States: 2020" U.S. Census Bureau, February 16, 2020, https://www.census.gov/data/tables/2020/demo/fertility/women-fertility.html#par_list_62.

4.  Yash S. Khandwala et al., "The Age of Fathers in the USA Is Rising: An Analysis of 168,867,480 Births from 1972 to 2015," *Human Reproduction* 32, no. 10 (October 2017): 2110–16.

5.  "Parenthood and Childbearing" (National Survey of Family Growth, waves 2011–2015), Centers for Disease Control and Prevention, June 6, 2017, https://www.cdc.gov/nchs/nsfg/key_statistics/a.htm#parenthood.

## Chapter Twelve: *The Road Not Taken—Cost and Choice*

Epigraph:  Ludwig von Mises, *Human Action: A Treatise on Economics* (New Haven: Yale University Press, 1949), 97; James M. Buchanan, *Cost and Choice: An Inquiry in Economic Theory*, vol. 6, *The Collected Works of James Buchanan* (Indianapolis: Liberty Fund Inc., 1999), 44.

1.  David Skarbek, *The Social Order of the Underworld: How Prison Gangs Govern the American Penal System* (New York: Oxford University Press, 2014), 2.

2.  Ibid., 3–4.

3.  Michael Pakaluk, "Socratic Magnanimity in the *Phaedo*," *Ancient Philosophy* 24, no. 1 (Spring 2004): 101–17.

4.  Skarbek, *Social Order of the Underworld*, 2–3.

5.  Pakaluk, "Socratic Magnanimity."

6.  Hannah Arendt, *The Human Condition*, (Chicago: University of Chicago Press, 1958), 247.

7.  Robert Frost, "The Road Not Taken," in *Collected Poems of Robert Frost*, ed. Edward Connery Lathem (New York: Henry Holt and Company, 1930), 131.

## Chapter Thirteen: *"The Planner of All Plans"—Hannah, Seven Kids, and Esther, Nine Kids*

1.  Niddah 31b.6, *Talmud: The William Davidson Edition*, Sefaria: A Living Library of Jewish Texts Online, https://www.sefaria.org/Niddah.31b.6?lang=bi&with=all&lang2=en.

2.   1 Samuel 2:8 (NRSVCE).
3.   1 Samuel 2:5 (NRSVCE).

## Chapter Fourteen: Me Doing Something Else—Danielle, Seven Kids

1.   Ron J. Lesthaeghe and Johan Surkyn, "When History Moves On: The Foundations and Diffusion of a Second Demographic Transition," in *International Family Change: Ideational Perspectives*, ed. Rukmalie Jayakody, Arland Thornton, and William Axinn (New York: Lawrence Erlbaum Associates, 2008), 83.

## Chapter Fifteen: "May I Ask Why?"—Steph, Six Kids

1.   Anne Morse, "Fertility Rates: Declined for Younger Women, Increased for Older Women: Stable Fertility Rates 1990–2019 Mask Distinct Variations by Age," U.S. Census Bureau, April 6, 2022, https://www.census.gov/library/stories/2022/04/fertility-rates-declined-for-younger-women-increased-for-older -women.html?utm_campaign=20220406msacos1ccstors&utm_medium=email &utm_source=govdelivery.
2.   Hans-Peter Kohler, Francesco C. Billari, and José Antonio Ortega, "The Emergence of Lowest-Low Fertility in Europe during the 1990s," *Population and Development Review* 28, no. 4 (December 2002): 641–80 at 646; Éva Beaujouan, Kryštof Zeman, and Mathías Nathan, "Delayed First Births and Completed Fertility across the 1940–1969 Birth Cohorts," *Demographic Research* 48 (March 2023): 387–420 at 392, https://www.demographic-research.org/volumes/vol48/15/48-15.pdf.
3.   Ibid., 392.
4.   Karel Neels et al., "Rising Educational Participation and the Trend to Later Childbearing," *Population and Development Review* 43, no. 4 (December 2017): 667–93, https://onlinelibrary.wiley.com/doi/10.1111/padr.12112.
5.   Claudia Goldin, *Career and Family: Women's Century-Long Journey toward Equity* (Princeton, New Jersey: Princeton University Press, 2021).

## Chapter Sixteen: "Plans to Prosper You"—Jenn, Six Kids

1.   Romans 8:28 (NRSVCE).

2. Jeremiah 29:11. Scripture taken from the Holy Bible, New International Version®, NIV®. Copyright © 1973, 1978, 1984, 2011 by Biblica, Inc.™ Used by permission of Zondervan. All rights reserved worldwide. www.zondervan.com The "NIV" and "New International Version" are trademarks registered in the United States Patent and Trademark Office by Biblica, Inc.™.

3. Catherine Pakaluk, "Morbid Safetyism," *First Things*, October 13, 2020, https://www.firstthings.com/web-exclusives/2020/10/morbid-safetyism.

4. Fyodor Dostoevsky, *The Brothers Karamazov*, trans. Richard Pevear and Larissa Volokhonsky (New York: Vintage Classics, 1991), 57.

## Chapter Seventeen: "People Matter"—Angela, Five Kids

1. Charles F. Westoff and Elise F. Jones "The End of 'Catholic' Fertility," *Demography* 16, no. 2 (May 1979): 209–17.

2. Andrew J. Cherlin, *Marriage-Go-Round: The State of Marriage and the Family in America Today* (New York: Vintage Books, 2010), 90.

3. For background on personalism, see Thomas D. Williams and Jan Olof Bengtsson, "Personalism," *The Stanford Encyclopedia of Philosophy* (April 27, 2022), ed. Edward N. Zalta, https://plato.stanford.edu/entries/personalism.

4. See Rhys Harrison et al., "Blindness Caused by a Junk Food Diet," *Annals of Internal Medicine* 171, no. 11 (December 3, 2019): 859–61, https://www.acpjournals.org/doi/abs/10.7326/l19-0361; Jack Guy, "Teenage Boy Goes Blind after Existing on Pringles, White Bread and French Fries," CNN, September 3, 2019, https://www.cnn.com/2019/09/03/health/poor-diet-blindness-scli-intl/index.html.

5. Levan Ramishvili, "Thomas Sowell: There Are No Solutions, Only Trade-Offs," YouTube, August 10, 2013, https://www.youtube.com/watch?v=3_EtIWmja-4. The quip is based on Sowell's full-length work in *A Conflict of Visions: Ideological Origins of Political Struggles* (New York: Basic Books, 2002).

## Chapter Eighteen: "Goodness and Light"—Leah, Five Kids

1. Fyodor Dostoevsky, *The Brothers Karamazov*, trans. Richard Pevear and Larissa Volokhonsky (New York: Vintage Classics, 1991), 57.

2. 1 Samuel 2:2 (NRSVCE).

3. 1 Samuel 2:21 (NRSVCE).

## Chapter Nineteen: *"The Lord Repays"—Self and Sacrifice*
Epigraph:   Sirach 35:12–13 (NRSVCE).

1.   Claudia Goldin and Lawrence F. Katz, "The Power of the Pill: Oral Contraceptives and Women's Career and Marriage Decisions," *Journal of Political Economy* 110, no. 4 (August 2002): 730–70 at 752, https://www.journals.uchicago.edu/doi/abs /10.1086/340778.

2.   See Matthew 16:25; Mark 8:35; Luke 9:24 and 17:33; and John 12:25.

3.   1 Chronicles 21:18–25 (NRSVCE).

4.   1 Samuel 1:27–28 (NRSVCE).

5.   1 Samuel 2:20 (NRSVCE).

## Chapter Twenty: *"He Didn't Know He Needed It"—Saving Our Lives*

1.   Hannah Arendt, *The Human Condition* (Chicago: University of Chicago Press, 1958), 247.

2.   Melissa S. Kearney et al., "The Puzzle of Falling US Birth Rates since the Great Recession," *Journal of Economic Perspectives* 36, no. 1 (Winter 2022): 151–76.

3.   Anne Case and Angus Deaton, "Rising Morbidity and Mortality in Midlife among White non-Hispanic Americans in the Twenty-First Century," *Proceedings of the National Academy of Sciences* 112, no. 49 (December 8, 2015): 15078–83; Stephan Collishaw et al., "Time Trends in Adolescent Mental Health," *Journal of Child Psychology and Psychiatry* 45, no. 8 (November 2004): 1350–62; Stephan Collishaw, "Annual Research Review: Secular Trends in Child and Adolescent Mental Health," *Journal of Child Psychology and Psychiatry* 56, no. 3 (March 2015): 370–93; Ramin Mojtabai, Mark Olfson, and Beth Han, "National Trends in the Prevalence and Treatment of Depression in Adolescents and Young Adults," *Pediatrics* 138, no. 6 (December 2016), https://doi.org/10.1542/ peds.2016-1878.

4.   Deborah S. Hasin et al., "Epidemiology of Adult DSM-5 Major Depressive Disorder and Its Specifiers in the United States," *Journal of the American Medical Association Psychiatry* 75, no. 4 (April 1, 2018): 336–46, https://pubmed.ncbi.nlm .nih.gov/29450462/.

5. Emily P. Terlizzi and Maria A. Villarroel, "Symptoms of Generalized Anxiety Disorder among Adults: United States, 2019," NCHS Data Brief no. 378, September 2020, https://www.cdc.gov/nchs/data/databriefs/db378-H.pdf.

6. Shefaly Shorey, Esperanza Debby Ng, and Celine H. J. Wong, "Global Prevalence of Depression and Elevated Depressive Symptoms among Adolescents: A Systematic Review and Meta-Analysis," *British Journal of Clinical Psychology* 61, no. 1 (September 2021): 287–305, https://pubmed.ncbi.nlm.nih.gov/34569066.

7. Sally C. Curtin, "State Suicide Rates among Adolescents and Young Adults Aged 10–24: United States, 2000–2018," *National Vital Statistics Reports* 69, no. 11 (September 11, 2020), https://stacks.cdc.gov/view/cdc/93667.

8. Elizabeth Arias, Betzaida Tejada-Vera, and Farida Ahmad, "Provisional Life Expectancy Estimates for January through June, 2020," Vital Statistics Rapid Release Report No. 10, National Center for Health Statistics, February 2021, https://stacks.cdc.gov/view/cdc/100392.

9. Andrea M. Tilstra, Daniel H. Simon, and Ryan K. Masters, "Trends in 'Deaths of Despair' among Working-Aged White and Black Americans, 1990–2017," *American Journal of Epidemiology* 190, no. 9 (September 2021): 1751–59.

10. Author's calculations based on average family sizes, birth spacing, and life expectancy. See "Table AVGW. Average Number of People per Family Household, by Race and Hispanic Origin, Marital Status, Age, and Education of Householder: 2022," in "America's Families and Living Arrangements: 2022," U.S. Census Bureau, November 17, 2022, https://www.census.gov/data/tables/2022/demo/families/cps-2022.html; Katherine A. Ahrens and Jennifer A. Hutcheon, "Birth Spacing in the United States—towards Evidence-Based Recommendations," *Paediatric and Perinatal Epidemiology* 33, no. 1 (January 2019): 1–4; Elizabeth Arias et al., "Provisional Life Expectancy Estimates for 2021: Vital Statistics Rapid Release Report No. 23," National Center for Health Statistics, August 2022, https://dx.doi.org/10.15620/cdc:118999.

## Chapter Twenty-One: "He Carries the Baby"—Saving Our Souls

1. "WSJ/NORC Poll March 2023," *Wall Street Journal* and NORC (National Opinion Research Center), March 2023, https://s.wsj.net/public/resources/documents/WSJ_NORC_ToplineMarc_2023.pdf.

2. Miller McPherson et al., "Social Isolation in America: Changes in Core Discussion Networks over Two Decades," *American Sociological Review* 71, no. 3 (June 2006): 353–75, https://journals.sagepub.com/doi/abs/10.1177/000312240607100301?ssource=mfc&rss=1&.

3. Henri C. Santos et al., "Global Increases in Individualism," *Psychological Science* 28, no. 9 (September 2017): 1228–39, https://journals.sagepub.com/doi/10.1177/0956797617700622.

4. Charles Murray, *Coming Apart: The State of White America, 1960–2010* (New York: Crown Forum, 2012).

5. Patrick J. Deneen, *Why Liberalism Failed* (New Haven: Yale University Press, 2018); Ibram X. Kendi, *Stamped from the Beginning: The Definitive History of Racist Ideas in America* (New York: Nation Books, 2016); Ezra Klein, *Why We're Polarized* (New York: Avid Reader Press/Simon & Schuster, 2020); Ben Sasse, *Them: Why We Hate Each Other—and How to Heal* (New York: St. Martin's Press, 2018); Nikole Hannah-Jones, *The 1619 Project: A New Origin Story* (New York: One World, 2021).

6. Aristotle, *Nicomachean Ethics*, II.1.1103a32–33, translation supplied by Michael Pakaluk.

7. Ibid., II.1.1103b21–22.

8. Aristotle, *Ethica Eudemia*, ed. R. R. Walzer and J. M. Mingay (New York: Oxford University Press, 1991), VII.1.1242b1–2.

9. Father Steve Boes, "The Story Behind 'He Ain't Heavy…,'" Boys Town Blog, June 9, 2017, https://www.boystown.org/blog/the-story-behind-he-aint-heavy; The same story with the crippled boy presented under a different name (likely a pseudonym) appears on pages 169–70 of Fulton Oursler and Will Oursler, *Father Flanagan of Boys Town* (Garden City, New York: Doubleday & Company, Inc., 1949). For a more complete description, with the 1921 photo, see page 30 of Thomas J. Lynch and Terry Hyland, *A Century of Service, A History of Healing: The Boy's Town Story* (Virginia Beach: Donning Company Publishers, 2016).

10. Luke 6:38, New Revised Standard Version Bible: Catholic Edition (Division of Christian Education of the National Council of the Churches of Christ in the United States of America, 1993).

11.  Hannah Arendt, *The Human Condition* (Chicago: University of Chicago Press, 1958), 247.

## Chapter Twenty-Two: Hannah's Children—The Future of the Nation

Epigraph:  Edith Stein, *Essays on Woman*, 2nd ed., rev., ed. Lucy Gelber and
          Romaeus Leuven, trans. Freda Mary Oben, vol. 2, *The Collected
          Words of Edith Stein* (Washington, D.C.: ICS Publications, 1996), 244.

1.  Brady E. Hamilton, Joyce A. Martin, and Michelle J. K. Osterman, "Births: Provisional Data for 2022: Vital Statistics Rapid Release Report No. 28," Centers for Disease Control and Prevention, June 2023, https://www.cdc.gov/nchs/data/vsrr/vsrr028.pdf.

2.  "Fertility Rates" (indicator), OECD (Organisation for Economic Cooperation and Development) Library, 2023, https://www.oecd-ilibrary.org/social-issues-migration-health/fertility-rates/indicator/english_8272fb01-en.

3.  Julian L. Simon, *The Ultimate Resource 2* (Princeton, New Jersey: Princeton University Press, 1996).

4.  Genesis 1:28 (NRSVCE).

5.  David Brooks, "The New Red-Diaper Babies," *New York Times*, December 7, 2004, https://www.nytimes.com/2004/12/07/opinion/the-new-reddiaper-babies.html.

6.  Charles F. Westoff and Norman B. Ryder, *The Contraceptive Revolution* (Princeton, New Jersey: Princeton University Press, 1977), Table II-3, referenced in Claudia Goldin and Lawrence F. Katz, "The Power of the Pill: Oral Contraceptives and Women's Career and Marriage Decisions," *Journal of Political Economy* 110, no. 4 (August 2002): 730–70.

7.  Ibid.

8.  Martha J. Bailey, "'Momma's Got the Pill': How Anthony Comstock and *Griswold v. Connecticut* Shaped US Childbearing," *American Economic Review* 100, no. 1 (March 2010): 98–129, https://www.aeaweb.org/articles?id=10.1257/aer.100.1.98.

9.  Jean-Baptiste Say, *A Treatise on Political Economy*, trans. C. R. Prinsep and ed. Clement C. Biddle (Philadelphia: Lippincott, Grambo & Co., 1855), section 1, book 2, chapter 11, https://www.econlib.org/library/Say/sayT.html?chapter_num=35#book-reader.

10. Lily Kuo and Xueying Wang, "Can China Recover from Its Disastrous One-Child Policy?," *The Guardian*, March 2, 2019, https://www.theguardian.com /world/2019/mar/02/china-population-control-two-child-policy; Andrew Jacobs and Francesca Paris, "Can China Reverse Its Population Decline? Just Ask Sweden," *New York Times*, February 9, 2023, https://www.nytimes.com/2023 /02/09/upshot/china-population-decline.html.

11. Kris James Mitchener and Christoph Trebesch, "Sovereign Debt in the Twenty-First Century," *Journal of Economic Literature* 61, no. 2 (June 2023): 565–623, https://www.aeaweb.org/articles?id=10.1257/jel.20211362.

12. Emre Tiftik, Khadija Mahmood, and Raymond Aycock, ed. Sonja Gibbs, "Global Debt Monitor: In Search of Sustainability," Institute of International Finance, September 19, 2023, page 1, https://www.iif.com/portals/0/Files/content /Global%20Debt%20Monitor_Sept2023_vf.pdf.

13. Author's calculations from U.S. Department of Education data. See "Private School Enrollment," National Center for Education Statistics, May 2022, https:// nces.ed.gov/programs/coe/indicator/cgc.

## Acknowledgments

1. Luke 1:46–48 (NRSVCE).
2. Psalm 84:3 (NRSVCE).
3. Ephesians 2:10 (NRSVCE).

# Index